P9-CBW-593

FUNDING
EVIL

How Terrorism
Is Financed—and
How to Stop It

Expanded Edition
with a new preface and epilogue by the author

RACHEL EHRENFELD

Bonus Books
Chicago and Los Angeles

09 08 07 06 05   5 4 3 2 1

ISBN (paper): 1-56625-231-8

The Library of Congress has cataloged the hardcover edition as follows:

Ehrenfeld, Rachel.
   Funding evil : how terrorism is financed—and how to stop it / Rachel
Ehrenfeld.
      p. cm.
Includes bibliographical references and index.
   ISBN 1-56625-196-6
   1. Terrorism—Finance. 2. Islam and terrorism. 3. Money laundering.
4. Drug traffic. I. Title.

   HV6431.E394 2003
   363.32—dc22

                                                                        2003016761

Bonus Books
875 North Michigan Ave., Ste. 1416
Chicago, IL 60611

Printed in the United States of America

To Nina, in appreciation

CONTENTS

FOREWORD

by R. James Woolsey

Rachel Ehrenfeld has done all serious students of this long war in which we are engaged a great service—by following the money. There are many terrorist affiliates: the governments of various rogue states; wealthy supporters in the Gulf and elsewhere; the Wahabi sect in Saudi Arabia; and a substantial network of criminal enterprises, such as drug cartels, which are ready and willing to make common cause with anyone who is the enemy of the West, of open societies, and pre-eminently of the United States.

In this meticulous and most readable work, a number of shibboleths are done serious damage. If you are one who is wedded to any of the following propositions, you will find substantial evidence that will shake your beliefs: that Shiite Islamists will not work with Sunni Islamists in support of terror; that religiously-rooted Islamists will not work closely with secular Arab nationalist organizations or secular rogue state governments in connection with terrorism; that there is a substantial distinction between the terrorist and the charitable wings of such organizations as HAMAS and Hizballah; that drug rings and other major international criminal enterprises have little to do with terrorism; that although corruption exists in the Palestinian Authority the amounts stolen are relatively small (millions not billions) and this has little to do with terrorism; that terrorist funding is a serious problem but not one that involves such places as Herndon, Virginia, and Charlotte, North Carolina.

On the contrary—there is ample evidence in this volume: that there is close cooperation on terrorism and its funding across both religious-secular and religious-religious divides; that the distinction between HAMAS's and Hizballah's charitable and terrorist wings, relied upon by European governments and many in the media, is not even a serviceable fig leaf; that there are close ties between the international drug trade and terrorism; that Yasser Arafat has become a billionaire, and a very successful funder of terror, by stealing from the Palestinian people; and that we have serious problems with terrorist funding from U.S. sources, due in part to a past reluctance to scrutinize adequately Wahabi and Islamist "charities" in the U.S.

Ms. Ehrenfeld does not stop with the descriptive. Her prescriptions for change in the last chapter deserve serious attention both because of the care with which she has made her case and because of the relatively small dent that has been made to date in blocking terrorists' access to their financial lifeblood. Theft and corruption in the Palestinian Authority cannot be rewarded as it is, in effect, now via funds from the UN (i.e. UNRWA, a substantial share of whose funding in turn comes from the U.S.) and the European Union. Saudi Arabia, through wealthy individuals, and Iran, through government policy, are the two heaviest hitters in funding terror—Ms. Ehrenfeld makes a solid case that it is time to take the gloves off with regard to both of these sources. Corruption, the drug trade, and money laundering operations—all used by terrorists, not only by criminals—also deserve increased international attention, she argues. She outlines international agreements with teeth, objective standards, and tough implementation—and how to utilize an existing index of Western companies that continue to trade with terrorist-sponsoring states.

Most importantly, Ms. Ehrenfeld ties the undermining of terror—quoting last year's excellent Report of the UN Development Programme and the Arab Fund for Economic and Social Development—to "strengthening personal freedoms and boosting broad-based citizen participation in political and economic affairs." In short, we need a strategy for this long war that not only cuts off terrorist funding but also dries up its sources, by convincing the good people of the Arab, indeed the whole Muslim, world that this is not a clash of civilizations but a war of freedom against tyranny. As we convinced Havel, Walesa, Sakharov, Solidarity, and many others behind the Iron Curtain during the Cold War, we must convince the decent citizens of all the nations that support terror, by whatever means, East and West, that this must change and that we are on their side and they on ours.

R. James Woolsey
Director of Central Intelligence, 1993–95

PREFACE TO THE EXPANDED EDITION

Early on the morning of January 23, 2004, I received an e-mail from a law firm in London. This was no ordinary message. It was a letter threatening to sue me for libel in a British court, for statements made in the original edition of *Funding Evil* about their client, Saudi billionaire Khalid bin Mahfouz.

The letter said that, contrary to allegations reported in this book, bin Mahfouz does not have now and never had "any involvement or association with the sponsoring of al-Qaeda," nor has he ever "knowingly financed terrorism of any description and vehemently den[ies] this."[1] Khalid bin Mahfouz's lawyers demanded:

- "An undertaking to the High Court in England not to repeat the same (or similar) offending allegations"
- "The withdrawal from circulation and destruction and/or delivery up of all unsold copies of the Book immediately"
- A public letter of apology
- A donation to a charity agreed upon by bin Mahfouz
- Payment of the legal fees involved[2]

I was not the first author that bin Mahfouz had threatened to sue, nor probably the last. At the time that this threat arrived, I was already aware that bin Mahfouz was engaged in "forum shopping," the latest legal tactic employed by him and other rich Saudis apparently seeking to skirt American justice and its freedom-of-speech principles:

"Some Saudis appear to be using the U.K. as a back door to silence their critics and repress free speech by threatening

> litigation, persuading publishers to back down rather [than] face
> years of expensive litigation—even if what they're publishing
> might in fact be true," said Trevor Asserson, who specializes in
> defamation in the London law office of Morgan Lewis & Bockius.[3]

Several wealthy Saudis are funding a cynical campaign to attack Americans' First Amendment rights by suing reporters who expose them under British libel laws. These are the same Saudis named in a trillion-dollar lawsuit tied to the September 11 terrorist attacks, the same Saudis who laugh all the way to Riyadh banks each time we fill up at the pump, and the same Saudis who have been identified by official statements and hearings in Congress as funders of al-Qaeda and HAMAS.[4]

Why British courts? In the U.K., a plaintiff can easily win a judgment because, among other things, he is not required to prove that the alleged libel was done with malice. Accordingly, Khalid bin Mahfouz, who is named in all the September 11 lawsuits, has threatened twenty-nine authors and publishers with libel suits in U.K. courts.[5] None have gone to trial. Instead, the defendants settled at an early stage because they could not, or would not, endure a lengthy and costly lawsuit; instead, they capitulated, apologized, retracted, and paid fines.

Since bin Mahfouz has a long track record of successful judgments by default, he clearly anticipates such a judgment against me too, relying upon his capability to pay for even the costliest legal proceedings—his lawyers seemed to assume that I would not have the financial means to defend myself.[6] This is not surprising given that in 2004 *Forbes* magazine listed bin Mahfouz as having $3 billion.[7]

Bin Mahfouz is the former owner of the largest Saudi bank, the National Commercial Bank (NCB),[8] and he established and funded a charity called the Muwafaq Foundation.[9] According to government officials in the U.S. and elsewhere (as documented in chapter 2), the NCB served as the major pipeline for terror financing. However, it has not been put on the official U.S. terrorist list. Neither has the Muwafaq Foundation, despite having been identified by the U.S. Treasury Department as providing logistical and financial support to al-Qaeda, HAMAS, and the Abu Sayyaf organizations.[10]

Bin Mahfouz himself has been accused of being involved in illegal activities in the past. A press release by New York District Attorney Robert Morgenthau on July 1, 1992, announced the indictment of "Sheik Khalid Bin Mahfouz, the chief operating officer of The National Commercial Bank of Saudi Arabia" for his involvement with BCCI, the Bank of Credit and Commerce International. Morgenthau pointed out that the significance of the indictment against bin Mahfouz is that "BCCI in 1986 needed additional capital to sustain and expand its operations. Mahfouz's name and money gave BCCI that capital."[11] As a result, "Mahfouz became a principal shareholder and director in the BCCI Group."[12] However, Morgenthau noted that "Mafouz's investment in BCCI later was secretly withdrawn, which resulted in a gross misstatement of the true financial picture of the bank. The scheme resulted in larger losses for depositors and others when BCCI's worldwide Ponzi scheme finally collapsed."[13] Morgenthau actually described the BCCI scam as a "rent-a-sheikh" scheme.[14] Bin Mahfouz denied all allegations but paid a fine of $225 million, and as part of the settlement with the government he was barred from any further activities in the American banking system. (Of course, just because he paid a $225 million fine does not necessarily mean that he actually did any of the things with BCCI of which he was—perhaps wrongly—accused.) In addition, his bank, the NCB, was forced to close its branches in New York and London as part of the same settlement.[15] The Board of Governors of the U.S. Federal Reserve, in a subsequent indictment on July 8, 1992, stated that "Mahfouz operated NCB with what he characterizes as an 'absolute authority.'"[16] This statement seems inconsistent with bin Mahfouz's claim that he did not know what was going on at

the National Commercial Bank, and therefore had no knowledge that
the NCB was used to funnel money to terrorist organizations.

Although the U.S. government did not list bin Mahfouz's Muwafaq
Foundation on its terrorist list, in a press conference held on October
12, 2001, when Yasin al-Qadi was added to the Designated Terrorist
List, he was described as "head of the Saudi-based Muwafaq Foundation, which transferred millions to Mr. bin Laden."[17] In addition, a
letter dated November 2001 from the Department of the Treasury to
the attorney general of Switzerland stated the following: "The
Muwafaq Foundation provided logistical and financial support for a
mujahidin battalion in Bosnia. The Foundation also operated in
Sudan, Somalia, and Pakistan, among other places. A number of individuals employed by or otherwise associated with the Muwafaq
Foundation have connections to various terrorist organizations. . . .
The Muwafaq Foundation also provided support to Hamas and the
Abu Sayyaf Organization in the Philippines." The letter went on to
say that "the Muwafaq Foundation also employed or served as cover
for Islamic extremists connected with the military activities of
Makhtab Al-Khidamat (MK) [which was absorbed in al-Qaeda and
was designated as a terrorist organization]. . . . A number of NGO's,
formerly associated with the MK, including Muwafaq, also merged
with al-Qaeda."[18]

Khalid bin Mahfouz, who established the Muwafaq Foundation in
1991, claims on his Web site that the foundation "was wound up between 1996 and 1998."[19] However, according to the *Guardian*, the
Muwafaq was possibly still active in the offshore haven of Jersey in
September 2001; as before, the foundation's lawyers denied that it
funded terrorism.[20] But, according to the Treasury Department's letter, the pattern of activity displayed by Muwafaq fit the pattern of
other "relief" organizations that worked in concert with terrorist
groups "and give[s] rise to a reasonable basis to believe that they
have facilitated terrorist activities."[21]

The 9/11 Commission Report, though it does not mention Khalid
bin Mahfouz by name, refers to the "Golden Chain," a "financial support network . . . put together mainly by financiers in Saudi Arabia
and the Persian Gulf states,"[22] which was responsible for Osama bin
Laden's "strong financial position in Afghanistan" from 1996 to
1998.[23] According to a court document cited as a source in commission's report, a list of the members of the Golden Chain was found in
the spring of 2002 in Bosnia during a raid on the offices of Benevolence International Foundation, a Saudi charity that funded terrorism.[24] According to the *Wall Street Journal,* "the Golden Chain list
was confirmed by U.S. officials and translated from Arabic by the Justice Department," and among the names listed are "billionaire
bankers Saleh Kamel and Khalid bin Mahfouz."[25]

No one has taken proceedings against bin Mahfouz all the way to
a final hearing to prove his much-denied connections with terrorism. A lot of people, many with access to high-level intelligence, have
made serious allegations, but due to national security concerns they
are not making all the evidence generally available. Thus, bin Mahfouz continues to protect himself by threatening libel lawsuits. But,
given the number of reports and investigations that point the finger
at him, one wonders why he has not been placed on the U.S. list of
terrorists.

Will the U.S. government add all those mentioned on the Golden
Chain list, including bin Mahfouz, to its terror list? Judging by the
9/11 Commission's precedent—probably not. This leaves me and
others who are trying to expose those that fund Islamist terror organizations to face the threat of costly legal action in British courts by
Khalid bin Mahfouz and his associates.

On October 19, 2004, Khalid bin Mahfouz commenced legal proceedings against me for libel in a British court. Despite the enormous
cost involved, I have decided to take it upon myself to challenge
Khalid bin Mahfouz and provide the U.K. court with evidence that

he, the Muwafaq Foundation, and the NCB have in fact supported al-Qaeda and HAMAS.

My challenge of bin Mahfouz carries even greater repercussions since Prince Turki, the Saudi ambassador to London, is alleged to have said recently that it's important that bin Mahfouz win because he "represents all of us [Saudi Arabia and the Royal Family]."[26]

So remember, this is a book the Saudis do not want you to read.

RACHEL EHRENFELD
NOVEMBER 2004

AUTHOR'S NOTE: The individuals and organizations described in this book as financial supporters of terrorism have been identified as such by law enforcement officials and other reputable sources. However, all the individuals and organizations mentioned have denied their involvement with terror financing.

PREFACE TO THE FIRST EDITION

At 8:45 A.M. on September 11, I was on the phone with Mike Gonzales, editor at the European *Wall Street Journal*. We were discussing the op-ed about financing terrorism I had written for the paper, which was to run the next day. The TV's regular morning chatter in the background suddenly changed and an anxious voice announced that a plane had hit the World Trade Center. We hung up and I rushed to my window, which has a clear view of downtown Manhattan and the World Trade Center. At first I saw smoke rising in the distance; before long a thick, black cloud had engulfed the Twin Towers. Later the sky turned black and the buildings disappeared altogether. I called Mike back—it was still possible to get a connection to Europe—and after describing the horrors outside my window I suggested a new lead for the op-ed; I knew instinctively that this was no accident, but a terror attack. And this is how my op-ed the following day began:

> The murderous terrorists who destroyed the World Trade Center towers in Manhattan and damaged the Pentagon, delivered a very clear and sobering message yesterday: The leader of the free world is vulnerable.
>
> Blame and responsibility for the most devastating terrorist attack in American history must be laid squarely at the feet of those who masterminded and perpetrated yesterday's mayhem. The security of the free world demands that they are identified and punished.
>
> And yet terrorism does not happen in a political vacuum. The policies pursued by Western nations impact directly on both the means available to terrorists and the motivations driving their

evil agendas. It is imperative that we assess what has gone wrong and begin to set those policies right.[1]

This is when the idea for this book emerged. It is my belief that the perpetrators of crimes of such magnitude are only the expendable foot soldiers; the true blame must lie with those who make their activities possible—the paymasters.

By now, the U.S. government has confirmed that al-Qaeda and other Islamist organizations have been raising money through charitable organizations, fundraisers in mosques, and legitimate and illegitimate businesses. They are also benefiting from sponsorship from states that provide money, arms, training camps, and safe haven. However, terror funds that derive from illegal drugs, the most valuable commodity in the world behind oil and arms, have received very little attention.

Identifying all the sources of funding for terrorism, and the methods employed in raising those funds, is what this book is about. It is also about what can be done to curtail and eventually to cut off funding for terrorism—the only way to prevent a horror like September 11 from happening again.

RACHEL EHRENFELD

JUNE 2003

AUTHOR'S NOTE: *Many of the names and terms used in this book originate in languages such as Arabic and Urdu that do not use the Latin alphabet. Therefore, they must be transliterated phonetically, and no universally accepted "correct" spelling exists. Although care has been taken to render these terms consistently throughout the text, quoted material from other sources may use alternate transliterations—for example, "al-Qaidah" for "al-Qaeda," "Hezbollah" for "Hizballah," or "Wahhabism" for "Wahabism."*

The text also uses the term "homicide bomber" to refer to terrorists who blow themselves up in order to murder their perceived enemies. Though many in the Western media refer to such attackers as "suicide bombers," there is nothing suicidal about their actions. Abd al-Aziz al-Rantisi, spokesman for the terror group HAMAS, explained the mind-set of the homicide bomber in a call for homicide bombings against U.S. forces in Iraq: "The enemies of Allah and the enemies of this people are cowards. They crave life, while the Muslims crave martyrdom. The martyrdom operations that shock can ensure that horror is sowed in the [enemies'] hearts, and horror is one of the causes of defeat. . . . In order to defend the homeland from the terrorist Crusader attack, there is a need for people who yearn for Paradise, and the shortest way to Paradise is death for [the sake of] Allah. Some of us should see the joyful and satisfied faces of the mothers in Iraq when they part from the fruit of their loins, who go off to the realms of honor, the realms of martyrdom." [2]

Acknowledgments

It would be impossible to list all the many people who assisted with resources and the preparation of this manuscript, and some have requested anonymity. I wish to convey my heartfelt gratitude to all of them, wherever they may be. The following have my special thanks:

Ziad Abdelnour, president of the United States Committee for a Free Lebanon, for your help in getting this project off the ground; Shalom Harrari, for your time and generosity; Yossef Bodansky, director of the Congressional Task Force on Terrorism and Unconventional Warfare, for your advice; Debra Bonner, for your constant help and encouragement, and Andrew Stromberg, for your faith in me; Ilan Berman, vice president for policy at the American Foreign Policy Council in Washington, D.C.—my special appreciation for your ready help, patience, and invaluable suggestions. Many thanks to Christopher Barder; Dr. Reuven Ehrlich, director of the Intelligence and Terrorism Information Center at the Center for Special Studies of the Israel Defense Forces; Steve Emerson, for access to materials at the Investigative Project in Washington, D.C.; Joseph Farah, publisher of WorldNetDaily, for your help; Ambassador Robert Gelbard, for your counsel; Yoram Hessel, former senior Mossad officer; and Dr. Daniel Kuhn and his wife Ziva, for your constant encouragement and friendship. Special thanks to Vijay Kumar; Dr. Josiane and Dr. Gil S. Lederman, for your kindness, assistance, and understanding; Matthew Levitt, senior fellow at the Washington Institute for Near East Policy; Dr. Steve Levy, for your unique ability to alleviate problems; Dr. Joseph Molyneux, former DEA special agent, adjunct professor of political science, American Military University, and vice president of security for a multinational corporation, my greatest appreciation for your many contributions and the long hours you have spent to assist me even from the other end of the globe. Heartfelt gratitude to Eytan Mottes, for your generous help, constant encouragement and care, excellent advice, and great cooking; Audna Nicholson, for your friendship and unfailing support; and the Prism Group, especially David Frankfurter. Many thanks to Richard Perle, for your help; Sol Sanders, for keeping me informed. And to James Woolsey, my most ardent thanks for your support, advice, and encouragement.

I want to warmly thank my editor, Devon Freeny, for doing a tremendous job patiently, thoughtfully, and diligently. Special thanks to Peter Miller, my agent, for understanding early on the importance of this project and continuing to pursue it relentlessly. And to my publisher, Jeff Stern, my appreciation for your foresight and encouragement, and for making this book possible.

I have been blessed with a team of committed and talented assistants and would like to express my gratitude to: Danielle Ramati—your devotion, energy, and skills proved utterly indispensable. Ilan Weinglass, for your eagerness and hard work. Ben Silverbush, for your help, and for saving the computer and the manuscript. Rhona Silverbush, for the long hours, dedication, and care. And my graphic artist, Julie Kim. Last but not least, special thanks to Andrea Swenson, my photographer, for being both talented and kind.

"We will direct every resource at our command to win the war against terrorists: every means of diplomacy, every tool of intelligence, every instrument of law enforcement, every financial influence. We will starve the terrorists of funding, turn them against each other, rout them out of their safe hiding places, and bring them to justice."

President George W. Bush,
September 24, 2001

CHAPTER ONE

How Did We Get Here?

There are experts who claim that terrorism does not require large amounts of money; when you "kill one, [you] frighten ten thousand," as the old Chinese proverb suggests. Individual terrorist acts do not in fact cost much—the attack on the World Trade Center is estimated to have cost only $500,000.[1]

But today's global terrorism requires money for much more than individual attacks. An expanding terror network must have enough funds to support:

- Recruitment
- Training camps and bases
- Housing and food
- Equipment, explosives, and conventional and unconventional weapons
- Forged identity and travel documents
- Intelligence gathering
- Communications among organizational components
- Bribery
- Day-to-day maintenance expenses of members awaiting commands to launch operations[2]

Terrorism also requires money for television, radio, print media, videos, and paid demonstrations to advance incitement against the targeted "enemy." Funding is needed to maintain the families of terrorists who are deployed as "sleepers"—who live undercover and do not support their dependents—as well as to compensate families of terrorists who are killed. The total cost of maintaining the global Islamist terror network is estimated to be in the *billions* of dollars.

To sustain these operations, sophisticated, multifaceted worldwide funding networks have been set in place over the past two decades. Funding sources for terrorism are:

- Governments such as Saudi Arabia and Iran
- Charitable organizations such as the Muslim World League (MWL) and the International Islamic Relief Organization (IIRO)
- Legitimate businesses operating as fronts
- The exploitation of financial markets, especially the unregulated commodity markets
- International trade, which converts cash into precious commodities such as diamonds and gold

Funding also comes from criminal activities such as:

- Extortion
- Smuggling
- Kidnapping
- Prostitution rings and trafficking in people
- Credit card fraud, identity theft, and counterfeiting.
- Pirating of videos, compact discs, tapes, and software

Unacknowledged is a major source of funding that comes from trade in illegal drugs such as heroin, hashish, cocaine, and methamphetamines.[3] "Terrorism Financing," a report published by the United Nations Security Council in January 2003, notes that "Saudi charities raise an estimated $4 billion in revenues and send abroad up to 20%."[4] The report identified Saudi charities and individuals as the major sponsors of al-Qaeda, but ignored al-Qaeda's revenues from criminal activities, and said nothing about the huge profits obtained by al-Qaeda from the illegal drug trade.[5]

NARCO-TERRORISM

"Terrorism and drugs go together like rats and the bubonic plague," said Attorney General John Ashcroft. "They thrive in the same conditions, support each other, and feed off each other."[6] Twelve of the thirty-six groups on the U.S. Department of State's Foreign Terrorist Organizations List have been identified as being involved in drug trafficking.[7] In October 2002 a Colombian courier for the Revolutionary Armed Forces of Columbia (FARC), which is funded mostly by drug trafficking, was arrested in the U.S. for having attempted to transport €182,000 (Euros) into the country; the money was confiscated. In another case, U.S. law enforcement derailed an al-Qaeda plot to exchange "9,000 assault weapons, such as AK-47 rifles, submachine guns and sniper rifles; 300 pistols; rocket-propelled grenade launchers; 300,000 grenades; shoulder-fired anti-aircraft missiles and 60 million rounds of ammunition," for $25 million dollars in cash and cocaine.[8] Attorney General Ashcroft said that the "toxic combination of drugs and terrorism," threatens U.S. national security.[9]

The nexus of terrorist groups and international criminal organizations is complex, linking money, geography, politics, arms, and tactics to create a mutually beneficial relationship. This nexus yields hundreds of billions of dollars in revenues worldwide—for 1992 alone, close to U.S.$1 trillion.[10] A decade later, with the exponential growth in drug consumption, U.S. experts estimate the profits to be as high as U.S.$2 trillion.[11] "It's so important for Americans to know

that the traffic in drugs finances the work of terror, sustaining terrorists," said President George W. Bush. "Terrorists use drug profits to
fund their cells to commit acts of murder."[12]

Not only are there no other commodities on the market today with
as high and fast a return, but the drug trade is also a triple-pronged
weapon that helps terrorists to:

- Finance their activities
- Undermine targeted countries politically and economically,
  and create crises in public health
- Recruit new members by citing drug use as an example of
  Western social degeneracy and arguing that such corrupt so-
  cieties must be destroyed

ORIGINS

Today there are sixty-nine major terrorist organizations in the world,
according to the U.S. Department of State's *Patterns of Global Terrorism 2002.* Of these, thirty-six are designated as Foreign Terrorist Organizations—and, of those, thirty-one are Islamist. (The Provisional
Irish Republican Army [PIRA] is the only other terrorist group on the
list that has a religious component.) How and why did terror—
traditionally directed within the terrorists' own borders and at their
own rulers—become the international plague it is today?

To understand terrorism in its larger historical, cultural, and economic context, it might be helpful to look eastward. A large gap lies
between the political and economic cultures of the West and the Islamic countries of the East—in which corruption plays an important
structural role. "Force and favors, as determined among individuals
through corruption, are the fundamentals of Arab and inter-Arab
politics," writes David Pryce-Jones. "Corruption among Arabs is
nothing more nor less than a daily functioning among every one of

the power challenge dialectic, and it is registering individual advances and retreats everywhere and at all times. Corruption plays a role approximating competition in a democracy. At the top of the social scale, corruption represents the power of the strong over the weak."[13]

Islamist rulers like the *mullahs* in Iran do not afford a high priority to improving their peoples' standard of living or human rights. In Afghanistan, when the Islamist Taliban seized power, we witnessed the spread of violence, the marginalization of women, and the persecution of all but like-minded Islamist fundamentalists. In other Arab countries where democracy has not taken root yet, such as Iraq and Libya, making use of violence must often seem the only way to try to effect change.[14]

Violence is central to the history and culture of the Islamist branch of Islam. A core tenet of the Islamist interpretation of Islam is that "the world is divided into two houses: the House of Islam *(Dar al-Islam),* in which Muslim governments rule and Muslim law prevails, and the House of War *(Dar al-Harab),* the rest of the world . . . ruled by infidels."[15] One reaches the House of Islam only through the House of War—that is, by the sword. According to the terrorism adviser of former Israeli premier Yitzhak Rabin, "Terrorism stems from cultural violence rooted in a perversely callous attitude toward human life and general disregard for the worth of individual rights."[16]

To paraphrase Carl von Clausewitz, terrorism for Islamists is the extension of both war and diplomacy by other means.[17] Not surprisingly, many Islamist régimes, as well as Arab dictatorships like Iran and Syria, use terrorism as a political weapon to achieve their goals and exert their influence externally. Saddam Hussein ruled Iraq with terror. He murdered and intimidated the Iraqi population, and funneled at least $9 million to finance homicide bombers in attacks against Israel, and to reward their families.[18] Documents found during Operation Iraqi Freedom revealed that Saddam not only funded terrorism, but also bought international political influence and public opinion, bribing foreign politicians and journalists alike.[19]

Dictators do not necessarily aspire to a literate, self-sustaining, and politically empowered citizenry. Instead, they concentrate on staying in power, using real or imagined external threats to rally the populace behind their régimes, viewing arms procurement as essential to maintaining their power base. Without democratic and economic development, the climate is not conducive to either progress or innovation. As the former Soviet dissident Natan Sharansky has said: "In a democracy, the leader has to be concerned about the well-being of his people. For him, war is always the last resort, because people want to avoid war at all costs. A dictator, however, does not depend on his people; the people depend on him. His primary goal, and greatest headache, is how to keep the people under control. To do so, he always needs an enemy, against whom he can constantly mobilize his people. The enemy can be an external one, an internal one, or if the dictator, like Stalin, is particularly adept, both external and internal concurrently."[20]

International Terror

Before September 11, terrorist groups most often attacked relatively small, select targets—political figures, airlines, multinational corporations—using conventional weapons of low lethality to achieve clearly defined goals that advanced their ideological or political objectives. Even though today's terrorists still target political leaders (e.g., three failed attempts in 1995 to assassinate Egypt's President Hosni Mubarak, and the IRA's attempts to blow up Ten Downing Street in the early nineties), they appear to prefer mass attacks on random civilians with the explicit intent of inflicting as much damage, high lethality, and international visibility as possible.

The new policy of targeting civilians was first presented publicly by Osama bin Laden in his February 1998 *fatwa* (religious edict). He said that any Muslim striving for God's rewards should "kill the Americans and plunder their money, wherever and whenever they find it."[21] This view was reiterated in an article written by Abu Aiman al-Hilali, a senior member of al-Qaeda:

> The citizens of the democratic western countries take full part in the decisions taken by their governments. The residents of those countries are not classified as "civilians" as they were classified during previous wars in history. In light of their influence on the decisions taken by their governments, they do not comply with the definition of "elderly, women and children" (who are immune from being targeted in terror attacks). . . . The western citizens who object to the actions of their governments are but a minority and lack substantial influence. They can not be separated from the entire population during an attack [by al-Qaeda].[22]

The Globalization of Terrorism

Most modern international terrorist organizations were trained, sponsored, and supported by the Soviet Union and its surrogates to help expand Marxism and Leninism.[23] To them, Communist domination meant the absence of national boundaries and the presence of a globalized Communist world order. According to the *Soviet Military Encyclopedia,* their objective was to conduct unconventional warfare to subvert and destabilize the targeted nations. The Soviets trained the PLO and various nationalists groups in guerrilla and terror techniques, and then used those groups to expand Soviet influence.

The Soviet Bloc continued to train PLO terrorists in countries as diverse as Cuba, Vietnam, South Africa, Bulgaria, and Hungary, until the Soviet Union's demise in 1991. All terrorists who were schooled by the Soviets or their allies received Marxist/Leninist indoctrination as part of their training.[24] Such indoctrination was also part of the training provided by the PLO in Lebanon, with the assistance of the Eastern Bloc, to terrorists from all over the world. In addition to training Middle Eastern terrorists, these camps also trained recruits from many different parts of the world, including Holland, Turkey, Japan, and Ireland. Instructors working for the PLO included East Germans, Hungarians, Bulgarians, and Russians. Eastern Bloc countries supplied material support like weapons and tanks.[25] The PLO oversaw these camps until it was expelled from Lebanon in 1982. Since then, Hizballah in Lebanon, supported by Iran and Syria, has taken over the training of terrorists.

The Soviets specifically linked drugs and terrorism as part of their strategy. The *Soviet Military Encyclopedia,* in its 1979 edition, provides a list of *measures to be used in peacetime* to promote Soviet foreign policy objectives. These measures include the use of "poisons and narcotics" as weapons against the West.[26] Involvement in illicit drug trafficking grew among terrorist organizations like the Revolutionary Armed Forces of Colombia (FARC),[27] the PLO in the Middle East, the Liberation Tigers of Tamil Eelam (LTTE) in Sri Lanka, and the Provisional Irish Republican Army (PIRA) in Ireland. This growing involvement in the illicit drug trade reinforced the alliance and intensified cooperation between nationalistic terrorist groups and criminal organizations.

In fact, terror groups that were trained by the Soviets and their surrogates all seem to have adopted this strategy. For example, Antonio Farach, a Nicaraguan diplomat and former member of the Sandinista régime, explained how the Sandinistas trafficked in drugs: "In the first place, drugs did not remain in Nicaragua; the drugs were destined for the United States. Our youth would not be harmed, but rather the youth of our enemies. Therefore, the drugs were used as a political weapon against the U.S. The drug trafficking [provided] a very good economic benefit, which we needed for our revolution. We wanted to provide food for our people with the suffering and death of the youth of the U.S."[28]

The PLO turned to international drug trafficking and criminal organizations as it began to globalize in the late sixties. Documents discovered in Lebanon in 1982, following the expulsion of the group, expose in minute detail how the PLO committed itself even in its earliest days "to alliances on the international scene" and "to bring about international measures, and especially UN resolutions . . . which will tighten the isolation of the Zionist and the American enemy."[29]

Ideological Transformation

Once the Soviet Union imploded and Islamist fundamentalism exploded, Communism was often replaced by the belief in radical versions of Islam, but the arena for terrorist operations remained the same—the international stage. Muhammad replaced Marx and Lenin, and radical Islam replaced the Socialist nationalist doctrines of the Arab revolutionaries. The collapse of the Soviet Union served as the catalyst for an alliance between radical Sunni and Shiite movements that helped to revive Islamist fundamentalism. Their new religious ideology offered divine guidance: suffering and frustration in this world were explained as trials on the road to martyrdom and paradise. The more the believer suffered and sacrificed, the richer would be his eternal reward. Improvement in technology and communications—and the increasingly heightened vitriol in Islamist rhetoric—only helped to make today's radical Islamist terrorists even more dangerous than their nationalist predecessors.

After his successful Islamic revolution in Iran, the Ayatollah Khomeini began calling for the unification of Muslims throughout the world, and for exporting his Muslim Revolution to wherever Muslims live so that Muslim domination could be achieved. "We are at war against Infidels," the Ayatollah told a large group of Pakistani military officers on a pilgrimage to Qom in January 1980. "Take this message with you . . . I ask *all Muslims* [emphasis added] . . . to join the Holy War. There are many enemies to be killed or destroyed. *Jihad* must triumph." He stressed that the "Iranian Experiment" should be followed, and that the realization of the true Islamic State should be carried out forcibly and without compromise.[30]

These plans for Islamic unification were accelerated by the Gulf War. The war helped the leaders of Islamist groups throughout the globe to enforce their vision that *Jihad,* holy war, is the only formula for protecting Islam from extinction by the West—led by the U.S. This opinion was and is repeatedly voiced by every Islamist leader. "Bush and Thatcher have revived in the Muslims the spirit of *Jihad* and martyrdom," wrote the Palestinian leader of the Islamic Jihad, Sheikh As'ad Bayyud al-Tamimi, on the eve of the Gulf War. He promised that all Muslims "will fight a comprehensive war and ruthlessly transfer the battle to the heart of America and Europe. . . . Islamic *Jihad* has the forces to carry out strikes in Europe and America."[31] Westerners might have considered statements like this to be pure rhetoric designed solely for domestic consumption, and might have dismissed them. But, to judge by events, the leaders of the international Islamist movement meant what they said.

The Legacy of Narco-Terrorism

Some Islamist terrorist organizations had early exposure to the Soviet drug-trafficking doctrine, and most depend upon revenues from illegal drugs, especially Afghan heroin sales, as their major source of funding. In 2001, Afghanistan produced 80 percent of the heroin sold in Europe, according to the U.S. Drug Enforcement Administration (DEA),[32] and more than 70 percent of the heroin that was sold worldwide. (Surprisingly, the report makes no mention of the fact that al-Qaeda benefited from the revenues generated by this trade.)

Moreover, despite the war in Afghanistan in 2001, and despite the presence of the International Security Assistance Force (ISAF), opium production for the year 2002 is estimated to have been between thirty-five hundred and four thousand tons[33]—up 10 percent from the year 2000. That quantity of opium, when refined, would yield 350 to 400 tons of heroin—amounting to an estimated profit, for 2002, of U.S.$6 billion.

From Afghanistan, heroin is moved to expanding international consumer markets through various routes:[34]

- To Europe through Pakistan and Turkey or the Balkans
- To the United States through Pakistan via the port of Karachi
- To Moscow through Pakistan, Central Asia, and Chechnya
- To Europe through the Central Asian Republics to Moscow and from there by air to Iraq[35]

Another route to Europe passes through Pakistan and from there to the Gulf States, Saudi Arabia, Egypt, and Lebanon.[36] All the countries through which the heroin is transferred are also affected by the growing number of people who are exposed and become addicted, and by growing criminal activity.

Terrorist groups that most benefit from the trade in heroin, cocaine, methamphetamines, and hashish include al-Qaeda, Hizballah, the Irish Republican Army (IRA), and the Revolutionary Armed Forces of Columbia (FARC).[37] For the year 2000, for example, revenues generated from illegal drugs for the FARC alone have been determined by U.S. experts to be at least $7 to $8 billion.[38]

From Drugs to Dollars

In January 2002, as part of the U.S. Drug Enforcement Administration's "Operation Mountain Express," members of a Hizballah drug ring were captured by U.S. and Canadian law enforcement. This action resulted in the arrests of three hundred people who had been selling methamphetamines in Detroit, Cleveland, Chicago, Phoenix, Los Angeles, San Francisco, and other cities in California. The DEA also seized $16 million in U.S. currency; 8 real estate properties; 160 cars; 181 pounds of methamphetamines; 30 tons of pseu-doephedrine, and 9 methamphetamine laboratories.

According to the DEA, a significant portion of the drug sales revenues had been sent to the Middle East to support Hizballah, HAMAS, and al-Qaeda terror operations. Some of the money had simply been carried to the Middle East in cash. The rest of the money had been laundered and then transferred to the Middle East.[39]

Money laundering has been defined as follows:

> The Money Laundering Control Act of 1986 makes it a crime for someone, knowing that the property involved in a financial transaction represents the proceeds of some form of unlawful activity, to conduct or attempt to conduct such a financial transaction which in fact involved the proceeds of a specified unlawful activity with the intent to:
> - promote the carrying on of specified unlawful activity;
> - conceal or disguise the nature, location, source, ownership or control of the proceeds of the specified unlawful activity; or
> - avoid a transaction report requirement under state or federal law.[40]

The former managing director of the International Monetary Fund (IMF) Michel Camdessus has estimated that the global volume of laundered money in 1999 amounted to between 2 and 5 percent of the world's gross domestic product—or approximately $1.8 trillion dollars. (This estimate, however, did not take into account the huge volume of money laundered through the businesses and charities of terrorist organizations; these funds were not yet considered suspect.)

Most money laundering operations are conducted through unregulated financial centers known as *Offshore Financial Centers* (OFCs). A 1999 International Monetary Fund report estimated annual global offshore assets at roughly $4.8 trillion.[41] These tax havens do not require either the owners of the accounts or the beneficiaries of the transactions to disclose their identities; nor do they require reports on any transactions. The OFCs have no uniform guidelines to identify suspicious transactions, no effective means of monitoring cross-border currency movements, and no requirements for maintaining financial records.[42]

OFCs include *shell banks* and *shell companies*—fictitious corporations that are created to conceal the identities of their owners, whose names never appear on the registration papers. Only the names of the local representatives or the "nominees"[43] are listed. The company's activities are couched in obscure and vague terms that satisfy lenient and permissive local requirements. Once money is safely deposited in such a "corporate" account, it can easily be transferred.

Another way to launder money is simply to convert cash into money orders. Since the proceeds of drug sales are usually in cash, members of U.S. terrorist cells can take the cash to banks and post offices to purchase money orders in sums smaller than $10,000. (Transactions in excess of $10,000 are reported to the government.) Members of terrorist cells then send the money orders overseas "to support their families," as countless immigrants in the U.S. do with legitimate money.

Money also can be laundered through systems similar to the Black Market Peso Exchange (BMPE) used by the Colombian drug cartels. According to the U.S. government's *2002 National Money Laundering Strategy:* "Typically, narcotics dealers sell Colombian drugs in the U.S. and receive U.S. dollars. The narcotics traffickers thereafter sell the U.S. currency to a Colombian black market peso broker's agent in the U.S. [at a discounted rate]." The Colombian BMPE then deposits the agreed-upon equivalent sum in pesos into the drug dealer's bank account in Colombia. U.S. dollars deposited in the Colombian peso broker's account in the U.S. are then sold to Colombian business-men, who use the dollars to import products from the U.S. into Colombia. The drug trafficker has succeeded in converting drug dol-lars into pesos without transferring the money abroad, and has also avoided U.S. reporting requirements.[44]

Terrorists and other criminals often call upon members of legiti-mate professions such as accountants and lawyers to help move and hide their money. "Money laundering is now an extremely lucrative criminal enterprise in its own right," stated the U.S. Senate Commit-tee on Government Affairs:

> The Treasury's investigations have uncovered members of an emerging criminal class—professional money launders that aid and abet other criminals through financial activities. . . . They are accountants, attorneys, money brokers, and members of other le-gitimate professions. They need not become involved with the un-derlying criminal activity except to conceal and transfer the proceeds that result from it. They are drawn to their illicit activity for the same reason that drug trafficking attracts new criminals to replace those who are convicted and imprisoned—greed. Money laundering, for them, is an easy route to almost limitless wealth.[45]

The "Super Hawala"

Terrorists also clandestinely transfer money through the *hawala*, an informal exchange in which payments are delivered without money actually being moved. Say you wish to transfer $20,000 to your friend in Karachi. Since you conduct business both here and in Karachi, someone gives you $20,000 here, and you arrange with your business contact in Karachi to give $20,000—or its equivalent—to your friend. Money never leaves the U.S., yet the funds are delivered. The process is totally untraceable.

There are even official *hawaladars* who conduct a *hawala* trans-action for a fee of 1 percent. The advantages of transferring money through the *hawala,* according to the U.S. government's *2002 National Money Laundering Strategy,* are the low overhead, the integration with existing business activities, and the ability to avoid taxation and foreign exchange regulations. A *hawala* transaction is often completed more rapidly than international wire transfers that involve corresponding banks. For customers in the U.S. who do not have a social security number or adequate identification, opening a bank account can be problematic. But the *hawaladar* requires only the customer's cash and some link for trust, usually one based on a cultural or ethnic relationship. The *Money Laundering Strategy* continues: "The anonymity and lack of paper trail also hide the remittance from the scrutiny of tax authorities. Lastly, some areas of the world are poorly served by traditional financial institutions, while the *hawaladar* may offer a viable alternative."[46] For terrorists, there could hardly be a system that is faster or more discreet.

Technology has enabled an even greater "super *hawala*" system to arise—one devoid of the ethnic or personal components that infuse traditional *hawala* transactions. Although the Bank Secrecy Act requires financial institutions to file reports and record transactions, improvements in technology permit "peer to peer" transactions to take place even without financial institutions. As the *Money Laundering Strategy* states, "Internet money transfers and new payment technologies such as 'e-cash,' electronic purses, and smart-cards based electronic payment systems, make it more difficult for law enforcement to trace money laundering activity, and easier for money launderers to use, move, and store their funds. These faceless transactions and the greater anonymity they may afford pose new challenges to law enforcement that must be addressed."[47]

Attempts to Stop Money Laundering

How well does the U.S. government stop terrorist money? Not very. To trace money—or commodities—that fund terrorism, the government tends to rely on sophisticated technologies such as special computer programs to detect suspicious transactions. However, since money is often provided to terrorists through legitimate businesses and institutions such as non-governmental organizations or even international aid organizations,[48] and through various charities, no amount of technology can detect where each dollar goes. Money is interchangeable; when there is a mix of legitimate and illegitimate funds how can anyone identify which dollar bill came from where?

On October 26, 2001, when it had become apparent that the laws in place before September 11 were not sufficient to stop the flow of money to criminals and terrorists, and on the premise that without money terrorists would not be able to operate, the U.S. Congress enacted the USA PATRIOT Act.[49] The new act better enabled the U.S. government to identify suspicious transactions, to trace money, and to stop the laundering of money. As part of this effort, the U.S. Treasury Department also established Operation Green Quest (OGQ)—a "multi-agency terrorist financing task force" that focuses on the coordination among all U.S. law enforcement agencies in "identifying, disrupting, and dismantling the financial infrastructures and sources of terrorist funding."[50]

Additionally, in July 2002, the U.S. government put into place its National Money Laundering Strategy (NMLS) to "deny terrorist groups access to the international financial system, to impair the ability of terrorists to raise funds, and to expose, isolate, and incapacitate the financial networks of terrorists."[51] Also, the United Nations Security Council adopted Resolutions 1373 and 1390, requiring member nations to join the U.S. in its effort to disrupt terrorist financing. And U.S. Government Executive Order 13244 was set in place to "block property and prohibit transactions with persons who commit, threaten to commit, or support terrorism."

In March 2003, to better coordinate the government's efforts to stop the flow of money to terrorists at home and abroad, the U.S.

Department of Treasury established a new "Executive Office for Terrorist Financing and Financial Crimes (EOTF/FC)."[52]

Nevertheless, although 166 countries had blocking orders in force, by April 2003 only $124 million in assets had been frozen—$88 million overseas and $36 million in the U.S.[53] According to frustrated U.S. intelligence sources, despite cooperation agreements, some European countries unfroze or released some of the assets on the grounds that the U.S. did not provide the requisite information to warrant the seizure. Moreover, a U.S. request to freeze Hizballah's assets was refused outright by Syria and Lebanon, who claimed that Hizballah is "a resistance group and not a terrorist organization."[54]

Anti-money-laundering laws, like any other laws, are effective only when they are implemented. Unfortunately, there seems to be little political will to apply and enforce existing laws—often because of stated "other political priorities" that come between the laws and their implementation.

Technological surveillance of financial transactions has yielded some positive results. However, most information received by U.S. intelligence about funds belonging to terrorist organizations has come from human sources, and not from the super-sophisticated electronic surveillance technology upon which U.S. intelligence is so reliant. A better way to intercept the money before it reaches terrorists would be to better identify the people who deposit it.

Legitimate Fronts

In addition to illegal businesses such as drug trafficking and money laundering, terrorist groups have established legitimate businesses that serve as covers for their illegal activities, provide employment to their members, generate additional income, and serve as ideal vehicles to launder money.

Money made through drug trafficking might be invested in farmland in South America, prime real estate in London, or hedge funds in the U.S. Perfect laundering vehicles are cash-and-carry businesses such as pizzerias and car washes—how can an investigator prove that any part of the profits was not generated by the legitimate business? Since the money is either laundered before it is invested or made legitimate afterward, its presence in legal enterprises makes it difficult to trace.

Moreover, the ability to integrate illegal funds into legitimate businesses helps provide those businesses with unlimited sources of money. This not only weakens the ability of law-abiding businesses to compete, but also severely undermines the economies in which they operate.

A recent example of a legitimate business that allegedly serves as a front for terrorist activities is Ptech, a computer software company in Quincy, Massachusetts. Ptech, which is privately held, uses artificial intelligence to provide organizations with a blueprint of their operations and tools to analyze their data.[55] Ptech was raided by U.S. federal agents on December 6, 2002. Apparently a secret owner of the company was Yassin al-Qadi, a Saudi millionaire. After September 11, al-Qadi was listed on the United States Treasury Department's Specially Designated Global Terrorist Entity List for allegedly funneling millions of dollars to al-Qaeda through the Muwafaq Foundation, a Saudi charity that he headed. Among the company's clients were the FBI, the FAA, the U.S. Air Force, the U.S. Naval Air Systems Command, the Department of Energy, and NATO. Federal agents involved in the case anonymously voiced their concern not only that Ptech was suspected of being a front for al-Qaeda, but that it was also using the software it had supplied to these agencies to access the government's data. Moreover, if the allegations against Ptech prove true, there is room for concern about Ptech's involvement in designing the Rocky Flats nuclear plant near Denver for the Department of Energy.[56]

Osama bin Laden's own legitimate fronts were first established in

Sudan in 1983.[57] His investments included: peanut and sunflower farms; a bakery; a furniture company; International al-Ikhlar Company, which produced honey and sweets; Bank of Zoological Resource, a cattle-breeding operation; and the Laden International import/export company. (In 1996 bin Laden was expelled from Sudan under extreme pressure from the U.S. and Saudi Arabia, and the Sudanese president Omar al-Bashir announced that his businesses were liquidated, but as late as 2001 his holdings in Sudan were estimated at about $30 million.)[58] Other al-Qaeda investments included an ostrich farm and shrimp boats in Kenya, agricultural holdings in Tajikistan,[59] and, according to U.S. and European intelligence sources, between fifteen and fifty cargo freighters around the world.[60]

Based on a U.N. report, the war on terrorism seems to have had little effect thus far on Osama bin Laden's fortune. "A large portfolio of ostensibly legitimate businesses," the *Washington Post* reported, "continue to be maintained and managed on behalf of Osama bin Laden and al Qaeda by a number of as yet unidentified intermediaries and associates across North Africa, the Middle East, Europe and Asia [and the United States]."[61]

Osama bin Laden's legitimate fronts make it easier for him to achieve his stated goal—to destroy the U.S. economy. As he said in a video released after the September 11 attacks, "It is very important to concentrate on striking the American economy with every possible means. Hit hard the American economy at its heart and its core."[62] The September 11 attacks were estimated by the end of 2002 to have cost the U.S. economy at least $135 billion.[63]

Where the Money Is . . . and How It Got There

If you want to move money in larger quantities, you need a bank. The bigger the bank, the easier it is to avoid scrutiny, especially when you regularly use the bank to conduct business transactions.

For instance, Osama bin Laden's financial officer in Sudan until

1996, Mustafa Ahmed al-Hisawi (AKA Sheikh Saeed), held an account at the Dubai Islamic Bank. In the months prior to the September 11 attacks, al-Hisawi deposited $148,895 into bank accounts in Dubai that were held by two of the September 11 hijackers. These accounts were in the Dubai Islamic Bank, as well as in Hong Kong Shanghai Bank (HSBC Holdings) and Citibank. The money was then wire-transferred to the hijackers' accounts in Sun-Trust Bank in Florida.

In 1999, the U.S. government had identified the Dubai Islamic Bank as having laundered money for bin Laden.[64] After September 11, SunTrust reported one of the suspicious transactions to the U.S. Treasury's Financial Crimes Enforcement Network.[65] Further, on September 25, 2001, Luxembourg's commission for supervising financial institutions cited the Dubai Islamic Bank as having links with Osama bin Laden and terrorism.[66] Despite all this, as of December 3, 2002, the Dubai Islamic Bank was still absent from the U.S. Specially Designated Nationals and Blocked Persons list.[67]

In another example, in 2002 the Israel Defense Forces discovered Palestinian documents in Ramallah indicating that the Amman-based Arab Bank had been a primary recipient of funds from Saudi Arabia, Syria, and Iran to be awarded to families of Palestinian homicide bombers.[68] The documents also revealed that Saudi charitable organizations had been transferring money through Arab Bank branches in the West Bank to organizations linked to HAMAS, also to be given to families of homicide bombers.[69] The Arab Bank was also used by Iran to funnel money to Fatah's al-Aqsa Martyrs Brigades for weapons, bomb-making materials, and other expenses, such as preparations for an attack that killed six Israelis.[70] In addition, the Arab Bank was identified by the Spanish authorities as having transferred money from the al-Qaeda cell in Spain to members involved in the September 11 attacks, and as having wired money to al-Qaeda members in Yemen and Pakistan.[71]

Yet another bank, the Saudi-owned al-Taqwa Bank, was identified by the Swiss authorities in 1995 as having links to terrorist organizations—but the Swiss authorities kept that information to themselves. Subsequently, in 1996, Italian intelligence also linked the al-Taqwa bank to terrorist groups: the Egyptian Jama'at al-Islamiyya, the Algerian Armed Islamic Group (GIA), and several Palestinian terror organizations.[72] Nevertheless, when in 1997 the FBI learned of the bank's activities,[73] the al-Taqwa Bank was allowed to continue its operations. It was only in November 2001 that the U.S. Treasury Department froze the assets of sixty-two individuals and organizations associated with al-Taqwa—or the Saudi charity al-Barakaat—on the grounds that these institutions provided fundraising, financial services, communications, weapons procurement, and shipping services for al-Qaeda.[74]

IN THE SPIRIT OF CHARITY

In the year 2000 alone Americans donated $133 billion dollars to humanitarian charities.[75] How much of it ultimately ended up funding the attacks on the World Trade Center and the Pentagon?

Charity is required of Muslims through a system called *Zakat*—an Islamic tithe specifying that at least 2.5 percent of one's income should be donated every year. Many charities, however, appear to have been diverting funds to terrorist groups for terror activities—including paying for homicide bombers, buying and manufacturing weapons, and funding training camps.[76]

Terrorist groups such as the PLO, al-Qaeda, HAMAS, and Hizballah have also established their own international networks of charities. In countries where governments do not provide adequate infrastructure or social services—not only in Muslim nations, but in countries worldwide—terror organizations such as the FARC in Colombia, HAMAS in the Palestinian territories, and al-Qaeda in Pakistan take advantage of this void to supply those services to people who would otherwise have no access to them. In return, the people offer their allegiance not to the government, but to the terrorists.[77] Unfortunately, alongside genuinely worthy causes such as building hospitals and supplying food, the groups pursue illicit activities such as purchasing weapons, establishing training camps, and paying families of homicide bombers. Their dual role possibly serves to legitimize and glorify terrorist activities.[78]

In Africa, for example, not only do hospitals supported by terrorist organizations serve the needy population (thus enhancing their image in the eyes of the locals), but they also provide an apparently legitimate way to obtain visas that make it easier for terrorists to infiltrate other countries.

Direct contributions from wealthy individuals also fund Islamist terrorists. It only takes a few such individuals to put into motion a great number of terror activities.[79] A disproportionately large number of these funders have been from Saudi Arabia—members of the royal family and individuals close to the Saudi government, all of whom claim their contributions went to "charity." The former chairman of the National Commercial Bank (NCB) in Saudi Arabia, Sheikh Khalid bin Mahfouz, for example, is alleged to have deposited tens of millions of dollars in London and New York directly into terrorist accounts—the accounts of the same terrorists who were implicated in the 1998 bombings of the U.S. embassies in Kenya and Tanzania, in which 224 people were killed, including twelve Americans, and more than four thousand were injured.[80] Mahfouz denies that he has funded terrorism.

STATE SPONSORSHIP

It was only after September 11 that the U.S. authorities made a serious effort to follow the money trail. Only then did the U.S. government openly acknowledge that Muslim charities—legitimate and illegitimate—were being used to collect money explicitly for a variety of illegal purposes,[81] and that *hawalas* were transferring millions to al-Qaeda and its affiliates. A vast illegal trade in commodities, such as gold and diamonds, was developing to hide terrorists' funds and launder their money. The spread of illegal arms and weapons of mass destruction internationally was persisting unchecked, and world-wide networks were producing illegal drugs and trafficking in them to fund terrorism. What the authorities did *not* acknowledge, how-ever, was the extent to which Saudi Arabia, Iran,[82] Iraq,[83] Pakistan,[84] Syria,[85] and Sudan[86] were sponsoring the most virulent terror net-works, such as al-Qaeda, Hizballah, and HAMAS.[87]

Before September 11, terrorism experts had considered the implo-sion of the Soviet Union to be the end of state-sponsored terrorism. These experts had turned their attention instead to transnational criminal organizations and had somehow managed to miss the growing cooperation between them and terror groups. They had also managed to overlook countries that were increasing their sponsor-ship of the fast-growing Islamist terror network.

Significant support to terrorist régimes such as Iraq and North Korea has been provided by international aid organizations, which sometimes deliberately do not control the use of their humanitarian aid. Such was the case with the "oil-for-food program" run by the UN in Iraq starting in 1991; in addition to at least $36 billion skimmed by Saddam Hussein,[88] billions of dollars more flowed into the coffers of governments, companies, and politicians in Russia, Egypt, France, Germany,[89] Jordan, China, the United Arab Emirates, and the United Kingdom.[90] For example, British Labour member of Parliament George Galloway established a charitable organization, the Mariam Appeal, allegedly "to save the life of Mariam Hamza . . . and to de-mand the lifting of the sanctions on Iraq which, we believed, were causing widespread suffering to the civilian population of Iraq."[91] However, according to a letter sent by the chief of Iraq's intelligence services to Saddam Hussein, Galloway planned to arrange visits of British delegations to Iraq and "to start broadcasting programs for the benefit of Iraq and to locate Iraq On Line for the benefit of Iraq on the internet and mobilise British personalities to support the Iraqi position."[92] For his efforts Galloway was apparently given at least $10 million, which was paid to his company "in co-operation with Mr. Galloway's wife, Dr. Amina Abu Zaid."[93] Once translated, the volumes of documents found in Iraq will no doubt reveal many more details about politicians, companies, and governments that aided Saddam Hussein's terror régime.

Saudi Arabia

State sponsorship continues to be one of the major forces sustaining Islamist terror organizations. The former head of the Saudi intelligence services, Prince Turki al-Faisal, for example, allegedly gave Osama bin Laden $200 million in 1998 to move to Afghanistan.[94] The money was intended to keep Osama bin Laden away from Saudi Arabia and to prevent him from overthrowing the Saudi royal family.

According to a report submitted to the president of the UN Security Council in December 2002, "One must question the real ability and willingness of the [Saudi] Kingdom to exercise any control over the use of religious money in and outside the country."[95] In the year 2000 alone, Saudi citizens' contributions to various Islamist groups amounted to $500 million.[96] Most of the money went to cover expenses such as salaries, pensions, and "terrorcare" services that included hospitals and schools—especially *ulemas* (religious teachers) and *madrasas*.[97] As Secretary of Defense Donald Rumsfeld pointed out: "There's a lot of money going into these so-called *madrasas*— and they aren't training people in mathematics or languages or sciences or whatever, humanities—they're training people to kill. They're training people to go out and kill innocent men, women and children. And we need to see that those schools are closed down, and we need to see that those schools provided [are] teaching the right things, so that people can live a constructive life in this world."[98] In *Wahabi* schools in the U.S., students are taught that "it is better to shun and even to dislike Christians, Jews and Shiite Muslims." Moreover, hurting and stealing from non-Muslims is permissible.[99]

Despite U.S. requests that the Saudi government take action to stop funding terrorist organizations and *madrasas* that breed hate, the Saudis have "in fact only taken 'baby steps'" in that direction.[100]

Saudi Arabia continues its efforts to enlist the Muslim population worldwide to the radical *Wahabist* way of life.[101] "The angry form of Islamism and Wahhabism in Saudi Arabia today is the soil in which anti-Western and anti-American terrorism grows," stated former CIA director R. James Woolsey.[102] *Wahabism* is the Saudi branch of Islam, established by Sheikh Muhammad bin Abd al-Wahab (1703/4–91). At its core is al-Wahab's decree that, in addition to the known Five Pillars of Islam, there is a sixth, hidden pillar: fighting the *Jihad* to spread Islam and to defeat its enemies.

According to scholar Daniel Pipes, "*Wahhabism* is the extremist vision of Islam that predominates in Saudi Arabia."[103] It is this version of Islam that has "pervaded the Saudi education system with its heavy doses of mandatory religious instruction" and that has "seeped outside the classroom through mosque sermons, television shows and the Internet, coming to dominate the public discussions on religion."[104]

The Saudi government English weekly *Ain-al-Yaqeen* bragged that the royal family and the Saudi Kingdom have spent billions of dollars "to spread Islam to every corner of the earth."[105] According to *Ain-al-Yaqeen*, the Islamic Center in Brussels, Belgium, received a total of more than $5 million; the Islamic Center in Geneva, Switzerland, receives annual support of close to $7 million; and the biggest Islamic Center in Europe, which the Saudis built in Madrid, Spain, received close to $8 million in total.[106] The Saudi Kingdom's efforts, under the leadership of King Fahd bin Abd al-Aziz, "has been astronomical, amounting to many billions of Saudi Riyals . . . [resulting in] 210 Islamic centers . . . more than 1,500 mosques and 202 colleges . . . and 2,000 schools for educating Muslim children in non-Islamic countries in Europe, North and South America, Australia and Asia."[107]

The Islamic Society of North America (ISNA) is the front organization through which the Saudis promote *Wahabism* in the U.S. In 2000, ISNA, through the North American Islamic Trust, funded 27 percent of the estimated 1,209 mosques in the United States, according to a report by the Council on American-Islamic Relations (CAIR).[108] Every fifth mosque has a full-time school and three quarters have a weekend school. According to this report, some thirty thousand adults and eighty thousand children attended a mosque's weekend school in the year 2000.[109]

From 1973 to the end of 2002, the Saudi Kingdom's spending to promote *Wahabism* worldwide (lately particularly in the West and especially in the U.S.) was estimated by Reza F. Safa, the author of *Inside Islam,* at $87 billion.[110] A major motive behind the Saudi royal family's funding of the proselytization and expansion of *Wahabism* throughout the world seems to be an attempt to hold onto its throne.[111] Ironically, it was also probably more the Saudi Royals' attempt to increase their influence than a desire to support democratic systems that led them to be among the major contributors to the first democratic elections held in the Muslim former Soviet republics, and the major sponsors of the Islamic political party, the Justice and Development Party (AKP), that won Turkey's October 2002 general election.[112]

In November 2002, *Newsweek* broke the story that Princess Haifa al-Faisal, the daughter of the late King Faisal and the wife of the Saudi ambassador to the U.S., had contributed tens of thousands of dollars to two of the World Trade Center homicide bombers. She claimed that she was deceived and that the funds were transmitted to the hijackers without her knowledge. The U.S. government tried to suppress the story for over a year, until on November 23, 2002, it was reported in *Newsweek* by Michael Isikoff and Evan Thomas.[113] In the meantime, the FBI investigation into this payment exposed another payment of $400,000, made by the Saudi embassy in the late 1990s to a Saudi-based charity, the International Islamic Relief Organization (IIRO), whose offices in Virginia were raided and shut down in March 2002. The IIRO was implicated in funding the 1993 World Trade Center bombing, as well as the 1998 bombing of the U.S. embassies in Kenya and Tanzania.

Even after the al-Qaeda attack in Riyadh in May 2003 that killed at least thirty-four people, including eight Americans,[114] the U.S. government does not seem eager to name Saudi Arabia as a state that sponsors terrorism, or to prosecute Saudi businessmen and organizations that fund terror.[115] The government is currently negotiating with the Saudis about whether or not to block the lawsuit brought by the families of the September 11 attacks "on the grounds that it could impair American foreign relations."[116]

Other States

Iran not only carried out *Jihad* against those within its borders who did not adhere to the Ayatollah Khomeini's version of fundamentalism;[117] it also expanded the *Jihad* internationally by funding likeminded organizations such as Hizballah. Iran opened training camps for terrorists and provided them with funds for terrorist attacks. Radical states such as Libya, Syria, Sudan, Pakistan, and Afghanistan soon followed the Iranian example, opening training camps and funding terror organizations—with or without the cover of religion.[118]

In contrast to Iran, Iraq, a secular state, initially fought for the unification of the Arab world through the message of Pan-Arabism—a secular movement that attempted to unite all Arab nations. It was only shortly before the outbreak of the Gulf War that Saddam Hussein added *Jihad* to Pan-Arabism in an apparent effort to gain more support in the Muslim world.

From its inception in 1964 until September 2000, Yasser Arafat's Palestine Liberation Organization (PLO) had historically been a nationalist movement. Arafat only embraced *Jihad* when he launched the September 2000 attack on Israel, apparently to distract the Palestinian population from their growing fury and daily frustration over the vast corruption and human rights abuses committed by his régime. Although Arafat claimed that the September 2000 attack on Israel was a popular uprising, the chief of the Palestinian Security Forces' political indoctrination department, Mazen Izz al-Din, said on Palestinian National Television on May 28, 2000, that the uprising was in fact anything but. "We have to be truthful and honest and spell it out," Mazen said. "One day history will expose the fact that the whole *intifada* and its instructions came from Brother Commander Yasser Arafat." The Palestinian Authority's communications minister, Imad Faluji, at a PLO rally in the Ein Hilwe refugee camp in South Lebanon on March 9, 2001, stated that Arafat and the Palestinian Authority had planned the current uprising during July 2000—a full three months before the attacks on Israel began.[119]

Igniting another war enabled Arafat to redefine the economic decline in the territories as "sacrifices" necessary to mobilize the Palestinians against the "Zionist enemy." Instead of fulfilling his promises to better the welfare of the Palestinian people through the creation of a viable, prosperous state, Arafat created terror both at home and abroad. "There are two kinds of Arab leaders," noted an Arafat aide, "those who have all power concentrated in their hands. And those who are dead."[120] Apparently initiating the war had helped Arafat to stay in power by deflecting attention from his refusal to accept a peace proposal that had been proffered by former U.S. president Bill Clinton and former Israeli prime minister Ehud Barak.

Sudan was added to the State Department's list of countries sponsoring terrorism in 1993, and had its assets frozen by the U.S. government for not complying with UN Security Council resolutions requiring them to end all support to terrorism. Despite these actions, Sudan continues to be a safe haven for terrorists, including members of al-Qaeda, Hizballah, Jama'at al-Islamiyya, Egyptian Islamic Jihad, Palestinian Islamic Jihad, and HAMAS.[121]

Statesmen argue the difference between "moderate" and "radical" Islamic states, but this distinction is often no more than a whitewash on the part of the West, in order not to inconvenience Western foreign policy—including the policies of the U.S. "Moderate" states like Algeria, Yemen, and even Egypt are known to aid terrorism abroad. They traffic in arms, abuse human rights, and promote incitement in the media against Jews, the U.S., and the West—all while understandably attempting to stem terrorism at home.

Oppression + Corruption = Terrorism

The precursors of state sponsorship for terror organizations are corruption, domestic terrorism, and the absence of democracy. Although there are claims that poverty pushes people into the arms of terrorists, the September 11 hijackers all belonged to the middle and upper middle classes. As President George W. Bush said: "Poverty does not make poor people into terrorists and murderers. Yet poverty, weak institutions and corruption can make weak states vulnerable to terrorist networks and drug cartels within their borders."[122]

The West has long been guilty of supporting the most repressive Third World régimes—despite evidence of their corruption and often abysmal human rights records. Of the 169 countries on the World Bank's list of recipients of development loans, 135 are afflicted with various degrees of systemic corruption. The disbursement of close to $400 billion in loans to these countries between June 1946 and June

2002[123] has done little to diminish this corruption. If anything, the money has only served to strengthen the corrupt systems.

Much of the money given to Third World countries seldom reaches its intended recipients; instead it often finds its way into secret off-shore bank accounts. Former Zairian president Mobuto Sese Seko, for example, who advised Zairian civil servants, "If you want to steal, steal a little in a nice way,"[124] looted the national treasury of $4 to $10 billion and fled to the French Riviera, leaving his nation bereft—only $4 million in Swiss bank accounts was frozen. In another example, Pakistani prime minister Benazir Bhutto's husband was sent to prison for abusing his status to increase the family wealth through government contracts—no money was recovered. Similarly, Philippine president Ferdinand Marcos and his wife Imelda made off with $5 billion from the Philippine people—only $2 billion was recovered. Former Indonesian President Suharto, along with his cronies and his family, in more than thirty-two years in office helped himself to $80 billion. No money was recovered, and the three Indonesian governments that succeeded him never tried seriously to retrieve it.[125]

To curtail the growing industry of terrorism it is mandatory to combat corruption and lawlessness, even though fighting them requires the cooperation of the very entities that most benefit from them.

WHAT IS TO BE DONE?

The U.S. faces a monumental challenge in its efforts to stop international corruption, international money laundering, and international terrorism. To make matters worse, despite the existence of the USA PATRIOT Act, and despite international conventions, few countries seem to be willing to cooperate fully with the U.S. Even those that do cooperate do so mainly because of their own security concerns. They often claim that the U.S. is not providing sufficient evidence to require action, or that cooperation might conflict with their own laws, especially their bank secrecy laws, and might discourage people from depositing money in their banks, thus hurting their economies.

Presenting the National Security Strategy of the United States of America in September 2002, President George W. Bush said: "The United States will continue to work with our allies to disrupt the financing of terrorism. We will identify and block the sources of funding for terrorism, freeze the assets of terrorists and those that support them, deny terrorists access to the international financial system, protect legitimate charities from being abused by terrorists, and prevent the movement of terrorists' assets through alternative financial networks."

The war on terrorism needs to be waged on all possible fronts; liberating Afghanistan and Iraq were necessary first steps. However, the most urgent task is to stop terrorist funding—especially that which is derived from the drug trade. The funding of this evil is enormous in scope, broad in diversity, ingenious in method, and aggressive in approach.

Funding Evil draws a roadmap illustrating how terrorist organizations—especially Islamist terror organizations—are funded. To identify the patterns of terrorist funding, the book exposes the primary groups and some of the individuals that give and receive money on their behalf. The book sheds light on how these activities have gone undetected for decades while terrorists have recruited thousands to their ranks and millions to their cause—amassing fortunes in the process.

Funding Evil shows how terrorism works, and ways to defeat it. In order to end its threat, we must cut off its funds.

"This nation can lead the world in sparing innocent people from a plague of nature. And this nation is leading the world in confronting and defeating the man-made evil of international terrorism."

President George W. Bush,
State of the Union Address,
January 28, 2003

CHAPTER TWO

The Islamist Plague: Al-Qaeda

THE INFECTION

During the Soviet invasion of Afghanistan (1979–89), the Russian military attempted to thwart the *mujahideen*'s ability to fight by exposing them to a biological agent known as glanders.[1] Glanders *(Burkholderia mallei)* is a highly infectious disease endemic to Africa, Asia, the Middle East, and Central and South America. No vaccine is available; only by identifying and eliminating the sources of infection can its spread be halted.[2]

Osama bin Laden fought against the Soviets with the *mujahideen*, so it is ironic that, according to U.S. intelligence sources, he may now be capable of using the same biological weapon to kill the infidels. More troubling than al-Qaeda's potential to spread such a disease, however, is the spread of al-Qaeda itself.

Al-Qaeda was established in Afghanistan in 1982 by the Palestinian sheikh Abdallah Yussuf Azzam and Osama bin Laden, the seventeenth of fifty-two children of a wealthy Saudi construction magnate.[3] The bin Laden family's wealth is estimated at about U.S.$5 billion; Osama bin Laden's share is said to be $300 million.[4] In the early 1980s bin Laden returned to Saudi Arabia to arrange for financial support for the *mujahideen,* utilizing his family contacts with King Fahd's brother, Prince Salman, and with Prince Turki, the current Saudi ambassador to the U.K., who was chief of Saudi intelligence for twenty-five years,[5] and who since the early eighties has continued to provide assistance to Osama bin Laden and al-Qaeda.[6]

Al-Qaeda was originally named Maktab al-Khidamat (MAK), or the Mujahideen Services Bureau, and was created to support the Afghans in their war against the Soviets. As part of its recruiting efforts, MAK set up offices in more than fifty countries to advance the internationalization of *Jihad.* Osama bin Laden, with political support from the Afghan government, expanded MAK by establishing the training facilities of Masadat al-Ansar, "the central base and home-away-from-home for the Arab *mujahideen* in both Afghanistan and Pakistan."[7] By 1985, this "base" had become known as *al-Qaeda,* and the offices that had been established by MAK became the center of al-Qaeda's global presence as a terrorist organization. In 1998, bin Laden also established the World Islamic Front to serve as an umbrella organization through which to launch *Jihad* against the "Jews and the Crusaders [Christians],"[8] in cooperation with groups such as the Algerian GIA (Armed Islamic Group), the Egyptian and Pakistani Jihad groups, the Abu Sayyaf organization in the Philippines, and the Palestinian HAMAS.

So far, bin Laden's terrorist cells have infected at least ninety-four countries around the world.[9] Al-Qaeda has spread stealthily, forging alliances with Muslim and non-Muslim terrorists alike, and with international organized crime. Its camps in Afghanistan and Pakistan have trained fifty to seventy thousand Islamic fighters from at least fifty-five countries.[10] It employs "sleeper" cells in many countries, and a largely invisible financial lifeline, to carry out operations on short notice.[11] U.S. deputy secretary of defense Paul Wolfowitz, testifying before the Senate, stated that "al Qaeda is not a snake that can be killed by lopping off its head . . . it is more analogous to a disease that has infected many parts of a healthy body."[12]

THE FOUNTAIN OF WEALTH

Although the war against the Soviets in Afghanistan ended in 1989, financial support to al-Qaeda from Islamic countries did not. The major funders of al-Qaeda have been the Saudis: the Saudi Arabian royal family (who give whenever they feel like it, and as much as they like) and the Saudi Kingdom;[13] charitable organizations based in Saudi Arabia and Gulf states; banks and financial networks; legitimate businesses such as real estate, publishing, software, and construction companies; and criminal activities such as credit card fraud and pirated compact discs, prostitution rings—and most of all illegal drugs, especially heroin from Afghanistan.[14]

Along with Pakistan, Saudi Arabia continued to finance the Taliban after they seized power in Afghanistan in 1989. The Saudis and the Pakistanis also continued to provide al-Qaeda members with safe haven and logistical support. In July 2002, Laurent Murawiec of RAND Corporation presented his findings to the Pentagon's Defense Policy Board: "The Saudis are active at every level of the terror chain, from planners to financiers, from cadre to foot-soldier, from ideologist to cheerleader."[15]

Despite recent denials from Saudi Arabia that it has been a major source of funding for the Islamists, the December 2002 report to the president of the UN Security Council stated that, over the past decade alone, Saudis contributed at least $500 million to al-Qaeda. Moreover, "most of this financial backbone is still at large and able to support fundamentalist organizations."[16] Much of the funding for al-Qaeda and other Islamist terror groups is widely alleged to come from two of the biggest banking and business families in Saudi Arabia: the al-Rajhi and bin Mahfouz families. (Both families deny that they funded terrorist organizations; both claim they gave to charity.) Both manage the intricate global infrastructure of businesses, investments, and charities, and the movement of money for Islamist groups.[17]

It is hard to determine the exact amount of Saudi Arabia's financial support and charitable donations to organizations that promote the Saudi political agenda around the world; it is even harder to determine how much Saudi money has gone to support terrorism. The Saudi government has stated that at least three hundred Saudi charities distributed more than $4 billion a year[18] in the 1980s, most to "Islamic activities." All together, according to an official Saudi report, "the total amount spent by Riyadh since then was pegged at SR281 billion or approximately $70 billion."[19] The Saudis claim they had no knowledge which charities sent money to whom, or how much they sent—since the government lacked controls to register such activities or to account for them (there is no corporate or personal income tax in Saudi Arabia). However, in 1994 a royal decree had already banned "the collection of money in Saudi Arabia for charitable causes without official permission. King Fahd set up a Supreme Council of Islamic Affairs, headed by his brother Prince Sultan. . . . The council was established to control the charity financing and look into ways of distributing donations to eligible Muslim groups."[20] In December 2002, under intense American political pressure, and after revelations that Saudi charities were heavily involved in the funding of terrorism, the Saudi government hired the Washington, D.C.–based public relations firm Qorvis Communications and launched a $20.2 million campaign to try to deny the fact that they sponsor terrorism and that Saudi charities are under government control.[21] The Saudis also used the opportunity to announce new measures to increase charity accountability and transparency; it remains to be seen if these will be implemented.[22]

The connections among members of the royal family, Saudi charities, financial networks, and individual contributors to al-Qaeda became further exposed in the lawsuit brought by the families of the victims of the September 11 attacks. For example, Prince Sultan[23] has allegedly championed anti-Western Islamist causes, including al-Qaeda, for years, and publicly supported and funded Osama bin Laden and al-Qaeda—both in his capacity as defense minister and as the chairman of the Supreme Council for Islamic Affairs, which oversees charities. Prince Sultan has also allegedly supported other organizations on the Treasury Department's Specially Designated Terrorist List, including charities and businesses.[24]

CHARITY FOR DEATH

Zakat, or charity, is an integral part of Islam. However, in Saudi Arabia—as in Kuwait, the United Arab Emirates, and other oil-rich Islamic countries—the governments control the charities and often make large contributions to them. Although most of these charities perform the humanitarian tasks for which they were originally created, a significant amount of money has been diverted, directly or indirectly, to fund terrorism, as has become apparent since September 11.

Saudi charities that are known to have funded al-Qaeda and other Islamist groups often have incestuous ties with one another. Although each charity has a different name and states a different mandate, most often they support the same cause—advancing *Jihad.* Among the charities that have been supported by the prominent Saudi banking families, the al-Rajhi and the bin Mahfouz, that have been identified in either a court of law or government reports as supporting al-Qaeda, are: International Islamic Relief Organization (IIRO); Rabita Trust (which changed its name to Aid Organization of the Ulema); Benevolence International Foundation (BIF); SAAR network organizations; Taibah International Aid Association; Global Relief Foundation (GRF); World Assembly of Muslim Youth (WAMY); Islamic African Relief Charity; Saudi High Commission (AKA Saudi High Relief Commission or SRC); Saudi Joint Relief Committee; Muwafaq (or "Blessed Relief")

Foundation; al-Haramain Islamic Foundation; Mercy International Relief Organization (Mercy); and the world's largest Islamic relief organization, which serves as the umbrella for the charities mentioned above, the Muslim World League (MWL). Bin Mahfouz denies that either he or his Muwafaq Foundation funded terrorism, and, again, he and the other Saudis involved insist they gave to charity—not to al-Qaeda.

Some of the most significant al-Qaeda-linked charities are profiled below.

The Muslim World League (MWL)

The Muslim World League was founded by, and is completely funded by, the Saudi government. Since its inception in 1962, it has expanded into at least one hundred branches in more than thirty countries. MWL is also the main body for other Saudi charities such as IIRO, Rabita Trust, and the SAAR Foundation Network. It is supported by Saudi government money and by the al-Rajhi and the bin Mahfouz families' global financial and business empires—though the parties involved, especially bin Mahfouz, deny any connection to terror.

The Pakistani branch of the MWL was created to support al-Qaeda. It was funded initially by Osama bin Laden, and later by the Saudi government. MWL's chief officers in Pakistan have had close ties to Osama bin Laden, and have supported some of al-Qaeda's operations, including attempts to obtain nuclear material.[25] Other branches of the MWL were created in the U.S.—one in Herndon, Virginia, and another in New York City. Although the MWL office in Virginia was raided and closed down in the spring of 2002, its New York office remains open.

The International Islamic Relief Organization (IIRO)

The International Islamic Relief Organization, one of the many arms of the Muslim World League, was established as a non-governmental organization in 1978 in Jeddah, Saudi Arabia, "in response to the increasing need to alleviate the suffering of human beings worldwide."[26] It is still financed by "the generous people of Saudi Arabia [the al-Rajhi and bin Mahfouz families], King Fahd, and the Royal family," according to IIRO's secretary-general, Adnan Basha.[27] He also noted that the IIRO "donated more than $60 million to the Taliban."[28] Incidentally, employees of the IIRO who also worked for the MWL and al-Qaeda have stated that they were employees of the Saudi government.[29]

The IIRO charity has used more than 70 percent of its funds to purchase weapons, thereby securing its status as a front for al-Qaeda's illegal activities (the rest of the funds were used for legitimate public works).[30] The Arabic periodical *Rose al-Yusuf* described the IIRO as "firmly entrenched with Osama bin Laden's al Qaeda organization."[31] The IIRO has also directly funded the Egyptian branch of al-Qaeda, the al-Jihad organization, and has moved money to, and received money from, one of its sister organizations, the International Relief Organization (IRO). The IRO, in turn, has financed the Success Foundation, which also allegedly received money directly from Khalid bin Mahfouz; both organizations appear to have sponsored al-Qaeda, HAMAS, and Hizballah. Official Palestinian documents discovered by the Israel Defense Forces in April 2002 list IIRO donations of at least $280,000 to Palestinian organizations that the U.S. has linked to HAMAS.[32]

Relations between the IIRO and al-Qaeda can be illustrated by the activities of the IIRO office in the Philippines. Osama bin Laden's brother-in-law Muhammad Jamal Khalifa headed the IIRO office in the Philippines and, in the early 1990s, cofounded the Philippine Abu Sayyaf terrorist organization. Khalifa served as Abu Sayyaf's chief adviser, overseeing its expansion, as well as that of the Philippine terrorist group the Moro Islamic Liberation Front (MILF). Khalifa, who was wanted by the Jordanian authorities for bombing a movie theater in Jordan in 1994, escaped to the U.S. and was extradited to Jordan, where he managed to stay out of jail. He was finally arrested in California in December 2001.[33]

The IIRO has been identified as a conspirator in:

- The 1993 World Trade Center bombing
- Plots to destroy the bridges and tunnels of New York City
- An attempt to blow up twelve American airliners simultaneously
- The 1998 bombings of the United States embassies in Kenya and Tanzania.

The IIRO was also involved in a conspiracy to assassinate former president William Jefferson Clinton and Pope John Paul II.[34]

After September 11, the U.K.'s Charity Commission "took the IIRO off its list of registered charities on grounds it did not function as one"—however, the U.S. did not. The IIRO offices in Virginia were raided by U.S. law enforcement in March 2002, but remain open. Apparently the Saudi Arabian government's denial that the IIRO has done anything other than to provide humanitarian aid to widows and orphans was persuasive enough for the U.S. government not to add the IIRO to its terrorist blacklist.[35]

SAAR Foundation

Another arm of the Muslim World League, the SAAR Foundation, was formed in the 1970s by Sulaiman Abdul Aziz al-Rajhi, the head of the al-Rajhi banking family—his initials are the name of the foundation. Like the IIRO and the MWL, the SAAR Foundation also opened offices in the U.S. SAAR was registered as a nonprofit organization in Herndon, Virginia, on July 29, 1983. In a pattern that has become common for organizations and financial entities affiliated with al-Qaeda, the organizations shared the same officers, and often even the same offices, with the MWL. In addition, the Virginia Secretary of State Corporate Records showed that SAAR's address in Herndon was registered as the address for more than one hundred SAAR-affiliated organizations—which had no offices, no staff, and no telephones—

but which were used to provide financial and logistical support for Osama bin Laden and al-Qaeda operations.[36]

SAAR's office in Tampa, Florida, was raided in 1995, following suspicions that SAAR activists in Florida were financing HAMAS and the Palestinian Islamic Jihad. Subsequent investigations by the FBI were described by a U.S. official close to the probe: "At the end of the day the progress can be best described as marginal." According to the same official, the investigation floundered because of the fear the probe would be seen as ethnic profiling.[37]

The SAAR Foundation, like other Muslim charities, did not hold fundraisers; yet, for 1998 alone, SAAR reported revenues of more than $1.8 billion—more than any U.S. charity has ever generated.[38] Among its donors were businesses such as the al-Rajhi family–owned Mar-Jac Investments and Mar-Jac Poultry; Reston Investments; York Foundation; and Safa Trust—all still registered and doing business in the U.S. By using fronts, the SAAR Foundation, through its investments in the U.S. in the 1980s, became one of the Washington Beltway's biggest landlords, as well as "one of South America's biggest apple growers."[39] Although it is reported that "the SAAR Foundation officially dissolved in December 2000," SAAR still continues its operations and has merely transferred its activities and officers to its sister organization, Safa Trust.[40]

Only in March 2002 were the SAAR network organization and the homes of its top executives raided by the U.S. government's joint terrorism task force as part of Operation Green Quest.[41] Documents seized during the raid reportedly show that money from these charitable organizations was sent to al-Qaeda cells around the world, most often through the international banking system. For example, U.S. authorities claim that SAAR transferred $20 million to al-Qaeda-linked offshore banks, and at least $9 million to another Saudi charity based in the Isle of Man. A U.S. official involved in the SAAR investigations commented, "Looking at their finances is like looking into a black hole."[42]

Saudi High Commission (SHC)

Another Saudi charity is the Saudi High Commission, AKA the Saudi High Relief Commission, which was founded by King Fahd's son Prince Salman bin Abd al-Aziz al-Saud in 1993. It is lauded by Saudis as "the largest fundraising effort in the Arab and Muslim world,"[43] but the exact amount of money the SHC has raised is unknown. What *is* known is that money the SHC claimed it sent to aid needy Muslims never reached them—not the $200 million that was sent to Bosnia-Herzegovina for the Muslims of Srebrenicia in July 1995, and not the $600 million that was sent to help rebuild the battered region following its civil war.[44]

When NATO forces raided the SHC offices in Sarajevo, they found a computer hard drive containing photographs of: the World Trade Center before and after the September 11 attack; the U.S. embassies in Kenya and Tanzania; and the USS *Cole*—as well as photographs and maps of Washington, D.C., with government buildings marked. NATO forces also found:

- Information about the use of pesticides and crop dusters to disperse chemical weapons and biological agents
- Instructions on how to forge State Department IDs
- Anti-Semitic and anti-U.S. propaganda designed for children
- Close to $210,000 worth of local currency
- Twenty-four vehicles with diplomatic plates that had been used to smuggle people and matériel into Bosnia-Herzegovina[45]

The NATO forces also found that the SHC branch in Sarajevo was employing an al-Qaeda operative, Sabir Lamar. He and five other operatives, from Algeria, had been involved in a plot to attack the U.S.

and U.K. embassies in Bosnia-Herzegovina. Lamar and his accomplices were arrested, and another member of the group, the Algerian Bensayah Belkacem, was identified at the time by NATO secretary-general George Robertson as having "direct links with al Qaeda and Osama bin Laden."[46] Moreover, when Belkacem was arrested at his apartment in Zenica, Bosnia, the authorities found forged passports and a mobile telephone listing for al-Qaeda's third-in-command, Abu Zubeida.

A subsequent audit of the SHC's Sarajevo office by the financial police of the Federation of Bosnia-Herzegovina Ministry of Finance revealed that its founder, Prince Salman, had "knowingly failed to take appropriate actions regarding the management and use of funds of the SHC in Bosnia Herzegovina." In addition, the investigators found that the SHC failed to account for $41 million that was missing from the SHC operating funds.[47]

Al-Rashid Trust (ART)

A Pakistani charity, the al-Rashid Trust (ART) was established as a welfare organization in Karachi in February 1996 by Mufti Muhammad Rashid. It not only advocates *Deobandi*, the same school of thought as the Taliban; it also promotes *Jihad*. "The holy war is an essential element of Islam," wrote Muhammad Rashid. "Any Moslem must carry the weapons, even in the mosque, if the need would be felt to make fire on a not-Moslem."[48]

Rashid and his organization have close ties to the Taliban, to Osama bin Laden, and to al-Qaeda, as well as to other Islamist organizations in Pakistan.[49] For example, ART has at least twenty-one branches in Pakistan, and runs many *madrasas* and mosques in both Afghanistan and Pakistan[50]—all used to recruit *jihadis*.[51] ART not only has established networks of hospitals and clinics to treat wounded terrorists, but also continues to provide financial and legal support to jailed Islamists around the world. ART also operates a network of bakeries (with an annual budget estimated at $4 million) that provides the organization with further income, employment for the locals, and bread for the poor.[52]

ART's funds reportedly come not only from Pakistan, but also from South Africa and the Middle East. ART collects contributions in mosques and through solicitations on a British Internet site, as well as through yet another charity, the Global Jihad Fund, which raises money for other Islamist groups as well.[53]

In the year 2000 alone, according to Pakistani sources, ART sent $750,000 in cash to Islamists in Chechnya, $36,000 to Islamists in Kosovo, and $34,482 in cash to the Taliban. In addition, ART is reported to support Islamist terrorism in Kashmir, India, and Central Asia.[54] Moreover, the organization shipped at least "U.S.$1 million worth of goods, food, medicine and other relief items into Afghanistan on a weekly basis," and sent "more than 70 truckloads of relief goods up to November 2001."[55] These truckloads turned out also to have been used for smuggling heavy weapons and ammunition—disguised as food relief—to the Taliban and al-Qaeda. In December 2002, Pakistani intelligence sources were quoted as saying, "It's nonsense to believe this has stopped."[56]

In September 2001, the U.S. Treasury Department placed ART on its Specially Designated Terrorist List for its involvement in financing and supporting international terrorism. However, since the organization was still operational as of January 2002, the U.S. request of the Pakistani government to freeze ART's accounts in local banks seems to have gone unheeded.[57]

Furthermore, it was in a *madrasa* compound owned by ART that the remains of *Wall Street Journal* reporter Daniel Pearl were found. Further investigations revealed that ART had been directly involved his abduction and murder,[58] and that Ahmad Omar Sayed al-Sheikh, who was in charge of the abduction, had been assisted by the Indian mafia to obtain false documents, arrange for safe houses, and launder drug money that was used for the operation. Ahmad Omar Sayed al-Sheikh was sentenced to death by hanging by a Pakistani court on July 15, 2002.[59]

EASY BANKING

As mentioned earlier, the bigger an international bank, the more easily it can be used to launder money. When the origin of the money appears legitimate, no attention is paid to its destination. The United States has recently made efforts to correct this problem—the USA PATRIOT Act helps enforce the identification of both depositors and recipients, and the Treasury Department's Specially Designated Global Terrorist Entity List names suspect banks and individuals. However, because many transactions are conducted outside the U.S., stopping the flow of suspicious funds proves to be a difficult task.

Below are some of the financial institutions that are known to have managed the flow of al-Qaeda's money.

Al-Rajhi Bank

The Saudi-based al-Rajhi Banking and Investment Corporation describes itself as "a major name in Saudi Arabia's banking and business world . . . contributing to the Kingdom's construction and development, and always operating within the framework of *Shariah* [Islamic law] principles."[60] Founded in Riyadh in 1987, it is one of the top ten Saudi companies, comprising 378 branches in Saudi Arabia. It also manages seventeen international subsidiaries located in offshore financial centers, mostly in Jersey and other U.K. locations, as well as in the Netherlands Antilles in the Caribbean.

It was the al-Rajhi Bank that held the accounts of al-Qaeda's European financial operative, Muhammad Galeb Kalaje Zouaydi, who used the bank to transfer funds "directly to the perpetrators of September 11, 2001,"[61] and to Islamist operatives in Bali. The al-Rajhi

Bank also transferred millions of dollars from Saudi Arabia to Madrid as part of a business conspiracy between Zouaydi and King Fahd's adviser and former minister of Waqf and Islamic Affairs in Saudi Arabia, Abdullah bin Abdul Muhsen al-Turki,[62] who is currently the secretary-general of the Muslim World League.

When the Kenyan police raided the house of Osama bin Laden's personal secretary in 1997, a member of the al-Rajhi banking family, Saleh Abdulaziz al-Rajhi, was reportedly discovered to have been involved with al-Qaeda. Saleh Abdulaziz al-Rajhi's businesses in the U.S. included American subsidiaries of al-Watania Poultry, one of the largest poultry businesses in the world; Mar-Jac Poultry; Mar-Jac Investments; and Piedmont Poultry.[63]

Executives of the al-Rajhi-owned Mar-Jac Investments and the al-Rajhi-funded SAAR charitable network seem to have attempted to influence U.S. politics by making contributions to the campaign of a former Democratic U.S. representative from Georgia, Cynthia McKinney, who accepted the money despite public statements these donors made in support of HAMAS and Hizballah.[64] (In addition, a $2,000 contribution to McKinney's campaign came from Floridian Sami al-Arian—the North American head of the Iranian-supported Palestinian Islamic Jihad. Al-Arian, who was indicted in February 2003,[65] seems to have used Iraqi and Saudi money to help al-Qaeda and the September 11 hijackers, according to U.S. investigators.)[66]

In short, the al-Rajhi Banking and Investment Corporation is still a primary bank that moves money for many of the interlinked charitable organizations that support al-Qaeda, such as the Muslim World League, the International Islamic Relief Organization, and the al-Haramain Islamic Foundation. The al-Rajhi family's Mar-Jac Holdings charity is a business partner of another family charity, the SAAR Foundation (see above). SAAR is said to have unlimited access to al-Rajhi funds: "If they wanted a few million dollars, they called the al-Rajhis, who would send it along."[67] Furthermore, despite the fact that a September 11 hijacker, Abdulaziz al-Omari, held an account at al-Rajhi Islamic Bank, the bank is missing from the U.S. Treasury's Specially Designated Nationals and Blocked Persons list.[68]

National Commercial Bank (NCB)

Another bank that was widely alleged to have been used as a vehicle to fund al-Qaeda's expansion is the National Commercial Bank. The first commercial bank of Saudi Arabia, it was founded in 1950 in Jeddah, Saudi Arabia, by Salim bin Mahfouz. Even though the Saudi government stepped in to control the bank in 1999, the bank reportedly continued to fund Islamist terrorism.[69] Its general manager and chairman until January 2003 was the founder's son, Sheikh Khalid bin Mahfouz, who held 30 percent of the Bank of Credit and Commerce International (BCCI)—a share equal to that "of the controlling shareholder . . . the ruling family of Abu Dhabi"—before it was closed down for corrupt practices in 1992. The former U.S. customs commissioner William von Raab has described BCCI as the "Bank of Crooks and Criminals International," and the U.S. Federal Reserve Board stated that "Mahfouz participated in the unsafe and unsound practices of BCCI."[70]

On July 8, 1992, bin Mahfouz was indicted by the Federal Reserve, not only for helping BCCI to violate American banking regulations, but also for assisting "BCCI in a number of transactions designed by BCCI to conceal its true financial condition and ownership from its auditors, regulators, creditors, and depositors."[71] Earlier, Khalid was indicted by a grand jury in New York City for having defrauded investors in the BCCI case; the indictment cost him $225 million, barred him from any further activities in the American banking system, and forced NCB to close its branches in New York and London.[72] According to Robert M. Morgenthau, district attorney of New York County, "BCCI was operated as a corrupt criminal organization throughout its entire 19 year history. It systematically falsified its records. It knowingly allowed itself to be used to launder the illegal income of drug sellers and other criminals. And it paid bribes and kickbacks to public officials."[73]

Although the Saudi authorities had reportedly been tipped off by U.S. intelligence in 1992 that Khalid was involved in the funding of terrorism, it was only seven years later, after the bank lost large sums of money, that the Saudi government was said to have audited both the NCB and Khalid. The audit, the very existence of which bin Mahfouz denies, reportedly revealed that, over a ten-year period, the bank's Zakat Committee had transferred $74 million to the IIRO and had channeled money from the Muwafaq (Blessed Relief) Foundation to al-Qaeda.[74] It also revealed that Khalid was in debt to the bank through loans that he had made to himself. These findings led the Saudi government, in 1999, first to detain bin Mahfouz,[75] and then to buy "a controlling 50% stake of NCB from Khalid for at least $1 billion," which reportedly the government then used to eliminate a portion of his debt to the bank. The bin Mahfouz family retained 34 percent of the bank.[76]

In January 2003, the Saudi government bought out the bin Mahfouz family by purchasing all their remaining NCB stakes for $1.8 billion, which was estimated to be "2.5 times book value"—in effect nationalizing the bank. According to U.S. financial analysts, this was how the Saudis swept under the carpet the bank's and Khalid's involvement in the funding of terrorism.[77] Khalid, who is said to be recuperating from an undisclosed illness in the Saudi Arabian resort town of Taif, maintains a 16 percent holding in Jordan's Housing Bank and controlling stakes in Lebanon's Crédit Libanais.[78]

Despite the reports alleging NCB's and Khalid's involvement in drug money laundering, illegal arms sales, banking fraud, and funding terrorism, dating back to his involvement to BCCI, many luminaries in U.S. business and politics continued to maintain their association with his family and with him.[79]

Al-Barakaat Exchange

The al-Barakaat Bank, headquartered in Dubai (which was one of only three governments that maintained diplomatic relations with the Taliban, along with Saudi Arabia and Pakistan), was actively involved in the funding of terrorism. It was founded in 1989 by a Somali financier and close friend of Osama bin Laden, Ahmed Nur Jimale.[80] Jimale had become familiar with the American banking system while working between 1979 and 1986 at the Saudi American Bank, founded in Jeddah by Citibank.

Al-Barakaat North America was headquartered in Dorchester, Massachusetts, with branches in Minnesota, Ohio, and Washington State. Al-Barakaat's ties in the U.S. extended to the Royal Bank of Scotland; PLC's Citizens Bank Unit; JP Morgan Chase and Company's Chase Manhattan; KeyCorp's Key Bank Unit; First Data Corp's Western Union; and Citigroup's Citibank and SunTrust Bank. In addition, al-Barakaat worked with the American branch of al-Baraka Exchange, which financed yet another al-Qaeda-affiliated business, al-Haramain Trading, in Egypt and Chechnya. Al-Barakaat, together with still another bank, al-Taqwa, raised, managed, invested, and distributed funds for al-Qaeda; provided terrorists with Internet services; secured telephone communications; and arranged for shipments of weapons.[81]

Al-Barakaat also used the *hawala* services of another Dubai bank, the al-Baraka Exchange, to transfer close to $1 million to the September 11 hijackers[82] through Western Union Financial Services. (Western Union was fined $8 million by New York bank regulators in 2002 for violating reporting requirements, enabling money laundering, and terrorist financing.)[83]

Former treasury secretary Paul O'Neill stated that "the al Barakaat companies are the money movers, the quartermasters of terror. At core, it is a *hawala* conglomerate operating in 40 countries around the world with business ventures in telecommunications, construction, and currency exchange. They are a principal source of funding, intelligence and money transfers for bin Laden." The bank was named a Specially Designated Global Terrorist Entity, and by executive order its operations were shut down and its assets frozen on November 7, 2001.[84]

Al-Taqwa Bank

Another bank, the al-Taqwa Bank in the Bahamas, was established in 1988 by a seventy-year-old naturalized Italian citizen, Youssef Nada, with significant backing from the Islamist political group the Muslim Brotherhood.[85] Founded in Egypt in 1928, the Muslim Brotherhood rejects Western values and calls for the establishment of a pan-Islamic state founded on the basis of *sharia*—Islamic law.[86] Nada was a key figure in the Brotherhood, as well as a construction magnate. He expanded al-Taqwa's operations to include companies in Switzerland, Liechtenstein, and Italy. Under Nada, the bank carried out its international financial activities in more than thirty countries, with a strong presence in the Middle East.

The al-Taqwa Bank's presence in the Bahamas—and the lack of its presence in Saudi Arabia—made it a perfect choice for al-Qaeda's money laundering activities: it looked just like any other international bank. Al-Taqwa Bank also worked with Islamist organizations such as the Muslim Brotherhood, HAMAS, and the SAAR Network—demonstrating the incestuous relationships among organizations that sponsor al-Qaeda.

The name of the Swiss branch of al-Taqwa was changed by its owner to the Nada Management Organization. Nada Management sponsored the Islamic Center in Geneva, which the Italian antiterrorist agency DIGOS (Division of General Intelligence and Special Operations) has described as "the most important financial structure of the Muslim Brotherhood and Islamic terrorist organizations."[87] In addition, one of the center's directors, Albert "Ahmed" Huber, a neo-Nazi who converted to Islam, "acknowledged publicly that he met with members of Osama bin Laden's terrorist network in Lebanon, as far back as 1995."[88]

In 1988, the al-Taqwa Bank also founded the Islamic Cultural Center of Milan, and paid its annual rent of $25,000. A board member of the al-Taqwa bank in the Bahamas, Sante Abdulawahab Ciccarello, was placed on the board of the Milan Center. U.S. Treasury Department officials have described the center as "the main al Qaeda station house in Europe, [that facilitated] the movement of weapons, men, and money around the world."[89]

The al-Taqwa Bank not only funded al-Qaeda, but also funneled money to HAMAS, to the Algerian Islamic Salvation Front and Armed Islamic Group, and to Tunisia's An-Nahda terror organization. Al-Taqwa also funded the Qatar Charitable Society (QCS), which opened offices in Albania, Azerbaijan, Bangladesh, Bosnia, Dagestan, the Palestinian territories, Pakistan, and Sudan. According to the U.S. government, the QCS played a role in financing al-Qaeda's 1998 bombing of the U.S. Embassies in Kenya and Tanzania. And, according to the Russian Interior Minister in 1999, QCS provided funding to al-Qaeda terrorists in Chechnya.[90]

In November 2001, when the Treasury Department shut down al-Barakaat Exchange, it also froze the assets of al-Taqwa and sixty-two organizations and individuals associated with the two groups.[91]

DRUG TRAFFICKING

A significant portion of the financing of many terrorist organizations stems from the illegal drug trade.[92] Ironically, even with the new focus on preventing terrorism, once a drug trafficker is apprehended with illegal drugs, the investigation usually focuses on the drugs in his possession and not on his possible involvement in terrorism. With evidence so readily available, the terrorist is more likely to be charged with drug trafficking, for which the penalties are less severe than those for involvement in terrorism.

Because of the steadily expanding consumer market, and because drugs are easily concealed and converted into local currency, they are likely to remain a major funding source for al-Qaeda and other groups.

Al-Qaeda & the Taliban

Heroin from Afghanistan—the world's largest heroin producer—provided the Taliban with an estimated $8 billion in 1999.[93] The Taliban government, together with al-Qaeda, had taxed the poppy growers and producers of opium base and heroin—often demanding gold—while al-Qaeda provided the growers with protection from warlords and other bandits who would otherwise have stolen their crops.[94] The Taliban, during a severe drought in the region in 1999, banned poppy cultivation, then used the ban to create a positive image for itself. However, the Taliban and al-Qaeda had stashed 500 metric tons of heroin in caves in the mountains of Afghanistan (tightly packed heroin does not lose its potency over a long period of time), and the United Nations Drug Control Program (UNDCP) estimated that, for the year 2000, the opium production ban resulted in a decrease of production of only 10 percent.[95]

Although the Taliban have since been removed from power, and despite the presence of the International Security Assistance Force (ISAF) in Afghanistan, both heroin production and prices in the country are on the rise.[96] DEA sources in Afghanistan report that, following the war, al-Qaeda gave large sums of money to Afghan farmers to increase their opium production. Heroin prices are not posted publicly, and depend on the purity of the product, but according to the World Bank's officials opium prices in Afghanistan "had risen from $100 a kilo to $500," in 2001. According to World Bank president James Wolfensohn, opium cultivation generated $1.4 billion in proceeds for 2001, "compared with the $1.2 billion international aid," that went to Afghanistan.[97] He went on to warn that "we should not forget the experience of Afghanistan is a proving ground for whether the international community can stay the course beside a fragile country as it builds itself up from the after-math of conflict"—referring to the liberation of Iraq.[98]

For the year 2002, opium cultivation is estimated to be up to 3,500 to 4,000 metric tons, which would yield 350 to 400 metric tons of heroin.[99] Such a quantity of heroin would generate about $6 billion—and most of that would certainly facilitate further destabilization of the region, financing al-Qaeda and other Islamist operatives.[100]

It was bin Laden who had managed the drug profits for the Taliban and arranged money laundering operations with the Russian Mafiya—operations so complex that they have been described as "an extended and octopus-like network that uses political names in Asia and in Africa in return for commissions."[101] Bin Laden's commission of 10 to 15 percent from these money laundering operations would have provided him with an annual income of about $1 billion.[102] Since the Taliban are no longer in charge, and since heroin production is up, it is likely that al-Qaeda's and bin Laden's shares in the profits from the heroin trade have only increased.

Under the Taliban, al-Qaeda would sometimes purchase the crops directly from the growers in Kandahar, Helmand, Nangarhar, Herat, and Badakhshan provinces, and deliver them to clandestine laboratories. Conversion laboratories would then refine the opium into both morphine base and heroin.[103] The conversion labs are still operational in southern Afghanistan, particularly in the Helmand province. They are also still operational in Pakistan, particularly in the Northwest Frontier province near the Afghan border.[104]

Al-Qaeda uses its global presence not only to distribute heroin to drug trafficking organizations, but also to exchange drugs for weapons. In November 2002, Attorney General John Ashcroft announced the arrest in Hong Kong of two Pakistanis and one naturalized American citizen from India—all al-Qaeda operatives. Prior to their arrest, surveillance had confirmed the defendants' connections to al-Qaeda through telephone records at their hotel. The three were arrested in Hong Kong as a result of a sting operation in which undercover FBI agents were offered 600 kilograms of heroin and 5 metric tons of hashish in exchange for four U.S.-manufactured Stinger shoulder antiaircraft missiles[105]—similar to the SAM missiles fired at a passenger plane in Mombasa, Kenya, in November 2002.[106] The al-Qaeda members, who met the FBI agents in a hotel room, said that the Stinger missiles were destined for their Taliban friends. (Although not in power any longer, the remnants of the Taliban are still active in Southern Afghanistan.)[107] The amount of heroin they offered the FBI agents had a wholesale value of approximately $12 million, and a street value of $240 million. Additional investigations revealed that their credit cards were linked to bank accounts used by al-Qaeda.[108]

Islamic Movement of Uzbekistan (IMU)

Al-Qaeda's drug trafficking business involves other terrorist groups such as the Islamic Movement of Uzbekistan, the stated purpose of which, like al-Qaeda's, is to turn the *sharia* into the law of the land. However, the head of the Kyrgyz National Security Council, Bolot Djanuzakov, states that Islam is "only a veil . . . [the IMU's] main aim is distribution of drugs."[109] Jane's Intelligence Review also notes that "the IMU is primarily concerned with financial gain [and] successfully used terrorism [to] secure" drug conduits.[110]

To this day, the IMU's major source of funding is derived from trafficking in Afghan heroin. When the Taliban ruled Afghanistan, al-Qaeda gave the IMU access to poppy-growing areas in northern Afghanistan for a fee. The IMU still uses the drug profits to fund its own terror operations.[111]

The IMU fought alongside the Taliban, and its leaders visited bin Laden frequently. According to Russian intelligence sources, bin Laden gave more than $35 million to the IMU in exchange for sniper rifles, communication devices, and night vision goggles. This well-funded organization pays its terrorists "between $100 to $500 in U.S.

bills" per month—in a region where the average minimum wage per month is equivalent to U.S.$4.90. Interpol's Criminal Intelligence Directorate estimates that "60% of Afghan opium exports were moving through Central Asia, and the IMU may be responsible for 70% of the total amount of heroin and opium transiting through the area."[112]

The Balkan Route

The geographic and ethnic makeup of the Balkan region has facilitated smuggling for centuries. The Balkan route was—and still is—used by al-Qaeda to traffic in illegal drugs and to smuggle al-Qaeda operatives into Europe. A report prepared by Macedonia's Ministry of the Interior in the spring of 2002 not only lists al-Qaeda's operations in the Balkans, but also names 370 al-Qaeda operatives in the area. According to Macedonian officials, al-Qaeda has two major cells that include fighters from Macedonia, Kosovo, Albania, Turkey, Saudi Arabia, Pakistan, Jordan, and Chechnya.[113] The Macedonian report details, additionally, how al-Qaeda-sponsored Islamist cells use Albania, Kosovo, Macedonia, Bosnia, Bulgaria, and Turkey as their heroin highway between Southeast Asia and Europe—to which the Balkans add their homegrown poppies and marijuana.[114]

According to UN and European law enforcement reports, Islamist groups in the Balkans, together with al-Qaeda operatives and local organized crime syndicates, run prostitution rings; traffic in illegal immigrants; smuggle illegal arms, oil, cigarettes, and alcohol; and launder money.[115] And a report in the Glasgow *Herald* states that Albanian Islamists and former Kosovo Liberation Army guerrillas have used $4 million in profits from Afghan heroin, which they sold in European cities, to purchase weapons, including SA-18 and SA-7 surface-to-air missiles.[116] The Albanian network, according to Yossef Bodansky, director of the House Task Force on Terrorism and Unconventional Warfare, "was headed by Muhammad al-Zawahiri, the engineer, brother of Ayman al-Zawahiri," the Egyptian pediatrician who is bin Laden's closest adviser.[117]

South America

Another center of illegal drug trafficking for al-Qaeda is the South American tri-border region— "a lawless jungle corner of Argentina, Brazil, and Paraguay. . . . Its borders roughly consist of the Argentine port city of Puerto Iguazu, the Brazilian city of Foz Do Iguacu in Parana State, and the Paraguayan city of Ciudad del Este."[118] This no man's land is the heart of Islamist terrorist activity in Latin America, and home to tens of thousands of Muslims, mainly from the Middle East. According to the spokesman for Paraguay's National Police in Ciudad del Este, Augusto Aníbal Lima, as of September 1994 "of all the Arabs in the area, only 273 are legally registered."[119] With its porous borders, numerous unguarded waterways, and more than one hundred unmonitored, hidden airstrips, and with only infrequent passport checks, the region has become a haven for arms dealers, drug traffickers, smugglers, counterfeiters, and terrorists.[120]

According to the CIA, al-Qaeda operates in the tri-border region, mostly by laundering money and conducting arms-for-drugs deals with Latin American terrorist organizations such as the FARC, the ELN (National Liberation Army), and the Peruvian Shining Path. According to Brazil's former national drug enforcement secretary, Jude Walter Fanganiello Maierovitch, al-Qaeda activities in the tri-border region include drug trafficking, arms and uranium smuggling, and money laundering operations, frequently in cooperation with Chinese Triads (criminal groups) and the Russian Mafiya.[121] Al-Qaeda's relationship with Colombian, Peruvian, and Bolivian drug traffickers also includes cocaine smuggling.

Al-Qaeda's involvement in Latin America's illegal drug trade was preceded by the activities of Afghan and Pakistani heroin traffickers, who had worked with the Colombian Cali cartel and the FARC. Not surprisingly, the Colombians' methods of poppy cultivation resemble those in Afghanistan, according to Colombia's former police chief General Rosso Jose Serrano. Pakistani and Afghan heroin traffickers, like al-Qaeda operatives, most often entered Colombia with false identification papers. In February 2002, Brazilian, Argentinean, Colombian, Paraguayan, and Bolivian authorities, who have searched suspected Afghan and Pakistani citizens, reported that many had been carrying several sets of false identification.[122]

PRECIOUS METALS & GEMS

To secure their sources of funding, and to cast as wide a net as possible, terrorists also use various commodities to invest their money and conceal its source. Recognizing this fact, the *2002 National Money Laundering Strategy* recommended that the U.S. Departments of Justice and the Treasury produce a report describing how precious metals and gems are used as a money laundering vehicle. The report will serve as a basis for a new strategy to challenge this aspect of terrorist financing.[123] In the meantime, however, terrorists continue to use gold, diamonds, and other valuable commodities to obscure and increase their wealth.

Gold

Like drugs, gold is a highly valued and internationally recognized commodity that terrorists, drug traffickers, and other criminals favor as a tool to launder money, "because you can melt it, smelt it, or deposit it on account with no questions asked."[124] It has no serial number, is not traceable in its various forms, can easily be converted to cash anywhere in the world, and can be deposited and transferred without any transaction report.

Following the Taliban takeover in 1996, al-Qaeda moved large quantities of gold into Afghanistan. To enhance its reserves, "the

Taliban collected taxes in gold from the heads of Pakistani and Indian trucking networks that hauled cargo through Afghanistan."[125]
Al-Qaeda, together with the Taliban, levied taxes on Afghan heroin
and opium producers—collecting the taxes in gold—and exchanged
drugs for gold. "The old networks of moving drugs and trading it for
gold, which they have done for years, is still operational," stated a
Pakistani intelligence source. "This is new money, not money
stashed away from before," but generated from the sale of opium
and heroin to Central Asian drug traffickers.[126] Al-Qaeda, like other
criminal organizations, also uses gold to launder money and sustain
its value. An al-Qaeda manual, found by the International Security
Assistance Force in Afghanistan in 2001, contains elaborate instructions on how to disguise and smuggle gold.[127]

U.S. intelligence sources suspect that al-Qaeda's financial network
is composed of former employees of the Bank of Credit and Commerce International. The bank had extensive operations in gold
smuggling, as well as in drug trafficking, money laundering, and illegal arms and diamonds trading.[128]

No sooner had the U.S. and the Allied Forces begun air strikes
against the Taliban in October 2001 than the Taliban and al-Qaeda
raided the vaults of the Afghani national bank, as well as local banks,
looting millions of dollars in cash and gold reserves. The gold and
money were smuggled across the border to Pakistan, and from there
to al-Qaeda accounts around the world. Much of al-Qaeda's gold was
moved to banks in Dubai, one of the world's least-regulated gold
markets.[129]

Dubai is conveniently situated in the midst of the Persian Gulf,
and is one of the seven emirates that merged to create the United
Arab Emirates in 1971. Dubai, known for its lack of any financial regulations, soon became a hub for terrorists, drug traffickers, and
money launderers.[130] It also was used by bin Laden and al-Qaeda to
launder money through its banks and its gold exchange.

Dubai was not the only place to receive gold from al-Qaeda and the Taliban. In August 2002, U.S. and European investigators discovered that large quantities of gold belonging to al-Qaeda and the Taliban had been moved from Pakistan to Sudan. "The bankers are the ones that move the money, and the bankers are not sitting in caves in Afghanistan," remarked a U.S. official.[131] The gold was hidden in other products and then shipped from Pakistan to Iran and Dubai, and from there flown by chartered planes to Sudan's capitol, Khartoum[132]—where, not coincidentally, Osama bin Laden lived from 1991 to 1996, and where he continues to hold business interests.

Although the United Arab Emirates banking authorities—as a result of American pressure—enacted anti-money-laundering laws in January 2002, they apply to their financial institutions but not to their *hawala* system or their gold exchange. Law enforcement sources expect that anti-money-laundering laws in the UAE and other Middle Eastern countries "will only increase the premium for 'cleaning' illegal money; [but] will not eliminate the laundering itself."[133]

Diamonds

When $240 million of al-Qaeda's assets were frozen by the U.S. government six weeks after the 1998 bombing of the United States embassies in Kenya and Tanzania,[134] Osama bin Laden's second in command, Ayman al-Zawahiri, wrote a letter instructing an al-Qaeda member to purchase diamonds, saying, "[diamonds] may well be a way out of the bottleneck and transfer our activities to the stage of multinationals [bringing] joint profit."[135]

Al-Qaeda was not the first Islamist terror organization to recognize the value of the illegal diamond market. Hizballah, through Lebanese diamond dealers in the Democratic Republic of the Congo (the Congo's diamond exports are valued at approximately $600 million annually, of which $420 million worth is exported illegally), purchased hundreds of millions of dollars worth of illegal diamonds from Zimbabwean and Congolese army generals.[136] Hizballah then resold the diamonds in countries such as the UAE, Mauritius, and India, where there are no regulations in place to govern their sale.[137]

Diamonds are easily hidden, difficult to trace, and exempt from traditional monetary and financial controls, and they retain their value. "Diamonds don't set off alarms at airports, they can't be sniffed by dogs, they are easy to hide, and are highly convertible to cash."[138] According to Mark van Bukste of the Antwerp Diamond Commission, "Diamonds are a form of currency. They are used to back international loans, to pay off debt, to bribe, and to buy weapons. Often, diamonds are a much better currency than money."[139]

Until July 2001, al-Qaeda would purchase diamonds from the Revolutionary United Front (RUF), the Liberian-backed rebels fighting for dominance in the West African nation of Sierra Leone. Al-Qaeda would buy the gems for less than market price, then resell them in Dubai, Mauritius, and India for a profit. The diamonds al-Qaeda bought were smuggled in small packets by senior RUF commanders from Sierra Leone to safe houses in Monrovia, where they were then exchanged for cash provided by diamond dealers from Belgium who were affiliated with al-Qaeda. For a fee, the Liberian government provided the security for all parties involved.[140]

Al-Qaeda's contact with the RUF came through Ibrahim Bah, a Libyan-trained Senegalese who had fought with Osama bin Laden against the Soviet invaders in Aghanistan in the 1980s. He later returned to Africa, where he became the major diamond dealer and weapons buyer not only for the RUF, but also for Liberian president Charles Taylor—all the while maintaining his contacts with al-Qaeda.[141]

The conduit for selling the diamonds, the ASA Diam diamond trading company in Antwerp, Belgium, was recommended to Bah in July 2000 by two al-Qaeda members: Samih Osailly and his cousin Aziz Nassour, a Lebanese diamond merchant. ASA Diam, which had been inactive for two years, agreed to manage al-Qaeda's gems, and within six months had made $14 million in profits.[142] Nassour, the diamond merchant, had been previously implicated by the CIA for his involvement in the illegal trade of diamonds and emeralds from the Congo and Zimbabwe on behalf of Hizballah. Nassour denied the charges from his safe haven in Beirut, but the United Nations subsequently banned him from international travel.[143]

When Sierra Leone's civil war ended with a peace treaty and democratic elections in the summer of 2001,[144] Nassour met with senior RUF commanders, who now operated from Liberia, and with the Liberian president's security chief to arrange for an even greater acceleration of mining operations, promising both to buy diamonds above the going market rate and to supply the RUF with weapons and medicine. After the meeting, a senior RUF commander faxed President Taylor: "Sir, we write to inform you of our present dealing with Mr. Aziz Nassour, that [sic] was introduced to us by Gen. [Ibrahim] Bah, upon your recommendation. Sir, we have agreed to sell all of our diamonds to Mr. Aziz Nassour through your offices." Al-Qaeda took advantage of thousands of former RUF rebels who were seeking employment to accelerate the diamond mining operations, thereby giving al-Qaeda control over most of Sierra Leone's and Liberia's diamond markets.[145]

True to their word, al-Qaeda representatives paid 15 to 30 percent over the going rate, thereby forcing regular merchants out of the market. They sold the diamonds through ASA Diam, generating millions of dollars for al-Qaeda. Even though ASA Diam ceased reporting its sales of diamonds to the Antwerp Diamond Center, Belgian investigators obtained records of the company's accounts and discovered transactions worth millions of dollars. Twenty million dollars had been withdrawn from the accounts just prior to the September 11 attacks—apparently to fund an al-Qaeda weapons-buying spree.[146]

Meanwhile, according to European investigators, al-Qaeda had also bought protection for their operatives from Liberian president Taylor. In the summer of 2001 Taylor received $1 million in cash in exchange for his consent to harbor al-Qaeda operatives. President Taylor's involvement in the illegal diamond trade, weapons smuggling, and terrorism was investigated by a specially appointed UN panel, which recommended that Taylor, his family, and senior members of his government be banned from international travel—a ban which was adopted by the Security Council in 2001.[147]

The al-Qaeda diamond trade also has a North American connection: Saudi businessman Yassin al-Qadi, whose apparent ownership of the Ptech software company led to the federal raid on its offices in December 2002 (see chapter 1). Al-Qadi, who is on the United States Treasury Department's Specially Designated Global Terrorist Entity List, also controlled New Diamond International, which, in turn, controlled nine million shares of the Nevada-based Global Diamond Resources. Al-Qadi was also a major investor in Vancouver-based MIT Ventures, a diamond mining and exploration company. He had investments in, and was a board member of, companies such as: the Saudi National Consulting Center, Qordova Real Estate Company, Cariba Bank in Kazakhstan, Himont Chemical in Pakistan, and Karavan Construction Company in Turkey.[148]

Al-Qadi's interest in real estate extended to the U.S., where he gave $820,000 to a HAMAS front organization to buy property that was rented out to generate income, and that could have been sold for a profit, in case the organization needed cash fast. It would be hard to find a more strategically placed individual to advance al-Qaeda's agenda—in the diamond trade and beyond.[149]

AL-QAEDA'S REIGN IN SPAIN

The ease with which al-Qaeda conducted its operations throughout the world is illustrated by the story of another of Osama bin Laden's brothers-in-law, a comrade-in-arms from the war against the Soviets in Afghanistan, Muhammad Galeb Kalaje Zouaydi (AKA Muhammad Ghalim Kalaji, AKA Abu Talha, AKA Abu Musab). Zouaydi was entrusted with the financial operations of al-Qaeda in Europe, and he managed this intricate web from the al-Qaeda headquarters in Madrid.

Zouaydi was born in Syria in 1961, graduated from Aleppo University in 1978 with a degree in mechanical engineering, and moved to Saudi Arabia in 1984. A year later, in Jeddah, he founded a household gifts company, "Mushayt for Trading Establishment."[150] The company was controlled from the start by the Saudi branch of the Muslim Brotherhood[151]—a group supported by the Saudi royal family.[152] In 1984, Zouaydi had also obtained Spanish citizenship and, with funding from Saudi Arabia, established businesses in Spain. These businesses served as covers for funding al-Qaeda operations not only in Spain, but also in Belgium, Italy, Germany, the Philippines, and Indonesia.[153]

In 1998, Zouaydi moved to Spain and expanded his investments into construction and real estate. Spanish authorities would later discover that Zouaydi laundered more than $2.5 million dollars through his companies over a five-year period. Between 1996 and 2001, Zouaydi's Saudi companies transferred at least $1,093,197 from Saudi Arabia through the al-Rajhi Bank to Spain, and from there to al-Qaeda's networks in Europe.[154] The authorities would also identify Zouaydi as a coconspirator in the multi-million-dollar money laundering operation that involved current Muslim World League secretary-general Abdullah bin Abdul Muhsen al-Turki.[155]

In addition, Zouaydi distributed at least $470,000 through

Mushayt for Trading Establishment to different individuals and organizations affiliated with al-Qaeda.[156] One of them, Mamoun Darkazanli, was described by the Spanish investigative judge Balthasar Garzón, who led the investigation into al-Qaeda's European operations, as "belonging to the most intimate circle of Mohamed Atta," the lead hijacker in the World Trade Center attacks.[157] "There was a double accounting system," noted one investigator, "and there was money that came from abroad and was mixed between the real business projects and the donations for jihad."[158]

Zouaydi's companies also functioned as fronts for arms trafficking, and generated large amounts of money through credit card fraud and the falsification of financial statements.[159] In addition to running al-Qaeda's financial operations in Europe, Zouaydi was also the head of the Kandahar City–based Jam'yah Ta'awun al-Islamia (Society of Islamic Cooperation), which had been founded by bin Laden in 2001, and which, after September 11, was placed on the U.S. Treasury Department's Specially Designated Terrorist List.[160]

Zouaydi's business partner, the head of al-Qaeda's Spanish cell, was also Syrian-born. Imad Eddin Barakat Yarkas, known as Abu Dahdah, was viewed by his Spanish investigators as "an intelligent, fanatic, and cold" leader.[161]

Abu Dahdah and his associates' favorite way of transferring money to operatives in Germany, Pakistan, Afghanistan, Lebanon, Yemen, and Bosnia was through the Amman-based Arab Bank—also the primary recipient of funds for Palestinian terror organizations from Saudi Arabia, Syria, and Iran.[162] Money that had been laundered by Abu Dahdah and Zouaydi through their Spanish businesses, together with "donations" from individuals and companies in Saudi Arabia, was sent directly to Muhammad Atta and the Hamburg cell to plan and finance the September 11 attacks.

Spanish investigative judge Garzón described Madrid as the epicenter for maintaining al-Qaeda's European cells from 1995 to 2001, and identified Zouaydi and Abu Dahdah as having been involved in the September 11 attacks, as well as in plans to blow up the U.S. embassy in Paris. The Spanish Unidad Central de Información Exterior (Central Unit for Foreign Information)—which had observed Abu Dahdah meeting with Muhammad Atta in the summer of 2001, during Atta's visit to Madrid in preparation for September 11—had been monitoring Abu Dahdah since he assumed the leadership of the "Soldiers of Allah" group in Madrid in 1995. To demonstrate Abu Dahdah's global networking on behalf of al-Qaeda, the Spanish Court's indictment described how "since 1996 . . . Abu Dahdah traveled more than 20 times to the United Kingdom, where he contacted prominent leaders of the *mujahideen* movement . . . he also traveled several times to Turkey, Belgium, Denmark, Sweden, Indonesia, Malaysia and Jordan. All these travels are made on behalf of the organization and in order to contact other members thereof."[163] The court further listed the Spanish cell's "gifts for Palestine" of €5,890.20 (Euros), which were given to the Hebron Muslim Youth Association, "an organization known to belong to the Palestinian terrorist organization Hamas."[164]

Co-opting and working with local terrorist groups is one of al-Qaeda's trademarks. Spanish and Moroccan security forces, along with the CIA, observed al-Qaeda cell members meeting with members of the Basque Fatherland and Liberty (ETA) terror organization. Apparently the meetings revolved around al-Qaeda's plans to use speedboats loaded with explosives to carry out homicide attacks against British and U.S. warships in the Strait of Gibraltar.[165] According to the investigators, the Spanish cell was "a hub of financing, recruitment and support services for al-Qaeda in Europe. It provided fake documents and refuge for terrorists in transit and raised money through credit card fraud, robberies and other crimes."[166]

The activities of this al-Qaeda cell were halted when Abu was sent to prison on November 18, 2001.[167] Spanish authorities arrested Zouaydi in Madrid on April 23, 2002.

CONTAINING THE DISEASE

Capturing such major al-Qaeda operatives is likely to curtail their activities, at least until they are replaced by others. This is true for the arrest of Sami al-Arian, a former computer science professor at the University of South Florida in Tampa. According to U.S. intelligence sources, al-Arian was one of al-Qaeda's most important U.S. operatives.[168] A review of his terrorist activity in the U.S. illustrates how Islamist operatives had united their efforts to fight the U.S. and Israel. Al-Arian, who joined the Palestinian Islamic Jihad (PIJ),[169] openly advocated the destruction of Israel and collected funds to help the PIJ carry out its terrorist activities against Israeli civilians. Later, he expanded his activities to support HAMAS and al-Qaeda, and used the World and Islam Studies Enterprise (WISE) and its sister organizations in the U.S. to serve as the "financial and strategic conduits" for these terrorist organizations.[170]

Throughout the 1990s, al-Arian continued his activities without any serious interruption, although he had been questioned several times by law enforcement. Yet not even his attempts to open an al-Barakaat Bank branch in Florida—with Saudi and Iraqi money—led the U.S. government to curtail his operations. According to U.S. intelligence sources, when Muhammad Atta failed to obtain a $1.1 million loan from the U.S. government with which to acquire crop-dusters, al-Arian and a coconspirator incorporated the Florida Baraka Exchange. This financial entity, which collapsed after September 11, apparently served to funnel money to the al-Qaeda hijackers who trained in Florida.[171]

The arrests of al-Arian and seven of his coconspirators on February 20, 2003,[172] was made possible by the enactment of the USA

PATRIOT Act. When prosecutors seek to indict suspected terrorists, the act allows them to access sources of information that were previously unavailable. RICO, the Racketeering Influenced and Corrupt Organization Act (passed in 1970), was also used to facilitate al-Arian's prosecution.

Two more arrests that occurred in early March could possibly affect al-Qaeda's financial ability in the U.S. and elsewhere. First came the arrest of Mustafa Ahmed al-Hawsawi on March 1 in Pakistan, together with al-Qaeda's chief of operations, Khalid Sheikh Muhammad. Al-Hawsawi "allegedly coordinated payments for the Sept. 11 attacks,"[173] and, according to U.S. terrorism expert Neil C. Livingstone, is "a big cog in the machinery that moves al Qaeda money around the Middle East."[174] The second arrest, on March 4 in Germany, was that of the Yemeni cleric Sheikh Muhammad Ali Hassan al-Mouyad, who used the al-Farooq Mosque in Brooklyn, New York, to funnel at least $20 million to Osama bin Laden. This is the same mosque that Sheikh Omar Abd al-Rahman used as a base for his activities before he was convicted for the 1993 World Trade Center bombing.[175]

These and other cases in which al-Qaeda and other terrorist operatives have been arrested and prosecuted in the U.S. seem to fulfill some of the intentions of the lawmakers behind the USA PATRIOT Act. "Today, Americans are safer because we have transformed the rules of engagement for investigating and prosecuting suspected terrorists within our borders," stated Attorney General John Ashcroft before the Senate Judiciary Committee.

However, it seems too early for the U.S. to congratulate itself for "winning the war on terrorism," as the Attorney General stated at the same hearing.[176]

By April 2003, of the seven-member al-Qaeda leadership, two had been caught and one was dead. Of the thirteen-member operational tier, five had been apprehended and five were dead. The rest were still at large.[177] In June 2003, Beirut was shaken by rockets launched from the Palestinian refugee camp Ein Hilwe, near the port city of Sidon in Southern Lebanon. Lebanese intelligence reported that the camp had been taken over in the past several years by more than two hundred al-Qaeda terrorists who arrived at the camp after the war in Afghanistan.[178] They imposed strict religious laws on the one hundred thousand inhabitants of the camp, and "they are taking the young boys and filling their heads with the glories of martyrdom for Islam"[179] and planning terror attacks and homicide bombing against Israel and the U.S. forces in Iraq.

Although U.S. law enforcement has had some successes of late, the more counterterrorism officials learn about al-Qaeda, the clearer it becomes: the organization has spread more widely and embedded itself more deeply than originally believed into the affairs of like-minded terrorist groups, sympathetic banks and charities, corrupt governments, and criminal organizations. Although the members of al-Qaeda are on the run, bin Laden still succeeded in executing a deadly homicide bombing attack in Riyadh in May 2003, killing more than thirty-four, mainly foreigners, including eight Americans.[180] His and al-Qaeda's followers are spread throughout the world, and the links they have forged—and the vast amounts of money these links help provide—promise that al-Qaeda members, perhaps under a different guise, will continue to threaten the U.S., the West, and anyone else who does not adhere to their repressive creed.

As with glanders, the highly infectious disease, identification and elimination are our sole means of defense. Only the identification and elimination of al-Qaeda's sources of funding—severing its financial artery—will help to prevent the spread of the Islamist plague.

*The current Mideast conflict was born out of
"the Oslo conceit that you could impose upon
Palestinian society a PLO thugocracy led by the
inventors of modern terrorism and then be sur-
prised that seven years later it exploded in
violence."*

Charles Krauthammer,
Washington Post, June 27, 2002

CHAPTER 3

The Palestinians

THE TERRORIST PROTOTYPE: THE PLO

The current techniques of terrorism financing are hardly new. They were refined over the course of three decades by the Palestine Liberation Organization (PLO), an umbrella group dedicated to the destruction of Israel and the establishment of a Palestinian state.[1] The PLO model not only established a precedent for other terrorist organizations, but also most likely served as inspiration for Osama bin Laden when he set out to create the financial infrastructure of al-Qaeda.[2]

The PLO was the first and, until al-Qaeda established itself in Afghanistan, the only terrorist organization that had its own territory—base of operation—first in Lebanon and later in the West Bank and Gaza. Even the use of "martyrdom" as a tool of terrorism was incorporated into the PLO agenda as early as 1978. And the PLO, like al-Qaeda later, enjoyed multi-state sponsorship. Two months after the Camp David agreement of September 1978, which ended the state of war between Egypt and Israel, ten Arab heads of state met in Baghdad and agreed to provide $3.5 billion annually to aid the PLO—and countries such as Syria, Lebanon, and Jordan—to continue their confrontation with Israel. Of a total of $250 million allocated annually to the PLO, $10 million was specifically designated for the "families of the martyrs."[3]

The PLO was formed by the League of Arab States in 1964. It engaged in terrorist activities from its inception, launching its campaign of terror against Israel on January 1, 1965, with an attack on Israel's National Water Carrier.[4] In 1974, the UN embraced the PLO by granting it observer status. This legitimization enabled the PLO to open offices worldwide, to obtain financial backing, and to increase its assets and income by a multiple of sixteen or seventeen between 1974 and 1981.[5] Over the years, the PLO received financial and political support from the Soviet Union and its satellites in Europe[6] (until the collapse of the Soviet Union in 1991), and from Latin America, Africa, members of the Arab League, and Third World countries.[7] Its wealth allowed the PLO to fund an international propaganda campaign, to gain great popularity, to increase its influence, and most of all to continue its terrorism and criminal activities with impunity.

In 1987 the U.S. declared the PLO a terrorist organization,[8] but a year later, in 1988, a presidential waiver was issued that "permitted contact" with it. Although the PLO is still officially a terrorist organization, the waiver permitting contact with it has remained in place.

The PLO has also been at the forefront of money laundering activities. The mid-1960s saw the development of money laundering as a tool to hide illegal sources of money.[9] These activities were facilitated for many years by corruption and hypocrisy worldwide, which have made illicit funds easy to launder and hide. Offshore banking centers, from Monaco, Nauru,[10] and Cyprus to Hong Kong and the Bahamas, as well as international financial organizations, have been used not only to launder money, but also to invest it.

Historically, the PLO has had nine principal sources of income:

- Official contributions from Arab states
- The Palestinian Liberation Tax Fund, a 3.5 to 5 percent tax on the income of all Palestinians worldwide
- Donations from wealthy Palestinians and international organizations such as the UN and the EU
- Support from charitable organizations
- Income from legitimate and illegitimate investments
- "Protection" charges paid by companies and states in order not to have terrorist acts directed against them
- Illegal arms deals
- Fraud, money laundering, counterfeiting, and other criminal activities
- Drug trafficking[11]

In 1983, six months after the PLO was expelled from Lebanon, it made an official decision, under the chairmanship of Yasser Arafat, to exploit the drug trade for funding. The decision was made at a secret emergency session of the Finance Committee in Algiers. The PLO treasurer at the time, Sallah Dabbagh, stated, "The entire future of the PLO operation for liberation may hinge on our exporting more drugs throughout the world."[12]

As James Adams observed in his 1987 book *The Financing of Terror:*

> An early lesson in the political impact of the drug economy on terrorist movements occurred in the Middle East with the Palestine Liberation Organization. The PLO has been one of the most successful terrorist movements of modern times, both in its ability to survive and in its accumulation of wealth. Inevitably, drugs have played a part in the investment portfolio.[13]

In 1983, a *Reader's Digest* article reported that "The PLO purchased an estimated 40% of its light infantry weapons with either heroin, hashish, or morphine base produced by PLO and Syrian controlled laboratories in Syria or in Lebanon's Beka'a Valley."[14] The U.S. Justice Department's *Special Report,* which was published in 1984, confirmed this information.[15]

The total amount of money accumulated by the PLO from its inception until the Oslo Accords has been estimated by a variety of sources. According to a 1990 CIA report, the PLO used drug trafficking, arms smuggling, and money laundering and counterfeiting to amass a fortune estimated between $8 and $14 billion.[16] In 1993 and 1994, the British National Criminal Intelligence Services estimated the total to be about $10 billion, with an annual income of $1.5 to $2 billion. The British report also noted that the PLO was, in fact, the wealthiest of the world's terrorist organizations.[17]

In 1995, the U.S. General Accounting Office (GAO) performed an investigation into this matter, but its findings were kept secret, apparently due to "national security reasons." Nevertheless, a source familiar with the investigation said that the report had found that Chairman Arafat and the PLO had indeed held "well over $10 billion in assets, even at a time when he was publicly claiming 'bankruptcy'."[18]

For decades the West has turned a blind eye to the PLO's fundraising endeavors, thereby allowing the PLO to continue operating freely both legitimate and illegitimate businesses. These ventures have laundered money for the PLO, which, in turn, has used the revenues to further its terrorist agenda. Although the great wealth of the PLO was an open secret, no one ever asked the organization to use its assets for the benefit of the Palestinian people. Nor was there ever a demand to account for the whereabouts of these assets. Meanwhile, the PLO's connections to international criminal organizations, drug cartels, and other terrorist groups, and to every rogue state, from Libya, Iran, and Iraq to North Korea and Sudan, set the pattern for other terrorist groups to follow.[19]

THE PALESTINIAN AUTHORITY

In 1993, under the Oslo Accords, the PLO established the Palestinian Authority (PA) to run all civil matters of the Palestinian people, except foreign relations and defense.[20] However, the change did not impede the illegal activities of the PLO or the newly established PA.[21] On the contrary, as the PA gained international legitimacy it abused this status to expand its criminal ventures, while at the same time it received financial support from Saudi Arabia, Iran, Iraq, and other Arab League member states, as well as from the international donor community, especially the EU, the UN, and the U.S.[22]

In September 2000, when the PA started to attack Israel, it also started to introduce religion into its political rhetoric; the PA added *Jihad* to its agenda to justify homicide bombings. As a result, the PA gained even more support financially and politically within the Arab/Muslim world, much as al-Qaeda did following the September 11 attacks. According to a soon-to-be-published report by Info-Prod Research, an economic research center, during the first year of the current Palestinian violence (2001), "the amount of money officially donated to the PA jumped 80 percent—from $555 million to $1.002 billion."[23]

FUNDING FROM THE EUROPEAN COMMUNITY

Since the Oslo Accords, according to the Palestinian Authority's own documents, it has received at least $4.5 billion from the international community to establish a viable administration and to develop the Palestinian economy.[24] By the spring of 2003, international aid to the PA reached at least $5.5 billion.

According to independent sources, by the end of August 2002 the PA had actually received a minimum of $4,938,868,000—or over $400 million more than had been accounted for. This figure includes $45

million per month from the Arab states until April 2002, after which
the amount was increased to $55 million per month, and €10 million
(Euros) per month from the EU to "help [the PA] meet urgent public
expenses, such as salaries for public sector employees."[25] Blaming Israel for the decline in the Palestinian Gross National Income following their attacks on Israel, the European Commission increased its
funding to the PA during 2000/2001 to $366 million.[26] After more
than two years of intensifying Palestinian terrorism, in October 2002
the European Commission approved an additional €29 million to
"support . . . Palestinian reform efforts," thus helping the Palestinians
to keep up their attacks against Israel.[27]

The EU began contributing €10 million a month to cover the
Palestinian Authority's salary expenses after Israel stopped transferring import tax revenue to the PA.[28] The transfer was required by the
1994 Paris Protocol, but Israel stopped making the payments because it suspected that the money was actually being used by the PA
to fund terrorism. In addition to the €10 million per month that the
EU had been giving for salaries, it had also transferred "more than
EUR 102 million" (for 2000/2001) for the Euro-Mediterranean Partnership program, MEDA.[29]

The MEDA program granted the PA a total sum of €340.9 million
for the years 2000 and 2001 for the stated purpose of "technical and
financial support measures to accompany the reform of economic
and social structures" in the West Bank and Gaza. This total included:

- €3.7 million for "NGO co-financing and co-operation"[30]
- €44.4 million from the European Commission's humanitarian aid office, with an additional €15 million allocated for
  2002[31]
- €22.9 million for food aid in 2001, with a projected €15 million for 2002[32]

- €3.4 million from the Common Foreign and Security Policy Budget[33]
- €4 million per year for "recurrent costs of the Education Ministry"
- €1 billion in loans and additional grants, and €500,000 from 1995 to 2000 for "monitoring Israeli colonising activities"[34]
- At least €422 million since 1994 to the United Nations Relief and Works Agency for Palestine Refugees in the Near East (UNRWA)[35]

Most of this money was allocated for economic development and reform, and yet the Palestinian economy declined dramatically over the same period. One wonders not only how the Palestinian Authority spent the €340 million, but also why the EU Commission continued to fund the PA despite so much evidence that its funding did little to reform either Palestinian institutions or the Palestinian economy.

Where Did the Money Go?

At the end of 2001, the Israel Defense Forces (IDF) discovered Palestinian documents that expose how the PA has been misusing international funds. The PA maintained a double reporting system, claiming it needed about $60 million per month for its salaries, when it actually needed only about $40.5 million. The balance—which amounts to $224 million for the year—is unaccounted for. The PA also used a low exchange rate for the dollar—3.7 sheqels, compared to the representative rate at that time of 4.4 sheqels—which created a surplus of $7.7 million.[36]

The PA's own documents also show that the PA deducts 1.5 to 2 percent from the salaries of all its security personnel. This sum, equivalent to $260,000 to $345,000 per month, is sent to Fatah, which is also known as the Palestinian National Liberation Movement and encompasses the terrorist groups Tanzim (originally the Fatah youth organization) and the al-Aqsa Martyrs Brigades.[37]

While both the U.S. and the EU classify the al-Aqsa Martyrs Brigades as a terrorist organization, Fatah is not recognized as such in Europe. Yet, according to the PA's own documents, the al-Aqsa Martyrs Brigades and the Tanzim are part of Fatah. For example, Fatah documents also have the logo of the al-Aqsa Martyrs Brigades on their letterheads, and PA documents contain letters from Fatah requesting payments for perpetrators of terror attacks.[38] Other PA records demonstrate cooperation between Fatah, HAMAS, and the Palestinian Islamic Jihad.[39] Moreover, ever since the attacks on Israel began in September 2000, the PA, HAMAS, and Palestinian Islamic Jihad have received millions of dollars from Iran, Iraq, and Syria, monies which were specifically designated for homicide bombings and other attacks against Israel.[40] The EU, while not refuting the evidence, tries to argue that Fatah is comparable to European trade unions: "This system [of deducting money from security personnel's wages to contribute to Fatah] is not dissimilar to the mandatory deductions from salaries for trade union members' fees in some EU countries."[41]

EU Funds for Terror

The Palestinian Authority's sponsorship of terrorism extends far beyond these wage deductions. But Chairman Arafat's signature, and orders in his own handwriting to pay thousands of dollars to families of "martyrs" from the PA's treasury—documents that have been authenticated by official Israeli, U.S., and German experts—have done little to convince the EU either to stop its funding of the PA's salaries or to admit that the money may have been misused.

PA documents from Arafat's compound show that money provided by the EU for PA salaries was actually used to pay $640,000 to $1 million per month to Fatah terrorists.[42] Also found were letters to Arafat from PA officials requesting that Fatah activists and other known terrorists who were not already on the PA security apparatus payroll be added.[43] One particular letter requesting to add twelve terrorists because "they are intifada activists who are wanted by the occupation authorities because of their deeds" bragged that "these are the best of the fighting brothers and activists in the blessed Intifada and they have an exceptional part."[44] The EU doggedly denies these facts, stating, "There is no evidence that any person involved in terror attacks has actually been recruited into the PA security services."[45]

A further form of EU direct support to Palestinian terrorists was revealed in January 2002, when a group of Palestinian terrorists who had been released from Israeli prisons visited Cairo, Egypt, as part of the EU-funded "Rehabilitation and Propaganda Program"—part of the "Rehabilitation Program for Released [Palestinian] Prisoners." The program had been launched in 1995 to help them "become integrated in society after their release," and had received additional support from countries friendly to the PA.[46] In press conferences held in Cairo, the prisoners accused Israel of "indiscriminate Nazi practices,"[47] and used this claim as a justification for continuing terror activities against Israel.

EU Denials

EU donations to the PA included demands for accountability. Similar demands have been attached to the EU's direct budgetary assistance since the PA's attacks on Israel began. But there was never reason to expect that the PA would meet any such stipulations, as Yasser Arafat made clear as early as July 1994:

> I refused and I will never accept!" Arafat said of the conditions imposed for economic aid. "I completely refuse any controls by anybody on Palestinian Autonomy, except the Palestinians themselves. We didn't finish military occupation to get economic occupation.[48]

Since money is interchangeable, and since the EU gave direct funding toward PA salaries and additional money to the PA Ministry of Finance for various projects, it is not unreasonable to assume that the PA allocated money received from the EU to fund terrorism.

Despite EU claims to the contrary, no real effort has ever been made to monitor how their money was spent. EU commissioner for external affairs Chris Patten is unwilling to investigate the PA's use of EU funds, stating that "I would like a committee of inquiry on these issues like a 'hole in the head'!"[49] But Patten also insists that "the commission has examined all documents that have been made available to us by the Israeli authorities. To date we have found no evidence that EU monies have been used by the Palestinian Authority to finance terrorist activities, or for anything other than their agreed purpose."[50] Patten maintains that "our aid has been carefully monitored. It has also been subject to strict conditionality."[51] His office has also stated that "the IMF conducts a close monitoring of the PA's fiscal situation on a monthly basis, covering *inter alia*, revenue developments, the evolution of employment, the wage bill, and non-wage current outlays."[52]

However, IMF staff members have directly contradicted Patten's claim on several occasions: "The Fund has not been monitoring spending under individual budget lines nor can it ascertain whether a particular spending commitment has been actually disbursed for the reported purpose. This is an auditing function that goes beyond the fund's present mandate."[53] As the director of the External Relations Department of the IMF, Thomas C. Dawson, reiterated in a letter to the *Wall Street Journal:* "The IMF does not 'monitor foreign assistance' to the Palestinian Authority. It simply provides the EU with information about broad developments related to its budget. It does not monitor or control every item in the budget."[54] The director of the IMF's Middle Eastern Department, George T. Abed, acknowledged that the IMF does not monitor the PA's spending, and stated that "with weak institutions and a budget of nearly $1 billion, there has, no doubt, been some abuse; the Palestinian Legislative Council itself has complained about this. The IMF does not and cannot control downstream spending by the various Palestinian agencies." Nevertheless, the IMF, much like the EU, does not want to be held accountable. "This matter remains between the Palestinian Authority and the donors," said Abed.[55]

On February 5, 2003, the European Anti-Fraud Office (OLAF) announced that it had begun an external investigation "in relation to allegations of misuse of funds donated by the European Union in the context of EU budgetary support to the Palestinian Authority."[56] This announcement followed a vote a day earlier by members of the EU Parliament, despite Patten's strong objection, to open a separate parliamentarian investigation into the EU's aid to the PA.[57]

The overwhelming evidence provided by the Palestinian Authority's own documents resulted in an initiative, beginning in 2002, by British European Parliament member Charles Tannock, to investigate how €540 million in aid given to the PA since 2000 has been spent. The proposal was met with fierce opposition led by Commissioner Patten, who personally lobbied members of the European Parliament not to support the initiative, even though "everybody has known for quite some time now that money [from the EU to the PA] ended up in the wrong hands," as an EU diplomat stated in May 2002—"Officially, however, they feigned ignorance."[58]

The EU argues that it will only accept that the money it sends has been funding terrorism if there are mechanisms in place to identify how each individual Euro is spent. However, since the EU Court of Auditors refused on November 5, 2002, to "certify the EU's [£]63 billion budget [or over U.S.$101 billion] for the eighth year running, admitting it can only guarantee that 5% of taxpayers' money is being spent properly,"[59] it is not surprising that the EU has been unable and unwilling to account for the whereabouts of money it gave to the Palestinians.

By the end of April 2003, after the appointment of Palestinian prime minister Mahmoud Abbas, the EU, still denying that their money was used to pay the salaries of members of the al-Aqsa Martyrs Brigades and other Palestinian terror groups, and blaming Israel for the economic hardship of the Palestinians, announced that it will "refocus" its aid. Instead of allocating money to pay the salaries of PA officials, the EU will target its €345 million in aid for the development of small enterprises and social services, for support emergency services, and for "technical assistance to facilitate implementation of reforms of public finance."[60] Commissioner Patten was pleased to note that the EU money has helped keep the PA as "a viable interlocutor for future negotiations" with Israel.[61] Indeed, it was largely EU money that supported Arafat's and the Palestinians' terror and propaganda campaigns. Allocating these new funds on promises that reforms are under way puts in doubt the sincerity of the EU declarations regarding "real reforms" in the PA. It remains to be seen how this new European aid is going to be spent.

The EU demonstrated its cavalier attitude toward Palestinian terrorism yet again on June 19, 2003, when an increase in homicide bombing attacks against Israel by HAMAS seemed to endanger European plans for the creation of a Palestinian state. British Foreign Secretary Jack Straw called on the EU to add HAMAS to its list of terrorist organizations and to block their funding. But, nineteen months after the U.S. put HAMAS on its designated foreign terrorist organizations list,[62] the EU declined to do the same.[63]

Other Sources

In addition to the EU's collective donations, according to Palestinian Ministry of Planning and International Cooperation, individual EU member states have donated at least $1,260,022,000 to the Palestinian Authority. Altogether, aid from Europe—including EU donations from 1998 to 2001—has totaled at least $2.52 billion.[64]

For 2002, the United Nations Relief and Works Agency was scheduled to have disbursed $521.7 million to the PA for the Palestinian people.[65] Of this, $110 million was to have come from the U.S.[66] The U.S. has also given $548,766,000 in direct aid to the PA, according to the Ministry of Planning and International Cooperation.[67] The total sum donated by the U.S. over the life of the PA, including the amount given through relief and development organizations, is $1.1 billion.[68] Further, after the 1998 Wye River Memorandum, which listed "steps to facilitate implementation of the Interim Agreement on the West Bank and Gaza Strip" discussed in previous agreements,[69] the CIA began training the Palestinian Authority Security Services.[70] The budget for this training is unknown, although in September 2002 an additional $20 million was allocated for training Palestinian security services.[71]

THE PALESTINIAN AUTHORITY'S INVOLVEMENT IN CORRUPTION

The corruption of the Palestinian Authority is endemic. The results of a 1997 investigation by the Palestinian Legislative Council (PLC), which were suppressed by Yasser Arafat but eventually leaked, revealed that according to Jarar Kidwa, head of the PA's financial monitoring institution, the PA had lost $323 million—40 percent of its annual budget for 1996—to corruption and mismanagement. The PLC report also implicated PA officials, some of whom still serve in its cabinet.[72]

In October 1999, the chairman of the PLC Budget Committee, Azmi Shuaibi, had harsh words for the PA at the Ninth International Anti-Corruption Conference in Durban, South Africa: "The recent corruption found in the PA is similar to the corruption that exists in the rest of the Arab countries' governments."[73] President George W. Bush finally acknowledged the PA's corruption when, in June 2002, he called on the Palestinians to change their leadership and bring reform, accountability, and transparency to the Palestinian Authority.[74]

U.S. national security adviser Condoleezza Rice stated, "Frankly, the Palestinian Authority, which is corrupt and cavorts with terror . . . is not the basis for a Palestinian state moving forward."[75]

The full extent of the Palestinian Authority and its leadership's income is impossible to determine, because it has been engaging in criminal activities since its inception. Notable among their legal and illegal sources of revenue are the following:

Palestinians Martyrs' Sons Enterprises (SAMED)

The PLO formed the Palestinians Martyrs' Sons Enterprises in 1970 to invest and develop its economic activities. SAMED was led by Ahmed Qurie, AKA Abu Ala, who is currently the speaker of the Palestinian Legislative Council.[76] He served directly under Yasser Arafat, who since the start of SAMED has signed the checks for all transactions and has therefore doubtlessly been aware of every detail.[77]

SAMED maintained a flexible accounting system that included bank accounts not identified as belonging to the PLO; instead, they were registered in the names of private individuals, including Qurie. The value of PLO investments in farms, industrial plants, clothing and weapons factories, real estate, newspapers, duty free shops, and airlines was estimated by the British National Criminal Intelligence Services (NCIS) in 1993 at about $10 billion.[78]

According to the U.S. House of Representatives Task Force on Terrorism and Unconventional Warfare (October 1991), SAMED has had an affinity for airport-related investments—which facilitated the PLO's procurement of forged travel documents and airline tickets.[79] The PLO has owned duty-free stores at airports in Nairobi, Kenya, and Lagos, Nigeria.[80] Through SAMED, it has also had investments in airlines from the Maldives to Nicaragua. Until 1993, SAMED also received approximately $50 million a year from the Palestinian Liberation Tax Fund.[81] Overall, in the 1970s and 1980s, the PLO, through

SAMED, earned an estimated $5 million *per day,* or nearly $2 billion per year[82]—which, according to the NCIS report, continued into the 1990s.

In December 1999, hackers broke into the PLO's computer system and discovered at least "5 billion pounds in numbered bank accounts in Zurich, Geneva and New York,"[83] as well as smaller sums in Europe, Asia, and North Africa. None of the accounts was registered to the PLO. The PLO records also reveal that it owned shares "on the Frankfurt, Paris, and Tokyo stock exchanges," including stocks in Mercedes-Benz, and that it owned property in prime locations in Paris, London, Geneva, and New York.[84]

Monopolies & the Palestine Commercial Services Company (PCSC)

Researchers have noted that "since the establishment of the PA, scores of monopolies have been created by Arafat and are being operated by individuals and organizations close to Arafat. These monopolies control and subvert almost every potentially profitable aspect of daily Palestinian life"[85]—including "basic goods such as wheat, cement, petrol, wood, gravel, cigarettes and cars."[86] In 2002, the scope of the revenues generated from PA monopolies was estimated at $300 million annually.[87] None of this money is accounted for.

Palestinian media investigations and sources within the Palestinian territories, as well as Palestinian documents found by the IDF, reveal that PA officials close to Arafat control various monopolies in the West Bank and Gaza:

- Arafat's personal economic adviser, Muhammad Rasheed, his communications adviser, Nabil Abu Rudaineh, and Arafat's wife, Suha, co-own pharmaceutical and apparel monopolies[88]

- Rasheed, together with another Arafat adviser, Hassan As-four, co-own an oil monopoly
- Nabil Shaath, the minister of planning and international co-operation, has a computer monopoly[89]
- Ahmed Qurie, speaker of the Palestinian Legislative Council and founder of SAMED, is a co-owner of cigarette, canned food, and dairy monopolies[90]

The economic arm of the Palestinian Authority, the Palestine Commercial Services Company, has monopolies in flour, oil, cigarettes, iron, and commercial sand, and the PA prohibits other companies from operating in these fields.[91] The PCSC also has "large minority stakes . . . in a Ramallah Coca-Cola bottler . . . and a myriad of other businesses, plus full ownership of a cement plant [worth $50 million in 2000] that had long enjoyed a government protected monopoly."[92]

The company has not been supervised by either the PA legislature or the Finance Ministry. Instead, it has been controlled by Muhammad Rasheed, who until December 2002 oversaw most of the economic activities in the PA territories.[93] PCSC was, until recently, the direct recipient of sales taxes—more than $500 million in the past two years alone, collected by Israel, but owed to the PA under the 1993 Oslo Accords.[94] The tax receipts had been placed by the Israeli authorities in a Tel Aviv bank, into an account controlled by Arafat and Rasheed.[95] The latest estimate of the value of the PCSC's holdings is at least $345 million in cash and equity.[96]

The injury to the Palestinian economy goes beyond the loss in revenues—the monopolies also stifle competition and result in higher prices for fewer products. Coupled with the fact the monopolies "are in the hands of Arafat's aides and they exploit their positions to extract high profits,"[97] the economic damage must be staggering.

Siphoning Off the Pension Fund

Pension funds for Palestinians working in the Israeli Civil Administration were transferred to the PA by the Israeli government. The PA
used part of these funds to pay the salaries of the inflated police
force it had created in violation of the Oslo Accords.[98] Other parts of
the pension fund were used for an investment in telecommunications. Together, these unauthorized expenditures amounted to $36
million. But, by September 1997, an additional $104 million had dis-
appeared; only $20 million remained in the fund.[99] Arafat's adviser
Muhammad Rasheed then "ordered the transfer of half of the remaining $20 million to a liquid account in a Gaza bank."[100]

Personal Corruption

The 1997 Palestinian Legislative Council investigation into PA corruption implicated both the minister of planning and international
cooperation, Nabil Shaath, and the minister of information and culture, Yasser Abd Rabboh. The report claimed that both men used
government money for personal purposes, and determined that
Shaath had embezzled ministry funds, transferring them to "accounts not subject to PA inspection." The report also demanded that
Shaath be removed from his position,[101] yet according to media reports he was allowed to keep both his position and his computer
hardware monopoly.[102] Shaath, in his role as minister of planning
and international cooperation, not only coordinates international
aid, but also has been the lead coordinator in the negotiations to reform the PA.

Personal corruption in the PA extends to the highest level—to
Yasser Arafat himself. Jawad Ghussein was secretary-general of the
Palestinian National Fund until 1996, and in August 2002 he told the
Haaretz newspaper that Arafat "took aid money and contributions
that were earmarked for the Palestinian people to his own

account."[103] Ghussein was in a position to know: for twelve years he had deposited $7.5 to $8 million each month into Arafat's personal bank account. By 1993, these deposits totaled $540 million.[104]

Similarly, taxes that Israel collects on imported goods go into four accounts in the Bank of Palestine and the Arab Bank of Gaza. According to a leaked IMF internal report, the account "is not under the control or supervision of the Palestinian finance ministry,"[105] but instead is under Arafat's personal control. At least half the money was put in the bank accounts to bypass the supervision demanded by international donors, to finance inflated security services and civil service payrolls, which had not been approved by the donors.[106] (A PA source had a different explanation, claiming that the money was there for emergency use.)[107]

Yasser Arafat wears three hats: he is the president of the Palestinian Authority, chairman of the PLO, and head of the Fatah terrorist organization.[108] As such, he controls the funds of all terrorist organizations under the PA umbrella. As of August 2002, Arafat's personal holdings included $500 million of the PLO's money; in all, his holdings were believed to total about $1.3 billion.[109] Experts estimate that this money is enough to:

- Feed three million Palestinians for a year
- Buy one thousand mobile intensive care units
- Fund ten hospitals for a decade

This would still leave $585 million to fund other social projects.[110]

The $1.3 billion figure does not include the large sums of money that Arafat was discovered, in December 2002, to have deposited into a Swiss bank account beginning in 1997. In that year, trusted adviser Muhammad Rasheed—assisted by Yossi Ginnosar, a former adviser to Israeli prime ministers Rabin, Peres, and Barak—opened a Swiss bank account for Arafat, for which Arafat and Rasheed were the only signatories. Swiss banks had been instructed by their government to prevent "political" money from entering the Swiss banking system, to prevent a repeat of the scandals that arose when the banks handled money belonging to dictators such as Ferdinand Marcos and Mobuto Sese Seko. But the bank Rasheed and Ginnosar contacted, Lombard Odier and Cie, evidently agreed to take Arafat's account after being assured that "in a few years' time, they will have billions at their disposal."[111] The account was opened with a $20 million payment. The memorandum for the account stated that "all its funds were the property of the Palestinian people."[112] Shortly thereafter, the account was worth $340 million,[113] but by March 2003 an investigation into the PA's missing assets identified only $300 million in this bank account. The "Valuation and Transparency" report, which was ordered by the PA's new finance minister Salam Fayyad, provided no explanation for the missing $40 million.[114]

Some of Arafat's corruption takes a simpler form—the outright theft of aid funds. For example, in June 2002 the Kuwaiti newspaper *al-Watan* reported that Arafat had diverted funds that were donated by Arab countries as aid to the Palestinians, depositing $5.1 million into his personal account.[115] Muhammad Rasheed invested some of these siphoned funds in the Jordan Cement Company on behalf of the Palestine Commercial Services Company, in order to profit from a rise in cement prices—ironically, due to the increased demand for building materials in a war the PA had created.[116]

After *al-Watan* exposed Arafat's theft, a member of the Palestinian Legislative Council from Nablus, Muawiya al-Masri, was interviewed by the Jordanian publication *al-Sabil*. He criticized Arafat's régime, and not for the first time; in 1999 al-Masri went public about the PA's corruption and was nearly killed in retaliation.[117] Undeterred, in July 2002 he spoke at length to *al-Sabil* about the endemic corruption of the PA and of Arafat in particular: "No minister can appoint a driver or a delivery boy in his ministry without the president's consent. . . . There is no institutional process. There is only one institution—the presidency, which has no law and order and is based on bribing top officials."[118]

Palestinian documents released in January 2003 show that the Palestinian Authority is involved in the systematic theft of medicine and food supplies donated to the Palestinian people by UNRWA and Arab countries. The IDF had complained about this to Arafat in 1996, after discovering food and medicine packages donated by UNRWA for sale in the markets of Tel Aviv. In turn, on advice from his financial adviser, General Fuad Shubaki, Arafat found a solution to the problem: "Both Arafat and Shubaki instructed the Preventive Security Service to confiscate all the food products from private shops and markets and to transfer them to stores belonging to the [PA] Ministry of Supply." Shubaki and Arafat's original plan to channel stolen food and medicine for PA's benefit had failed, so instead a senior Fatah leader in Gaza and a confidant of Arafat, the PA's minister of supply, Abu Ali Shaheen (nicknamed the "Minister of Theft" by the Palestinians) continued to steal the supplies and to sell them on the black market.[119]

In a region full of autocratic régimes, however, Arafat's corruption is consistent with that of his neighbors. As Abd al-Wahab al-Effendi, a Sudanese scholar, wrote in a recent article about corruption in Arab régimes published in the London-based Arabic daily al-Hayat:

> Corruption of the Palestinian Authority and other Arab regimes is actually a necessary condition for fulfilling the role imposed upon them—to serve foreign interests and subjugate the peoples. Were the PA to give full authority to the Palestinian parliament and the legal apparatuses, and were it to obey popular will and spend its grant funds and income on education, health, services, and reviving the economy, what would be left for bribing the activists and intellectuals with appointments to ministries and the security apparatus?[120]

The article concluded: "Under the existing regimes, the fight against corruption is like fighting . . . Catholicism in the Vatican."

THE PALESTINIAN AUTHORITY'S INVOLVEMENT IN CRIME

Counterfeiting

Under the PA's control, according to the Israeli police, massive merchandise counterfeiting enterprises are still flourishing, "making millions of dollars a year," with royalties going to "senior Palestinian Authority figures."[121] The merchandise includes Microsoft and other companies' software, compact discs, DVDs, clothing, cosmetics, and books. These activities are executed in cooperation with HAMAS and other Palestinian terrorist organizations, which share in the profits with the PA's leadership.[122]

The PA has also been counterfeiting Israeli, Jordanian, and Kuwaiti currency.[123] For example, in April 2002 the IDF found "large quantities" of counterfeit Israeli currency in denominations of 50-, 100-, and 200-sheqel notes, in Arafat's compound in Ramallah.[124]

Shakedowns

According to confidential Palestinian sources,[125] arbitrary charges for traffic violations, demands of large bribes, kidnapping for money, and extortion of 70 to 90 percent of the income from private businesses, are rampant in the PA. The PLO employed similar methods when it was headquartered in Lebanon.

Palestinian and Israeli sources report that Muhammad Dahlan, former head of the PA Preventive Security Service in Gaza, supplemented his salary by collecting "more than a million shekels per month in protection money (from suppliers of oil, cigarettes, etc.), kickbacks for issuing licenses . . . and (since 1997), border-crossing-fees."[126]

Jibril Rajoub, the head of the Preventive Security Service in the West Bank, was reported to have extorted protection money from oil distributors, to have received kickbacks from the Jericho casino (until it was closed), and to have stolen intellectual property, presumably in concert with the other counterfeiting rings operating out of the PA territories.[127]

Automobile Theft

Jibril Rajoub and his men are also implicated by the Israeli police as having been involved in car theft networks.[128] Car theft from Israel is prevalent among Palestinians, frequently with the connivance of senior PA officials. According to reports by the Israeli police and eyewitnesses, cars stolen from Israel receive special license plates issued by the PA.

The Israelis have accused former PA police commissioner Ghazi Jabali of having licensed thousands of stolen cars from Israel, for a charge of $7,000 for a permanent license, until the PA fired him for having embezzled $20 million from the PA. Despite Jabali's illegal activities, Arafat proceeded to appoint him as a PA adviser on police affairs.[129] This should comes as no surprise, because al-Bahar, the company Jabali ran to produce the forged license plates, was owned by Yasser Arafat's wife, Suha.[130]

More on the Palestinian Authority's Support for Terrorism

Statistics provided by the Israeli Foreign Ministry in the fall of 2002 show that, since the beginning of the Palestinian attacks on Israel in September 2000, one homicide bomber from the Palestinian territories has been sent to Israel every five days. At the time of this writing, Palestinian terrorists have committed 16,899 attacks against Israel, killing 757 Israelis and injuring 5,222 more.[131] In January 2002, Yasser

Arafat declared in an op-ed in the *New York Times* that he opposed the killing of innocent civilians. Since then, attacks on Israelis have steadily escalated[132]—with Arafat's approval and funding.

Extensive evidence not only exposes the waste and corruption of the Palestinian Authority, but also further demonstrates the extent to which the PA funds and supports terrorism, both directly and indirectly. PA documents, receipts, and photocopies of checks confirm the transfer of hundreds of thousands of dollars from the PA budget to the families of members of the al-Aqsa Martyrs Brigades, and even to relatives of HAMAS terrorists—despite Arafat's continuing denials of cooperation with HAMAS.[133] At times, payments were ordered either directly by the Palestinian Ministry of Finance, or by Arafat's own office. At other times they were made from the Preventive Security Service's budget, in clear violation of the original purpose for which the service was first created—which was to prevent terror.[134]

For example, on July 19, 2001, the Palestinian Ministry of Finance issued two payment orders, both for the terrorist Tzafut Udah Rachmi, for his involvement in planning terrorist attacks against Israel—one payment for the sum of $15,000, the other for $2,500. The Arab Bank branch in Gaza paid both of these amounts on August 8, 2001.[135] Again, on July 28, 2002, Arafat personally ordered the Palestinian Ministry of Finance to pay the mortgages for the families of two terrorists, Jahad Alamarin and Awal Alnamera, who had been employed by the Preventive Security Service in Gaza, and who had been killed in terror attacks against Israel. Arafat had also ordered the Ministry of Finance to pay $2,000 to each of the families of the "martyrs."[136]

Additional PA documents show that Yasser Arafat, in his own handwriting, ordered the PA Ministry of Finance to pay $9,000 to the "El-Farouk" rental car company in Gaza for a car which had been driven by the son of a senior HAMAS operative in Gaza, and which had been bombed by the IDF on September 18, 2001. The rental company, instead of demanding the money from HAMAS, asked Arafat to cover the damage. By ordering the payment, Arafat not only misappropriated the PA's money, but also—despite his denials—sponsored a HAMAS terrorist. This payment also reveals how the Palestinian Ministry of Finance covers the routine operational costs of HAMAS.[137]

Under Arafat's direction, the PA's Preventive Security apparatus became not only an organization that perpetuates instead of preventing terror, but also a producer of large quantities of arms. A similar change occurred in other PA security services, including General Intelligence and Arafat's personal guard, "Force 17." According to Preventive Security documents and testimony by Preventive Security officers apprehended by the Israel Defense Forces, the arms were distributed to "all the terrorist organizations operating in the Gaza Strip."[138] These arms are distributed in an ongoing and generous manner to organizations including the Palestinian Islamic Jihad, the Popular Resistance Committees, and HAMAS, which use the arms for daily attacks against Israeli targets along the Gaza Strip.[139]

Moreover, on January 2003, the leader of HAMAS, Sheikh Ahmed Yassin, announced publicly that "the PA had aided the Palestinian terrorist organizations to carry out terrorist attacks against Israel. 'The Palestinian Police force has, several times, aided fighters to perpetrate their actions.'"[140]

Palestinian terrorists on the PA payroll include:

Marwan Barghouti

Despite his arrest and indictment for the murder of twenty-six Israelis, this former head of the terrorist organization Fatah/Tanzim in the West Bank continues as of this writing to receive a salary of $2,500 per month from the PA.[141] In addition to his personal involvement in these murders, Barghouti has allocated special funds for terrorists and has signed checks to pay for attacks against Israel—all with Arafat's explicit approval.[142]

Barghouti, together with Fa'ak Kana'an, who was the head of Fatah in Tulkarm and also on the PA payroll, sent letters[143] requesting Arafat's approval to pay terrorists through the PA's security apparatus payroll, and to reward them additionally with bonuses for their attacks on Israelis. Arafat provided his approval.[144]

Further evidence of Marwan Barghouti's personal involvement in terrorist activities was provided in an Israeli court ruling in January 2003, which stated that Barghouti "authorized the execution of the attack"—a homicide bombing—on the Sea Food Market restaurant in Tel Aviv in March 2002, which killed three people and seriously injured dozens.[145] Barghouti also received $20,000 from Yasser Arafat "for purposes of funding training facilities"[146] for terrorists. He also assisted terrorists in committing homicide bombings—he interviewed them, and participated in their training. In addition, he obtained weapons, including explosives, that were given to homicide bombers, and financed the acquisition of other weapons. After the Israelis arrested Barghouti, Arafat approved a payment of $1,200 to arrange for "spontaneous public demonstrations" to protest the arrest.[147]

Nasser Awis

Barghouti's deputy Nasser Awis served as the link between him and the Tanzim in the West Bank and Gaza. He has been identified in PA documents not only as the head of the al-Aqsa Martyrs Brigades in Samaria, but also as an officer in the PA General Intelligence and General Security apparatus; he received his salary from the PA.[148] Since January 2002, Awis has been responsible for attacks that have killed twenty Israelis and wounded at least 120. Awis was also engaged in the acquisition, production, and smuggling of heavy weapons systems.[149] He was captured by the IDF in April 2002,[150] and a year later was convicted on fourteen counts of murder and other charges,[151] and sentenced to fourteen life sentences plus fifty years.[152]

Fuad Shubaki

The former PA chief financial officer and a close friend and confidante of Arafat, Shubaki established two arms smuggling networks, one from Iraq and Iran, and another from Jordan and Egypt.[153] Shubaki not only allocated $80,000 for a heavy arms factory to produce artillery rockets for the al-Aqsa Martyrs Brigades[154] but also was directly involved in organizing funds for another arms smuggling operation from Iran on the ship *Karine-A*.[155]

It was only after the *Karine-A* was intercepted by the Israeli Navy and the arms smuggling operation was exposed in January 2002 that—under the weight of American pressure—Shubaki was finally imprisoned in a PA facility in Jericho. PA documents captured by the Israeli Defense Force in Gaza in February 2003 reveal that the July 2002 appointment of Brigadier General Mahmoud Awdallah as Shubaki's replacement was arranged by Shubaki himself and ordered by Arafat, in defiance of strong objections in the PA. The documents also reveal that, despite Subaki's official replacement, and despite U.S. and U.K. supervision, Shubaki continues to direct the Financial Directorate of the Palestinian General Security service from his "jail" in Jericho. He conducts his business by cell phone.[156]

THE PA & THE FOSTERING OF HATE

As the Palestinian Authority provides money and support for the current perpetrators of Palestinian terrorism, it also encourages the spread of violence to a new generation, through the dissemination of violent, hateful propaganda. On many public, well-documented occasions, Yasser Arafat himself has encouraged children to become *shahidis* (homicide bombers), and, as of this writing, has repeated his promise to continue the armed struggle against Israel.[157]

According to statements by former Arafat deputy Mahmoud

Abbas, now the Palestinian prime minister, Palestinian children are given 5 sheqels (about U.S.$1) for each pipe bomb they throw.[158] In January 2003, the UN Security Council protested the use of children as homicide bombers. The UN under-secretary-general, Olara Otunnu, declared, "We have witnessed both ends of these acts: children have been used as suicide bombers and children have been killed by suicide bombings. I call on the Palestinian authorities to do everything within their powers to stop all participation by children in this conflict."[159] Otunnu then called on the Israeli authorities to "abide fully by the international human rights and humanitarian legal obligation concerning the protection, rights, and well-being of Palestinian children." But the Palestinian Authority still has not been listed as a party of concern regarding its use of Palestinian children as homicide bombers.[160]

Such incitement not only runs counter to the Oslo Accords that Arafat signed in 1993, agreeing to "strive to live in peaceful coexistence and mutual dignity and security,"[161] but also runs counter to the Joint Declaration by the European Parliament, the European Council, and the European Commission Against Racism and Xenophobia, which states that the EU:

> Considers that incitement to racism, as well as the dissemination and promotion of any type of revisionist thesis concerning the Holocaust or denial that the Holocaust took place, should be considered a criminal offence at Union level and calls on all the Member States accordingly to adapt their legislation against the perpetrators of acts of racism.[162]

The Palestinian Authority is also obligated by treaty to end such messages, as the preamble to the Oslo II Interim Accord distinctly states:

> The government of Israel and the PLO reaffirm "their mutual commitment to act, in accordance with this Agreement, immediately, efficiently and effectively against acts or threats of terrorism,

violence or incitement, whether committed by Palestinians or Israelis."[163]

The Palestinian education system is funded by the international
donor community through the United Nations Relief and Works
Agency (UNRWA). The agency's total budget for 2003 alone was
U.S.$405 billion.[164] The UNRWA employs at least eighteen thousand
Palestinians in more than 250 schools it operates in the West Bank
and Gaza Strip.[165] But UNRWA-paid teachers, in UNRWA-built
schools, are teaching from textbooks with anti-Semitic, anti-Israel,
and anti-coexistence indoctrination. The following are examples
from Palestinian educational materials:

- A seventh-grade textbook includes a question referring to
  the poem "The Shahid," in which students are asked, "Which
  of the following is the meaning of the expression 'honorable
  death'?" The answer choices are: "Death from illness, Sudden
  death, [or] Martyrdom (shahada) while defending the
  homeland."[166]
- From a seventh-grade textbook, *National Education:* "Question: how many of the Palestinian villages have been destroyed and replaced by imperialist settlements?"[167]
- Maps of Palestine do not include Israel. This seems to be, in
  effect, an effort to deny the nation's existence.[168]
- In the al-Amari refugee camp in Ramallah, in a UNRWA-run
  school, there were posters displayed prominently "glorifying
  suicide attacks, armed struggle, and the leaders of the terrorist wing of Hamas"[169]

UNRWA

UNRWA's involvement in the fostering of hate extends beyond the
propaganda in its schools' textbooks. UNRWA representative Saheil
Alhinadi praised homicide attacks in a speech he gave in July 2001.[170]

And an intelligence report from December 2003 details how the UN social club in Gaza would hold meetings of the terrorist organization Tanzim, and how, in the UNRWA-run refugee camps, Palestinian terrorists store ammunition in UNRWA schools and smuggle arms in United Nations ambulances. "When we came into this refugee camp [Jenin]," stated Israeli deputy prime minister Natan Sharansky in April 2002, "to the place where for years no army and no soldier had entered, it became clear that practically every house, and almost every window, was booby-trapped, that the struggle would be very hard." He continued, "Overwhelmingly, almost everybody who was discovered until now was a soldier with arms, with weapons in their hands and some with explosive materials, suicide bombers."[171]

The UNRWA spokesman, Paul McCann, protested that "our school teachers and doctors aren't the ones to root out Hamas."[172] However, Palestinian and Israeli sources agree that the UNRWA refugee camps are staffed mostly by members of HAMAS, which also runs the camps' workers "union."[173] As former U.S. ambassador to Morocco Marc Ginsburg reported, "The refugee camps indeed are not policed by anyone but the Palestinian Authority. With the United Nations Relief and Works Administration personnel administering the lion's share of the programs, but other organizations, including extremist Islamic organizations, operate freely in the camps."[174]

When the Israelis searched camps run by the UNRWA, they discovered "illegal arms caches, bomb factories, and a plant manufacturing the new Kassam-2 rocket, designed to reach Israeli population centers from the West Bank and Gaza."[175]

USAID & PASSIA

On August 28, 2002, Julie Stahl of CNS News reported that U.S. aid money is funding at least one group that engages in pro-Palestinian propaganda in the U.S. and in Europe. Since 1997, the United States, through the U.S. Agency for International Development (USAID), has given $1.2 million to the Palestinian Academic Society for the Study of International Affairs (PASSIA). The group, according to Stahl, "teaches Palestinians how to lobby, raise money for political causes and win favorable media coverage and support."[176] One assignment was to prepare a fundraising proposal for information booklets on the "al Aqsa Intifada." In other publications, PASSIA advocates the right of return for Palestinian refugees to all of Israel, which would be tantamount to destroying Israel by demographically overwhelming it.[177]

HAMAS: ISLAMIC JIHAD & PALESTINIANS

The greed and corruption of the Palestinian Authority has created a void in the essential services provided to the Palestinian people. In many cases, that void has been filled by the Palestinian Islamic Resistance Movement, also known as HAMAS. HAMAS consists of both a military wing and sociopolitical wing, and the latter is involved with activities such as building hospitals, running health clinics and schools, and aiding the poor.

The military wing, however, has been engaged in countless terrorist attacks against Israel, including hundreds of both attempted and successful homicide bombings. But HAMAS does not kill only Israelis or Americans;[178] it has also executed at least forty Palestinians whom it alleged had collaborated with Israel.[179] According to President George W. Bush, "Hamas is an extremist group . . . it is one of the deadliest terrorist organizations in the world today."[180]

HAMAS was founded by Sheikh Ahmed Yassin in 1987 for the stated purpose of waging *Jihad* to liberate Palestine and to establish an Islamic Palestine from the Mediterranean Sea to the Jordan River.[181] Sheikh Yassin has often publicly stated his support of homicide bombing. During a rally in support of Saddam Hussein and Iraq, which was held in the Jabalya refugee camp in Gaza in January 2003, Yassin called on the Iraqi people to "become human bombs, using belts and suitcases aimed at killing every enemy that walks on the earth and pollutes it."[182] A crowd of three thousand HAMAS supporters carried slogans calling for "Death to USA" and "Victory from Jerusalem to Baghdad."[183] (HAMAS had opened an office in Baghdad in 1999.)

HAMAS's funding stems from Iran, Saudi Arabia, the Gulf States, the United Arab Emirates, Syria, and Iraq; from the U.S., Canada, and the tri-border region of South America; and even from al-Qaeda. Despite religious differences between HAMAS and some of its sponsors—such as Iran, which contributes $3 to $30 million per year[184]—millions of dollars are channeled to HAMAS by Muslim governments to continue its *Jihad.*

HAMAS's U.S. Connection: The Holy Land Foundation (HLF)

In December 2001 President George W. Bush announced the freezing of the assets of the Holy Land Foundation of Richardson, Texas, a tax-exempt, American-based charity that had sent money to HAMAS. According to the president, "Hamas has obtained much of the money that it pays for murder abroad right here in the United States . . . it raised $30 million from people in America last year."[185]

The HLF, whose declared revenues in the U.S. for the year 2000 exceeded $13 million,[186] was the charity most responsible for raising funds for HAMAS in the U.S. and Canada. Documents found in the offices of the HAMAS-affiliated Tulkarm Charity Committee include its correspondence with the Holy Land Foundation regarding the funding of various projects. The Charity Committee received HLF money through the Tulkarm branch of the Arab Bank, which is headquartered in Amman, Jordan[187]—the same bank through which the al-Qaeda cell in Madrid transferred money to the September 11 hijackers.

The HLF was founded in 1989 with offices in Texas, California, New Jersey, and Illinois; it described itself as the largest Muslim charity in the United States.[188] HLF collected donations for HAMAS in the

U.S. while masquerading as a humanitarian and charitable organization. The funds were then wired to HAMAS charitable conduits in the West Bank and Gaza, which then transferred the funds to HAMAS operatives, including homicide bombers and other terrorists.[189] According to President Bush, "Money raised by the Holy Land Foundation is used by Hamas to support schools and indoctrinate children to grow up into suicide bombers. Money raised by the Holy Land Foundation is also used by Hamas to recruit suicide bombers and to support their families."[190]

In 1993 in Philadelphia, the FBI monitored a meeting held by the HLF with high-ranking HAMAS officials.[191] According to the FBI, "It was decided that most or almost all of the funds collected in the future should be directed to enhance the Islamic Resistance Movement [HAMAS] and to weaken the self-rule government [in Israel]."[192]

The Holy Land Foundation's fundraising efforts on behalf of HAMAS were already recognized in 1997, when the Israeli police raided the organization's Jerusalem headquarters and arrested its director, Muhammad Othman, for having distributed money to families of HAMAS homicide bombers.[193] Representatives of the Holy Land Foundation do not deny this, but claim that "the money is given on the basis of need and not the political affiliation of the deceased."[194] A U.S. government document "established that these funds were used by Hamas to support schools and indoctrinate children to grow up into suicide bombers."[195]

Moreover, support for homicide bombings is advocated in HLF documents: "Is it not out of honesty and sincerity that we all be brothers to the martyr's widow? Should we not stand by her and compensate her children for what they lost by their father's martyrdom?" proposed an HLF fundraising letter from 1988.[196] In another HLF appeal from March 1993, the pledge card read: "Yes. I can and want to help needy families of Palestinian martyrs, prisoners and deportees."[197] An HLF brochure distributed at a Dayton, Ohio, conference in December 1996 stipulated that at least one thousand families have benefited from a relief program provided by HLF that was "aiding distressed families of detainees, deportees, martyrs and other impoverished families to be uplifted to a more mainstream life."[198]

Days before the September 11 attacks, a California-based Internet company, Infocom, which had been founded with HAMAS money and which had shared office space, personnel, and board members with the Holy Land Foundation, was raided by the FBI, and its assets were frozen. However, the HLF itself continued to operate. One month before the government finally closed down the foundation, the FBI wrote in a memo about the HLF that it had "concluded that the foundation had been designated by top Hamas officials as the movement's primary fund-raiser in the United States."[199] The FBI had known about this foundation since at least 1993; why had they taken so long?

The Holy Land Foundation's fundraising activities were not limited to the United States. In 1998, the South African National Intelligence Agency reported that a Canadian aid organization in Ontario, the "Jerusalem Fund," had been funneling money to the Holy Land Foundation office in Richardson, Texas, from where it was then transferred to HAMAS in the West Bank and Gaza. "The Hamas infrastructure in Canada forms part of the infrastructure in the United States," the report maintained; it added, "The Jerusalem Fund operating in Ontario is a source of funds for the Holy Land Foundation in the United States."[200] The report further noted that, in addition to HAMAS, the Jerusalem Fund also supported Islamists in Iraq, Kosovo, Lebanon, and Turkey, and that since 1991 it had raised $350,000 to $400,000 annually.[201]

HAMAS in Europe: The al-Aqsa Foundation

The European conduit for HAMAS is the al-Aqsa Foundation. The group "operates around Europe, including the Netherlands and Belgium,"[202] said Ronny Naftaniel, director of the Center for Information and Documentation on Israel (CIDI) in the Hague. According to Naftaniel, a Palestinian named Muhammad Amar, who is currently the head of the foundation in Germany, also directs the al-Aqsa Foundation office in Holland, from where it raised €600,000 in 2000, mostly from cities in the Netherlands with large Muslim populations. Despite international recognition that HAMAS is a terrorist organization, Holland's General Intelligence and Security Services (AIVD) claim that "there is no proof that this money is used for terror activity, since Hamas also directs social and cultural activity."[203] Germany shut down its al-Aqsa Foundation offices in August 2002.[204]

The al-Aqsa Foundation has still another branch in South Africa. It uses its Web site to advance incitement with photos of homicide bombings, to solicit funds for HAMAS terror activities against Israel, to provide medical assistance to wounded terrorists, and to promise "proper" Islamic education to nursery and primary school children.[205] The Web site lists It'ilaf al-Khayr (Union for Good), located at Nat West Bank in London, as the primary recipient of donations.[206]

HAMAS Banks

In addition to contributions from charities and individuals, HAMAS also received $20 million in 1998 to open the al-Aqsa Islamic Bank in the Palestinian territories. The funds came from both the owner of the Saudi al-Baraka Bank, Saleh Abdullah Kamel, and from a subsidiary of al-Baraka, the Jordan Islamic Bank. Kamel had also provided significant financial infrastructure to Osama bin Laden in Sudan beginning in 1983.[207]

The HAMAS-owned al-Aqsa Bank also "embarked on joint projects with Citigroup, intertwining itself with Citibank's Israel division. Soon, al-Aqsa and Citibank shared a single database for Israel. Money deposited into al-Aqsa accounts in Europe or other parts of the Middle East became accessible from Israel [to HAMAS members] though Citibank chapters."[208] By the time Citibank severed its relations with al-Aqsa, based on advice from Israeli authorities as well as from the U.S. Treasury Department, at least $1 million had been transferred through Citibank into the al-Aqsa Bank on behalf of HAMAS.[209]

Another bank that was used to move money to HAMAS was the Saudi-owned al-Taqwa Bank. It had been identified as being involved with HAMAS as early as 1997, when deputy assistant secretary of the Treasury Department, Jamie C. Zarate, told Congress that the "$60 million collected annually for Hamas was moved to accounts with Bank al Taqwa."[210]

By late June 2003, senior U.S. government officials had announced that they were investigating "Account 98" funds—specially designated Saudi accounts that go to fund charitable organizations in the West Bank and Gaza—under suspicion that the money went to fund HAMAS and other Palestinian terror organizations. The Saudis claimed they never give directly to the Palestinians and that the money was monitored by international organizations. However, Palestinian documents prove otherwise.[211]

OTHER PA TERROR ALLIANCES

Evidence of cooperation between the Palestinian Authority and HAMAS has already been discussed, but the PA also has other terrorist allies. Terrorists who were trained in the PLO camps in Lebanon, Libya, and Sudan in the 1970s and 1980s forged an alliance with the PLO that carried over to the PA. Even organizations with opposing ideologies have all found common ground, and have been known to cooperate financially and logistically in the interest of advancing terrorism. Some examples of groups with ties to the PA are:

Palestinian Islamic Jihad (PIJ)

The Palestinian Islamic Jihad[212] carried out joint terrorist operations against Israeli targets with the al-Aqsa Martyrs Brigades, HAMAS, and Fatah, from their center of operations in Jenin's refugee camp.[213] The PIJ's major sponsors are Hizballah, Iran, and Syria.[214] The PIJ leader in Gaza, Abd Allah al-Shami, confirmed the connection and expressed "the hope that the PIJ and Hamas would coordinate their activities in the future."[215] The PIJ has, as well, claimed responsibility for homicide bombings in Israel.[216]

Irish Republican Army (IRA)

The PLO's connection to the IRA dates back to the 1970s and 1980s, when PLO and IRA operatives trained together in Libya and Lebanon's Beka'a Valley. However, the IRA's active involvement with the PLO was noted only in March 2002, when a sniper shot to death ten Israelis and wounded scores of others. The sniper left behind a bolt-action rifle—a practice that has been identified as an Irish Republican Army trademark.[217]

A second incident with IRA fingerprints was uncovered after the Israeli incursion into Jenin in May 2002. Paul Collinson, a British explosives expert working with the Red Cross, identified hundreds of explosive devices found there and noted that "the pipe bombs found in Jenin were exact replicas of those in Northern Ireland."[218] The *Daily Telegraph* quoted a U.S. government official as saying in response: "If there was clear and convincing evidence that the IRA has been training Palestinians in bomb-making techniques, then we are facing a grave and grievous situation for the IRA. It would surely lead to a reassessment of whether the IRA should not be put on the designated list of terrorist organizations with a global reach."[219] Recent revelations about al-Qaeda's training methods have also been identified as carrying some of the IRA's trademarks.[220]

INTERNATIONAL AID FOR PALESTINIAN TERROR

Iraq

Until the U.S. liberation of Iraq, the nation's support for, and encouragement of, Palestinian terrorism came directly from Saddam Hussein, and was distributed through three entities that his régime directed in the Palestinian territories: the Arab Liberation Front (ALF), the Palestinian Liberation Front (PLF), and the Palestinian branch of the Iraqi Baath party. These organizations operated according to instructions from Iraq and received generous Iraqi financing. Palestinian documents show that, from June 2002, the ALF branches in Gaza received $40,000 per month[221]—in an area where the average wage is less than $2 a day.[222]

Saddam funded homicide bombings and attacks on Israel committed by any and all Palestinian terror groups. According to PA documents, Iraq had apparently transferred at least $35 million to Palestinian terrorists for homicide bombings in Israel.[223] Families of homicide bombers received $25,000 (as of March 2002), while families of other terrorists attacking Israel received $10,000.[224] Grants from Saddam were often distributed in public ceremonies, such as a rally that ALF and the Baath party arranged in Gaza in August 2001. During the rally, the families of two homicide bombers each received $15,000, "according to the Decision of Commander Saddam Hussein . . . in appreciation of their bravery."[225]

In January 2003, Arafat, who was pressured by the U.S. to stop terrorist attacks against Israel, ordered the PA to confiscate $420,000 that had been sent from Iraq to the families of Palestinian homicide bombers.[226] A member of the pro-Iraqi Palestinian Liberation Front protested that "this is the biggest scandal ever."[227]

Saddam continued to fund Palestinian terrorism even after the war in Iraq had begun. His agents in the West Bank and Gaza Strip distributed at least $250,000 to families of homicide bombers in public ceremonies while crowds chanted, "Oh, beloved Saddam, we are ready to sacrifice our blood for you."[228]

In April 2003, U.S. Marines discovered a Palestinian Liberation Front training camp near the Diallo River in southwest Baghdad. The well-equipped facility, which was built twenty-five years ago, was outfitted to train at least six hundred people at a time. Documents found in the camp included correspondence with the PLO and showed that Iraq provided weapons to the PLF "as late as January 2003."[229]

Discoveries during the Iraq war confirmed U.S. allegations that Saddam Hussein also had close ties to al-Qaeda. The extent of the relationship remains unknown at the time of this writing; however, "more than 100 al Qaeda terrorists are believed to have been in Iraq before the start of the war,"[230] and documents found at the Iraqi intelligence headquarters confirmed that the al-Qaeda-Saddam connection had existed since at least 1994.[231] After U.S. forces took over the terrorist training camp operated by the radical Iraqi group Ansar al-Islam in northern Iraq, a Special Forces officer described the materials found in the camp as "the Al Qaeda mobile curriculum."[232] Al-Qaeda instructors helped the group in the training of not only Iraqis, but also terrorists "from Algeria, Sudan, Syria, Morocco, Tunisia, Qatar, Saudi Arabia, Germany, Spain, Italy and Canada."[233] The camp had a factory that produced "the poison ricin and a topical cyanide poison."[234]

Saudi Arabia

Saudi Arabia, like Iraq, also publicly supports homicide bombing in Israel. In September 2000, Saudi Arabia conducted two telethons for the specified purpose of raising funds for the families of Palestinian homicide bombers. When the first telethon raised only $10.8 million for the "Palestinian martyrs," King Fahd ordered another one, urging "Saudis, expatriates, and private companies to contribute generously."[235] The Saudi minister of the interior, Prince Nayef bin Abd al-Aziz, also called for contributions, proclaiming that this telethon "is a continuation and assertion of the kingdom's support [for the *intifada*]."[236] The second telethon's take included donations of $2.7 million from King Fahd, $1.35 million from Crown Prince Abdullah, and $800,000 from Defense Minister Prince Sultan—and totaled $163.3 million. Altogether, the two telethons raised $174 million for families of homicide bombers, including members of HAMAS and the al-Aqsa Martyrs Brigades.[237] Other Gulf states—the United Arab Emirates, Bahrain, Qatar, and Kuwait—held similar events, from which they raised $94 million.[238]

Saudi funding, however, did not come solely from the telethons. "Prince Sultan affirms [the] Kingdom's Support for the Palestinian Intifada," reported a Saudi embassy press release; $40 million had already been given to "the families of those martyred" and additional "worthies."[239]

Saudi Arabia also created the Saudi Committee for the Support of the al-Quds Uprising, based in Riyadh and run by interior minister Prince Nayef.[240] Overall, this committee "reported the transfer of $55.7 million mostly to the families of suicide bombers and to the families of imprisoned or injured Palestinian militants."[241] The methods by which these funds were transferred and where they ended up are unknown. However, documents found in the offices of the Tulkarm Charity Committee record in great detail the payments to 102 HAMAS terrorists who were killed in "martyr operation[s]."[242] The family of each listed terrorist received $5,340, according to the Saudi committee's documents.[243] They listed each "martyr" and the manner in which each one died, including eight that had lost their lives while perpetrating homicide bombings.[244] In another instance, the Saudi Committee transferred money to Palestinian prisoners in the Megiddo prison in Israel. It is unknown how it was transferred.[245]

The latest Saudi contributions, in April 2003, came from two sources: about $500,000 (the first installment of the year) from the "popular committee for assisting the Palestinian Mujahideen," headed by Prince Salman bin Abd al-Aziz, the governor of Riyadh;[246] and $1 million from $32 million the Saudi Committee for the Support of the al-Quds Uprising has earmarked for this purpose.[247]

In December 2000, in an apparent attempt to obtain some of the Saudi money, Yasser Arafat complained to the Saudis that they had not transferred funds to the PA, but had instead sent it directly to HAMAS and its associates.[248] He further asked permission to send a committee to Saudi Arabia to discuss ways to verify that their money would reach its "real beneficiaries."[249] When the Saudi interior minister declared on January 7, 2001, that 123,750,000 riyals had been "paid in support of the families of Intifada al Quds fatalities, prisoners, wounded and disabled, as well as needy Palestinian families,"[250] Arafat responded with a handwritten letter marked "very important," instructing his deputy Mahmoud Abbas and the PA representative in Saudi Arabia to "please inform me where did this money go to and who received it since the martyrs and wounded received nothing."[251]

SOME THINGS NEVER CHANGE

From the Oslo Accord until the end of 2002, the Palestinian Authority received more than $5 billion in aid; this translates to $1,330 per Palestinian. In comparison, the Marshall Plan to rebuild Europe after World War II provided each European with only $272 in today's dollars. By March 2003, international aid totaling $5.5 billion in unmonitored funds has done very little for the Palestinian economy— between 60 and 75 percent of the Palestinian people have to survive on less than $2 a day. According to the latest World Bank report, in 2002 alone $40 million in aid were transferred each month to the PA, while "the gross national income of the Palestinians in 2002 shrunk 40 percent in relation to 2000."[252]

The Oslo Peace Accord that Yasser Arafat signed in 1993, which created the Palestinian Authority, was supposed to bring peace and prosperity to the region. Instead, lack of accountability for funds throughout the years has enabled Arafat to create a full-fledged terrorist state, perpetuating the suffering of both the Palestinian and the Israeli people. According to testimony before the Armed Services Committee:

> Rather than prepare his people for peace, he has indoctrinated them for war. He has praised suicide bombers as "martyrs" and repeatedly has called for a jihad (holy war) to liberate Jerusalem. Arafat, the veteran terrorist, has created an environment in which terrorists flourish.[253]

By the year 2000, when Arafat could not get what he wanted through a "peace process" he reverted to a "war process" and initiated a campaign of violence against Israel.[254] Continued funding from Arab states and the international community maintains Arafat in power in spite of his public support of Saddam Hussein, his support of terrorism, and his persistent use of homicide bombing. Moreover, despite the "war on terrorism" and ongoing Palestinian violence, Arafat and his Palestinian Authority have never been identified as a terrorist entity.

But President George W. Bush does recognize the need for serious changes in Palestinian leadership. In June 2002, he outlined his vision for peace in the Middle East, stating that "when the Palestinian people have new leaders, new institutions and new security arrangements with their neighbors, the United States of America will support the creation of a Palestinian state whose borders and certain aspects of its sovereignty will be provisional until resolved as part of a final settlement in the Middle East."[255] To pursue his vision, in December 2002 his administration presented the Road Map—a peace plan for Israel and the Palestinians, pushed forward by the EU, that would lead to a Palestinian state. The Road Map is subject to both sides' adherence to the conditions listed in the plan. As President Bush later reiterated:

> The Palestinian state must be a reformed and peaceful and democratic state that abandons forever the use of terror. The government of Israel, as the terror threat is removed and security improves, must take concrete steps to support the emergence of a viable and credible Palestinian state, and to work as quickly as possible toward a final status agreement. As progress is made toward peace, settlement activity in the occupied territories must end. And the Arab states must oppose terrorism, support the emergence of a peaceful and democratic Palestine, and state clearly that they will live in peace with Israel.[256]

Along with the Road Map, a "Quartet" was formed by the United States, the United Nations, the European Union, and the Russian Federation, to oversee the establishment of two independent states living peacefully side by side by the year 2005.[257]

Apparently to appease Arab states on the eve of the war to remove Saddam Hussein, and pressured by the Europeans and UN secretary-general Kofi Annan, President Bush repeated his intention to publish a plan for the implementation of the Road Map.[258] Although, by the first week of March 2003, the U.S. administration appeared ready to postpone the plans for a settlement between Israel and the Palestinians until after the war with Iraq was settled,[259] the discussions never stopped. However, on April 2, 2003, following a meeting with the EU representative, Arafat canceled any further talks with the U.S. and Israel regarding the Road Map, claiming that the U.S. was not a "legitimate partner while it is destroying Baghdad."[260] Clearly, Arafat had no intention of following the president's plan. Yet, the very next day, the Quartet met again in Brussels to continue the work on the road map.[261]

The EU, the UN, and the Russian Federation continue to pursue the Road Map, despite clear violations of all agreements signed thus far by Arafat and the Palestinian Authority, including their failure to institute real structural reforms. EU commissioner Christopher Patten has described Arafat as an "indispensable" partner, and to help him the Europeans devise cosmetic "reforms." The appointment of a Palestinian prime minister is the most recent example.[262] When Arafat named Mahmoud Abbas (AKA Abu Mazen), who on March 10, 2003, was approved by the Palestinian Legislative Council, this act was praised as a "real" change.[263] But Abbas, the secretary-general of the Executive Committee of the PLO, is no moderate; he is in fact a Holocaust denier whose book *The Other Side: The Secret Relationship Between Nazism and Zionism* asserts that the Holocaust claimed fewer than a million Jewish lives, and that even those deaths were the result of a Nazi-Zionist conspiracy.[264]

Arafat chose Abbas, his longtime deputy, because he had followed Arafat's lead since the inception of the Palestinian Liberation Organization in 1964. "If someone thinks that by appointing a Prime Minister—even with someone as important as Abu Mazen who has had an historic role in the PLO—that Chairman Arafat will disappear, he is mistaken," commented Ahmed Tibi, an Arab-Israeli member of the Israeli parliament.[265] Moreover, according to a Palestinian official, the appointment was conditional—Abbas had to agree that "Arafat would remain the supreme commander of [the] security forces and retain the final word on peace talks."[266] In addition, Arafat has the power to name or fire the prime minister.[267] Even a draft of a new constitution for a future Palestinian state, which was published in the Palestinian daily *al-Ayyam* on January 20, 2003, preserved the status of the "president"—Arafat—as the central executive authority.

Since its inception, the PA, led by Arafat, has consorted with, harbored, financed, and armed terrorist groups. Now, with the appointment of Arafat's "yes man" as prime minister, they show no signs of change. Discussions of a new Road Map serve only to give Arafat and

the PA more time to perpetuate more terrorism, and more funding to
do so, partly from the EU.

Reform Attempts: Salam Fayyad

In the summer of 2002, President Bush issued a strong condemnation of Arafat and his leadership following a wave of terror attacks
against Israel. Because of that condemnation, and because official
Palestinian papers that were discovered documented Arafat and the
PA's involvement in financing terrorism and misappropriating funds,
on June 9 Arafat was forced to appoint a new minister of finance:
Salam Fayyad, a former IMF official who, assisted by outside experts,
began an attempt to overhaul the corrupt system.

Fayyad has managed to consolidate all PA ministries' known in-
coming funds into a single account, which is supervised by him and
by a nonprofit organization called the Democracy Council. The
council was officially appointed by Fayyad and approved by the
Palestinian Authority and the Palestinian National Council. The
Democracy Council's role is to track down all PA assets; however,
only $600 million in PA assets have been identified.[268] A major im-
pediment is the fact that only assets owned by the PA after December
31, 2002, are investigated. No PA assets or funds held before that date
come under scrutiny.[269] Thus, the millions that have been siphoned
away from the Palestinian people by Arafat and the Palestinian Authority will probably remain a secret.

The Democracy Council prepared a report containing "financial
and corporate details about the PNA's investments and commercial
activities," which was released on March 3, 2003.[270] The report made
public seventy-nine commercial investments and a listing of bank
accounts that were formerly controlled by the Palestine Commercial
Services Company. It identified corrupt practices such as the mo-
nopolization of the cement industry, and the fact that "agents or employees of various agencies of the PA, which were identified . . .

routinely demand cash payments in order to facilitate the import and transportation of cement into Gaza. For example, agents from the security forces regularly request payment for loading and off-loading."[271] However, no names are mentioned, despite mountains of evidence in the PA's own documents, which reveal in minute detail how the cement racket is run—and who runs it.[272] Asked about the lack of details and names in the report, the lead auditor responded, "That will be dealt with by somebody else."[273]

In addition to the work of the Democracy Council, Standard and Poor's is supervising how the tax remittances transferred by Israel to the PA are being allocated. However, few of its accountants are known to speak or read Arabic, the language in which the books are kept.[274]

Thus far, Minister Fayyad has failed in his efforts to hold the different PA ministries accountable for the businesses they independently own and operate. Similarly, although Fayyad has attempted to change the PA's practice of disbursing payments in cash, thus enabling the funding of terrorists, he has been thwarted by Arafat, who continues to authorize the transfer of funds to the terror infrastructure in the PA—including payments to the al-Aqsa Martyrs Brigades and to the owners of metal workshops that produce the Kassam rockets used to attack Israeli targets.[275]

Fayyad has also proven unable to end Arafat's direct payments to terrorists held in Israeli prisons and to their families. Likewise, Fayyad failed to stop Arafat's payment of $2,000 to the foreign minister of Cyprus, in support of expelled Palestinian terrorists that Cyprus had agreed to take in.[276]

Moreover, Fayyad did not succeed in eliminating the 15 percent "tax" imposed by the PA on their employees. This money, which is unaccounted for in the PA budget, goes to Fatah.[277] An indication of how the money is used can be gleaned from Fatah's official statement boasting the success of its newly designed and domestically produced rocket, the al-Buraq, which was fired by the al-Aqsa Martyrs Brigades on February 24 against Israeli civilians.

In a further subversion of the minister's authority, Arafat's treasurer in the Finance Ministry, Sami Ramlawi, returned to his post after having been fired when Fayyad took office. Ramlawi, on Arafat's orders, hands out cash payments to security forces.[278]

The marginalization of Fayyad and Abbas, the failure to remove Arafat from the leadership of the PA, the Palestinians' continuing involvement in terror activities against Israel, and the vocal daily demonstrations in the West Bank and the Gaza Strip in support of Saddam Hussein and against the U.S, led House Majority Leader Tom DeLay "to warn against treating the Palestinian Authority as a trustworthy negotiating partner. . . . 'Negotiating with these men . . . is folly, and any agreement arrived at through such empty negotiations would amount to a covenant with death.'"[279]

Predictably, the creation of a Palestinian prime minister has reinvigorated the EU push for an Israeli-Palestinian settlement. And there was some reason for optimism; the appointment of a new government could have led to a much-needed transition in the PA's affairs.[280] But the transformation of this corrupt régime will take time, and unless Arafat, who is still supported by the EU and still holds the ultimate power in the PA,[281] is removed from power, terrorism will go unabated and true reforms—instead of crony politics—will continue to elude the Palestinian people.

For now, Arafat continues to control the PA's five major security forces,[282] while Prime Minister Abbas has stated that the Palestinian people are not giving up their armed struggle. "It is our right to oppose," he told the *Alsharak Alawast* newspaper. "The Intifada must continue . . . using any means necessary."[283] Hours after the new Abbas government was announced, a homicide bomber, a member of the al-Aqsa Martyrs Brigades, killed three Israeli civilians and injured at least fifty-five others in an attack next to the American embassy in Tel Aviv.[284] On May 10, 2003, during U.S. Secretary of State Colin Powell's visit to Israel and the Palestinian territories to discuss the Road Map, terrorists from the al-Aqsa Martyrs Brigades, harbored by Arafat in his headquarters in Ramallah, murdered an Israeli civilian.[285] At the same time, instead of arresting these terrorists, the new PA cabinet moved to *legitimize* their actions by paying them an official monthly salary of $200, allegedly "to keep them under control."[286]

On May 19, 2003, as negotiations on the Road Map continued, Israelis suffered four Palestinian terror attacks in just two days. This led some Israeli government officials to state that, since Abbas is unable or unwilling to stop the terror attacks, and since Arafat is the leader of the terror groups, Arafat must be expelled—but Prime Minister Sharon vetoed the idea. In reaction, Arafat called Fox News to say that he is "committed completely to the peace" and that he, Arafat, still holds a leadership role. Neither Abbas nor any other Palestinian official challenged him, and more terror attacks against Israelis followed.[287]

Under these circumstances, pushing the Road Map forward and rewarding Arafat's PA with statehood proves to the Palestinians and to other terrorists that terrorism pays. Despite the PA's ongoing terror attacks on Israelis, and despite Arafat's continuing involvement, the U.S. has already provided the PA with $125 million in aid for 2003 "to create jobs, rebuild the infrastructure and revive their economy."[288] And on May 25, 2003, under heavy American pressure, the Israeli government approved the Road Map, with some conditions.[289] While the Palestinians continue their murderous attacks, the U.S. still pressures Israel to progress with the plan. According to Secretary of State Colin Powell, "We must not let this latest terrorist outrage derail the path to peace."[290] Would his comment be the same had these ongoing terror attacks occurred not in Israel but in the United States?

Arafat made his own Road Map clear in his June 6, 2001, interview on Radio Palestine: "War is a dream, peace is a nightmare," he said. As long as Arafat remains in charge, no real change or reform will be possible in the Palestinian Authority.

"Hezbollah may be the A-team of terrorists. While Al-Qaeda may be actually the B-team."

U.S. Deputy Secretary of State Richard Armitage,
September 5, 2002

"In the past, when the Marines were in Beirut, we screamed, 'Death to America!' Today, when the region is being filled with hundreds of thousands of American soldiers, 'Death to America!' was, is, and will stay our slogan."

Hizballah Secretary-General Hassan Nasrallah,
March 2003

"We in the Hizballah are very proud that America, the Great Devil, accuses us of being a terrorist party."

Hizballah Secretary-General Hassan Nasrallah,
August 2000

CHAPTER FOUR

The "Party of God": Hizballah

In 1974, while conducting missionary work among the long-oppressed Shiite Muslim minority in Lebanon, Imam Musa Sadr, a Lebanese Shiite educated in Iran, founded a social organization called "the Movement of the Deprived" *(Harakat al-Mahrumin),* in order to further his "continuous struggle until there are no deprived people left in Lebanon."[1] A year later he added a military wing, AMAL,[2] which fought together with the Lebanese National Movement and the Palestinian refugees in Lebanon "against the projects of partition and settling the Palestinians in Lebanon."[3] When an Islamic revolution brought Shiite leader Ayatollah Khomeini to power in Iran in 1979, Sadr and his organization began receiving support from the Iranian government.

In 1982, after the Israelis invaded Southern Lebanon to expel the terrorists of the PLO, members of Iran's Revolutionary Guard arrived in Lebanon. Their mission was to help create a movement that would participate in the *Jihad* (holy war) against Israel—while adhering to Khomeini's brand of Shiite Islam. Within the year, under the guidance of the Revolutionary Guard, members of the Iranian government, military leaders, a group of Shiite clerics, and the Lebanese supporters of AMAL, "the Disadvantaged on Earth" had been incorporated into a new group: Hizballah, the "Party of God."[4]

From Hizballah's inception, it had deep ties to both Iran and Syria—taking orders from Iran, and establishing a "military" wing in Syria with Damascus' political, military, and financial support.[5] Its spiritual leader was Sheikh Muhammad Hussein Fadlallah Mahallatiin, who to this day serves as the chief *Mujtahid* (arbiter of Islamic Law) of Lebanon's Shiite community and spreads his terrorist ideology to Shiite Muslims around the world.[6] Hizballah's leadership advocated the use of violence and terror as valid and important devices to attain the organization's political objectives.[7] Hizballah's goals included the establishment of Shiite Islamic rule in Lebanon and the liberation of all "occupied Arab lands," including Jerusalem. Their goals also encompassed the destruction of the U.S. and Israel, as well as the elimination of Jews worldwide.

Hizballah assumed control of the terrorist training camps of the ousted PLO, and Iran's Revolutionary Guard and Ministry of Intelligence continued the international terrorist agenda that had been established during the PLO's reign. They sent instructors to Lebanon to assist in training operatives from terrorist groups the world over. According to the testimony of U.S. Representative Dick Armey, organizations that Hizballah has trained in Lebanon include "al-Qaeda, Al-Jihad, Hamas, the Japanese Red Army, Abu Nidal's organization, Force 17, New People's Army, the IRA, Chechen rebels, Fatah, the Red Brigade, Palestinian Islamic Jihad and the Medellin Drug Cartel."[8]

At first, Hizballah focused its efforts against Israel and Israeli targets. Assisted by Iran and Syria, the organization established an extensive military network in Lebanon, first in the Beka'a Valley area, then later in Southern Lebanon and in Shiite neighborhoods of Beirut.[9] The West chose to ignore repeated warnings that this brand of terrorism would spread internationally. Before long, Hizballah was carrying out an ambitious campaign of terrorist bombings and other attacks, orchestrated by the head of Hizballah's "external security apparatus," Imad Mugniyah.[10]

Mugniyah was the mastermind behind a number of high-profile acts of terror:

- The bombing of the U.S. embassy in Beirut in April 1983, in which sixty-three people died
- The bombing of the U.S. Marine barracks in Beirut in 1983
- The bombing of the U.S. embassy annex in Beirut in 1984
- The 1985 hijacking of TWA Flight 847, in which an American was executed
- The 1985 abduction of four Soviet diplomats, one of whom was killed
- Also in 1985, the abduction, torture, and death of CIA Beirut station chief William Buckley[11]

According to the Russian Foreign Intelligence Service (SVR), Mugniyah also served in the 1980s as a bodyguard for PLO Chairman Yasser Arafat. The Russians have also reported that Mugniyah was involved "in the planning of the September 11, 2001 attacks on the United States," and was "also a close associate of Osama bin Laden."[12]

As Hizballah began its campaign of international terror, the Islamists' infrastructure in Western Europe was expanding dramatically. Islamists had arrived in Europe to rally around the Ayatollah Khomeini during his exile in Paris in the 1970s. When he subsequently rose to power, he rewarded them with lucrative Iranian-controlled businesses—legal and illegal—in locations such as Europe and West Africa. By the mid-1980s, Shiite Hizballah loyalists in Western Europe had quietly and effectively infiltrated local Muslim communities with the subversive aim of converting them to Khomeini's version of Islam, and of eventually gaining control over those communities.[13] Countless legal and quasi-legal institutions—including religious, cultural, and economic groups—were established to conceal these dormant Hizballah networks; to finance their activities; to serve as a source for future recruitment of European-based terrorists; and to provide financial support for their attacks.[14]

HIZBALLAH TODAY

During its first decade in Lebanon, Hizballah was not officially part of the country's political system. But, in 1992, Hizballah began participating as an official party in Lebanon's parliamentary elections. At present, Hizballah holds 11 of the 128 seats in the Lebanese Parliament, enabling it to claim that it has a legitimate "political" wing. However, Lebanon is not an independent country; it has been, and continues to be, controlled by the Syrians ever since they invaded it in 1975.[15] Therefore it is only with Syria's permission that Hizballah controls and governs both Southern Lebanon and the Shiite ghettos in Beirut. Syria also provides Hizballah with military logistical support and weapons, which are used primarily to attack Israel.[16]

In 1996, after the reorganization of Iran's intelligence services and the establishment of the "Supreme Council for Intelligence Affairs" under the direct supervision of then–Iranian president Ali Akbar Hashemi Rafsanjani, "Hizballah International" emerged to advance the Islamic Revolution and to destabilize the West.[17] As a result, the name *Hizballah* is now "used to signal strong sponsorship and control by Iran for any terrorist organization, whether it is local, such as Hizballah of the [Persian] Gulf and Hizballah Palestine, or international, such as Hizballah International."[18] Hizballah's power and influence led to such an expansion of its activities that it became necessary to form "an organization of secondary level groups working on the local level led by regional functionaries."[19]

Hizballah's terror network is said to comprise about five thousand trained terrorists within Lebanon, who are armed with "tanks, artillery, anti-aircraft guns and missiles—lots of missiles . . . about 10,000 short-range missiles and rockets that can strike much of Israel."[20] After the Israeli seizure of Iranian arms aboard the ship *Karine-A* in January 2002, Hizballah intensified its efforts even more vigorously to transfer weapons to the Palestinian Authority and its network of terror organizations. According to Hizballah leader Hassan Nasrallah, "transferring weapons to the Palestinians is one of [Hizballah's] greatest most important obligations."[21] By conservative estimates, Hizballah's international network includes at least fifteen thousand operatives[22] in cells in the U.S., Canada, Argentina, Paraguay, Brazil, Belgium, Britain, France, Germany, Spain, Switzerland, Indonesia, Malaysia, and throughout Africa.[23]

Along with its terrorist activities, Hizballah, like many other Islamist terrorist organizations, also provides social services such as free hospitals and schools,[24] from which most of its foot soldiers are recruited. Hizballah publishes newspapers and magazines, and even owns a television station, al-Manar, which broadcasts incendiary anti-Semitic, anti-Israeli, anti-Western, and anti-U.S. invective to more than ten million Arabic-speakers throughout the Middle East and Europe.

The group's highest governing body, Hizballah's Consultative Council (the *Majlis al-Shura*) has been led since 1992 by Secretary-General Hassan Nasrallah, who assumed power after his predecessor, Abbas Mussawi, was killed by the Israel Defense Forces.[25] Nasrallah is considered a hero for having forced Israel's withdrawal from Lebanon in 2000, as well as for having continued to escalate the ongoing campaign of attacks against Israel.[26] However, Nasrallah's international notoriety as the leader of Hizballah—considered generally to be the most dangerous terrorist organization today—did not stop UN Secretary General Kofi Annan from publicly meeting and shaking hands with him in Beirut in June 2000.[27]

Hizballah's Wealth

Western intelligence sources estimate Hizballah's operational budget to be approximately $200 to $500 million annually.[28] The money comes from a variety of sources, including:

- At least $120 million annually from Iran, and a smaller amount from Syria
- Support from charitable organizations
- Donations from individuals
- Proceeds from legitimate business

Hizballah also derives profit from illegitimate businesses such as:

- Illegal arms trading
- Cigarette smuggling
- Currency counterfeiting
- Fraud
- Robbery
- Operating illegal telephone exchanges
- Drug trafficking[29]

The following sections will examine these sources of Hizballah's financial power.

STATE SPONSORSHIP: IRAN & SYRIA

The director of the Congressional Task Force on Terrorism and Unconventional Warfare, Yossef Bodansky, writes, "Ultimately the key to effective terrorism in and out of the Arab world is firmly in the hands of the two main sponsoring states—Iran and Syria."[30] These two states pursue a consistent strategy of encouraging and inflaming the Palestinian *intifada*, of providing the Palestinians political and propaganda backup and support, and of providing practical assistance in the carrying out of terrorist attacks inside Israel. Iran transfers large sums of money via organizations such as Hizballah and the Islamic Jihad, which rely on the banking systems of the Syrians and the Palestinians.[31]

In addition, a connection among Iran, Hizballah, and Sudan was formally established during the historic 1991 meeting in Khartoum between Iranian president Hashemi Rafsanjani, and the Sudanese Islamist leaders General Omar Hassan Ahmad al-Bashir and Sheikh Hassan al-Turabi.[32] This coming together of the otherwise ideologically opposed Sunni and Shiite radical groups was the result of their common desire to expand the Islamic revolution. Soon after, Iran provided about $20 million to establish training camps for Hizballah and other Islamist organizations in Sudan.[33] Sudan thus became the Mecca of basic training for Islamist terrorists worldwide.

Iran

In an interview granted to *al-Awsat* in March 1996, Hizballah Secretary-General Hassan Nasrallah openly acknowledged receiving funds from Tehran to support the group's terror activities against Israel.[34] For years, Hizballah received $60 to $100 million annually from Iran,[35] a sum that, at the end of 2001, was increased to $10 million per month, to provide more assistance to the Palestinians in their attacks against Israel.[36] However, the value of the aid is considerably higher than $120 million a year, if one takes into account the other forms of support that Iran provides to Hizballah: weapons, explosives, facilities, organizational aid, instructors, political support, and diplomatic immunity.[37]

Virtually all Iranian-supported entities, such as student associations; humanitarian foundations; scholarships; international organizations; bankers and other officials; and international transport companies, receive formal instructions directly from Tehran. From beneath the cloak of these fronts, Iran and its allies have formed a solid network with which to conduct international terrorism.

Iran funds terrorist activities through international companies that have been established by the Shiite international commercial élite, that are controlled by Hizballah leaders, and that recycle the funds through Western banks. The Shiite international élite also provides venture capital to establish small businesses such as shops and restaurants within the émigré community—these not only generate revenue for Hizballah, but also serve as fronts from which to recruit new terrorists.[38]

The Ahl al-Bayt (House of the Prophet) Islamic Cultural Center in Paris, for example, serves as a meeting and recruitment spot for Hizballah. The center's activities are funded by Lebanese import/ export companies run by Hizballah sympathizers in Beirut and Paris.[39] French intelligence sources report that the center also operates a religious bookstore that is used for covert communications between Iran and Hizballah, and between members of Hizballah.[40]

In another example, soon after the Ayatollah Khomeini took over the Iranian government in 1979, an Iranian company called "International Metro" was established, with its headquarters in London and a transportation office in Geneva. Fifty-one percent of International Metro was owned by SAVAMA—the Iranian security services—and the remaining 49 percent was held by the owner of the Bank of Credit and Commerce International (BCCI), Agha Hasan Abedi.[41] International Metro was in fact a front for SAVAMA. It, in turn, established other companies with different names throughout Europe also to serve as fronts for illegal business.

In 1981, in a move to further the Islamist agenda, and as an investment for the future of the Islamic Revolution, the Council of Ministers in Iran appropriated 1 billion riyals—approximately $270 million—to send Hizballah members as students to the West.[42] In the early 1980s, Iran's ambassador to London, Muhammad Reza Narachan, established secret Iranian intelligence and terrorist cells in Great Britain. When Hizballah threatened to take aim at British government buildings in November 1984, a Hizballah member explained, "We have people in place. They are just waiting for orders."[43]

Iran and Hizballah have also increased their activities among Muslim communities in Africa, assisted by the large Lebanese Shiite community in West Africa, especially in Sierra Leone, which, by the end of the 1980s, had become a hub of terrorist activities. Iranian and Hizballah operatives were also assisted by the former Soviet intelligence apparatus, the KGB, and its Eastern European surrogates, as well as by Libya, which provided diplomatic fronts and commercial, financial, cultural, educational, religious, and media networks. Hizballah used Sierra Leone to disguise its acquisitions of sophisticated weapons systems and electronic equipment. Moreover, by the end of 1987, according to the Task Force on Terrorism and Unconventional Warfare, Hizballah sympathizers controlled about 90 percent of Sierra Leone's gold and diamond production, plus exports.[44]

In Lebanon, Tehran maintains contact with Hizballah through the Iranian embassy in Beirut,[45] and through frequent visits by Hassan Nasrallah to Iran. Nasrallah has met regularly with Iran's key leaders, including the Ayatollah Khomeini (until his death in June 1989), former president Hashemi Rafsanjani, and current president Muhammad Khatami. Iranian leaders make no secret of their support. On one visit in October 1999, Khatami praised Hizballah as "a liberation movement" that defends "the freedom, Islamic and Arabic dignity of the occupied land."[46] Soon after, Tehran began direct flights to Beirut's airport to deliver large quantities of advanced weaponry, including Sagger anti-tank missiles, long-range Katyusha rockets, rocket launchers, mortars, anti-tank mines, and other explosives.[47] These shipments are still being sent in addition to the regular Iranian arms transfers via Damascus, Syria.

In the spring of 2000, Iranian intelligence took steps to consolidate all Palestinian terrorist organizations into a single Secret Islamic Revolutionary Army, with Hizballah's expert operative Imad Mugniyah at the helm, to help Arafat plan his September 2000 attacks on Israel.[48] In mid-July, Ali Akbar Velayati, Iran's former foreign minister—and adviser to Iran's current "supreme leader," Ayatollah Ali Khamenei—"met with key Palestinian terrorist leaders—the leader of the Popular Front for the Liberation of Palestine General Command (PFLP-CG), Ahmad Jibril, Colonel Abu Musa of the anti-Arafat branch of the PLO, and three HAMAS leaders who were being sheltered in Damascus . . . and gave them a total of $3 million to take the initial steps toward fulfilling the new *Jihad* plans."[49] In late July, Iran arranged "a meeting in Afghanistan between Osama bin Laden's new 'Lebanon team' . . . and a Palestinian delegation."[50] As a result, al-Qaeda terrorists were sent to Lebanon for intensive training by Hizballah in "the laying of ambushes, bomb construction and diffusing techniques, local booby-trapping techniques, and clandestine communications," as well as in the forging of documents.[51] At the same time, with Hizballah's help, al-Qaeda operatives were smuggled into the PA-controlled territories to help train members of HAMAS, the Islamic Jihad, the PFLP-CG, Arafat's al-Aqsa Martyrs' Brigades, and other Palestinian terror organizations.[52] Iran also funded—and still funds—terrorist groups such as the Egyptian Jama'at al-Islamiyya, the al-Jihad, and the Algerian Armed Islamic Group (GIA).[53]

In a deal brokered by Hizballah's Imad Mugniyah, Iran began transferring arms directly into the West Bank and Gaza. Two shipments—one on the ship *Karine-A,* from Iran, and another on the boat *Santorini,* from Lebanon—were foiled by the Israeli Navy in January and May 2001, respectively.[54] Hizballah also sent Palestinian terrorists, injured in attacks against Israel, to Tehran for medical treatment, where they were recruited by Iran's intelligence service and given advanced military training to carry out further attacks against Israel.[55]

Iran used Hizballah to carry out terrorist attacks against Israeli
and Jewish targets, such as the bombing in Buenos Aires, Argentina,
of the Israeli embassy in 1992, and the bombing of the Jewish Community Center there in 1994; 165 people died in both attacks, and
hundreds more were wounded. It was not until July 2002 that the former Argentinean president Carlos Menem was exposed as having
covered up Iran's connection to the attacks. According to a former
Iranian intelligence agent, Abolghassem Mesbahi, who defected to
Germany in 1996, Menem "received $10 million from Iran while pres-
ident of Argentina in exchange for helping cover up Tehran's . . . participation in [the] July 18, 1994, bombing of a Jewish community
center in Buenos Aires."[56] The planning of the attack, according to
Mesbahi, had been coordinated by Hizballah operatives in cooperation "with members of the Argentine police, corrupting them or
threatening them to collaborate with the attack."[57] Mesbahi reported
that the $10 million bribe had been transferred from a Swiss account
jointly controlled by Iran's former president Hashemi Rafsanjani and
the son of the late Ayatollah Khomeini[58] to Menem's numbered account in Bank Degroof Luxembourg in Geneva.[59] Both Menem, who
is of Syrian descent, and the Iranian government have denied the allegations. However, Interpol has identified the bank account, and the
Argentinean government has been pursuing the investigation.[60]

In February 2003, an Argentine court issued warrants against current Iranian leader Ayatollah Ali Khamenei and twenty other high-
ranking Iranian officials for their involvement in the 1994 bombing
of the Jewish Center in Buenos Aires. Khamenei cannot be arrested,
because as the leader of Iran he enjoys immunity. However, once out
of office he can be brought to justice.

Despite perceived differences in ideology, Iran also harbors "several hundreds of al Qaeda operatives" that fled Afghanistan after its
liberation in 2001.[61] According to an Israeli intelligence report, the
group includes bin Laden's son Saad, "Saif al-Adel, an Egyptian who

is on the FBI's list of the most wanted terrorists," and bin Laden aide Abu Hafs. Reportedly, Iran is assisting them to plan anti-Western and anti-Jewish attacks.[62]

The Iranian government has denied the claims.[63] But Iran's role in international terrorism has led the U.S. Department of State to denounce it as the "most active state sponsor of terrorism . . . in the international arena."[64]

Syria

After Bashar Assad ascended to the presidency of Syria in 2000, replacing his late father, Hafez al-Assad, the country's support of Hizballah increased.[65] "Syria is more proactive in sponsoring terrorism today than it was under Hafez al-Assad. Bashar has dropped the whole pretense—any pretense of his father's caution," testified former FBI counterterrorism intelligence analyst Matthew Levitt to the House International Relations Committee in September 2002.[66] Furthermore, according to intelligence sources, "The Bashar Assad regime not only allows Hizballah to carry out terror attacks from Lebanese territory, as one of its expressions of support for the Intifada, but also provides direct aid to Hizballah, a step from which Assad Sr. refrained (the Syrians provide Hizballah with rockets which have a range of dozens of kilometers)."[67]

In addition to sheltering and financing Hizballah, and transferring Iranian weapons to the group, Syria supplies it with arms from its own stockpiles, including thousands of long-range rockets.[68] Moreover, Damascus provides assistance worth millions of dollars to Hizballah in the form of training facilities, as well as logistical and technological support for attacks against Israel.[69] In an interview on Syrian TV in June 2002, Hassan Nasrallah praised Syria for remaining a "safe haven to *jihad* . . . the geographical and political refuge adopting the resistance movements in the region."[70] In addition to using Hizballah as its primary agent against Israel, Syria has increasingly been providing safe haven, finances, arms, and training to al-Qaeda, and Palestinian terrorist organizations such as the PFLP, HAMAS, and Islamic Jihad.[71] On January 1, 2002, Damascus radio broadcast that "Syria has turned its land into a training camp, a safe haven and an arms depot for the Palestinian revolutionaries."[72]

Iran, Syria & Hizballah's Support of Palestinian Terrorism

"The Palestinian Islamic Jihad [PIJ] is a fruit from the bountiful tree of the leader Khomeini,"[73] declared Dr. Ramadan Shalah, PIJ's secretary-general, at a meeting with the president of the Palestine National Defense Association in Damascus on August 3, 2002. Shalah, who took responsibility for having planned the homicide bombing carried out in Megiddo, Israel, earlier that year, operates out of Damascus, as do other terrorists. Damascus is the center from where Syria and Iran, through Hizballah, control and direct the terrorist activities of PIJ, HAMAS, and the Popular Front for the Liberation of Palestine General Command inside Israel and in the Palestinian territories. Evidence of Iranian money transfers equaling $400,000 to HAMAS's Az al-Din al-Qassam Battalions was found in Palestinian intelligence reports dated December 2000. A transfer of $700,000 from Iran, according to the same reports, was designated to "'support the Hamas military arm inside' and to encourage suicide attacks." The reports also state that "the Hamas leadership in Syria maintains contacts with the Az Al-Din Al-Qassam Battalions in the PA regarding the carrying out of military attacks against Israeli targets."[74]

According to an October 2001 statement by Jibril Rajoub, the head of the PA's Preventive Security Service, Hizballah, HAMAS, and PIJ activists had been meeting in Damascus "in order to increase the joint activity 'inside,' with the aid of Iranian money."[75] These meetings apparently took place "after an Iranian message had been transferred to the HAMAS and PIJ leaderships, according to which they must not allow a calming down [of the situation] at present." Rajoub's report went on to say, "What is required now is to carry out suicide attacks against Israeli targets in Gaza, in the West Bank and inside Israel."[76]

Syria has also been actively involved in building up HAMAS capabilities. Twenty HAMAS operatives arrested in Israel in 2001 testified that they had been students recruited "during their studies in Syrian, Yemenite, Sudanese, and other Arab universities. The students were located by the Hamas HQ activists in Damascus and sent for training in Syria and in Lebanon [in Hizballah camps]."[77] The HAMAS operatives reported that their training had included:

- Intelligence gathering
- The use of arms
- Kidnapping
- Preparation of explosive charges and explosive belts
- "The techniques of carrying out terrorist attacks against civilians and military targets"[78]

The HAMAS cells to which these terrorists belonged had carried out "two suicide attacks in Netanya in April and May 2001, in which 8 Israeli civilians were killed and more than 100 wounded."[79]

Hizballah's involvement in exporting terrorism was exposed again in May 2003 when a Hizballah explosives expert, Hamed Muslam Musa Abu Amra, was arrested by the Israeli Navy on board the Egyptian fishing boat *Abu Hassan,* which was on its way to Gaza.[80] The boat was loaded with explosives and bomb-making materials, including thirty-six computer disks containing elaborate instructions on how to assemble the most deadly bombs. The deadly cargo included videotapes demonstrating how homicide bombers should position themselves in order to increase the death toll. The Hizballah operative was on his way to establish "a school for terror" in the Gaza strip at the request of and in coordination with a close associate of Yasser Arafat, a senior Palestinian naval police officer.[81]

According to Palestinian intelligence documents discovered by the Israelis in Jenin in 2002, money transferred from Iran and Syria to Palestinian terrorist groups is used for "preparation of terrorist attacks in Israel, support of the families of dead and detained terrorists, arms procurement, and the purchase of dedicated equipment for terrorist attacks such as IDF uniforms."[82] In March 2003, on the eve of the war in Iraq, Syrian President al-Assad further boosted Palestinian terrorism when he transferred "$4.94 million to the account of al-Aqsa and al-Aqsa uprising." The money was deposited in the Islamic Bank for Development.[83]

By 2002, Iraq was also rumored to have been helping arm Hizballah. These rumors were substantiated in January 2003, when Western intelligence sources reported that a shipment of 122 mm missiles armed with chemical warheads from Iraq had reached Hizballah in Lebanon.[84]

CHARITY

Hizballah fundraising efforts seem to employ a different framework than most other Islamist organizations. Through its "political" wing in Lebanon, Hizballah coordinates fundraising operations in North and South America, Africa, Europe, and Asia.[85] In addition to its major state sponsorship, members of Hizballah raise funds through mosques and at special events from donations—sometimes given voluntarily, sometimes by extortion.[86] According to terrorism experts, Hizballah's financial support in the U.S. comes primarily from Detroit, New York, Boston, and Los Angeles—cities with large Shiite communities. In Detroit, for example, Hizballah operates through four charitable organizations: the Islamic Resistance Support Organization, the Educational Development Association, the Good Will Charitable Organization, and the al-Shahid (the Martyr) Association.[87] Yet U.S. government officials and U.S. terrorism experts rarely identify "Hizballah's charities" by name; rather, official statements only mention "Hizballah's funds" in general—"Hizballah benefit far more than does Al Qaeda from money flowing out of the United States."[88]

Hizballah operatives also extort "charitable donations" from Lebanese immigrants in the United States, Canada, and South America, threatening—and delivering—harm to Muslims who do not "donate." These funds are transferred to support terrorism through Hizballah-affiliated organizations (the identities of which so far have not been made public) and through other vehicles for moving money.[89]

In Canada, where Hizballah was outlawed only in December 2002, the organization raised money mainly through the al-Shahid Association in the greater Toronto area, Montreal, and Ottowa—homes to large Shiite communities.[90]

The Ivory Coast is the hub of Hizballah's African fundraising operations. In South Africa, Zaire, and Senegal, Hizballah often operates through affiliated local Muslim organizations such as the People Against Gangsterism and Drugs (PAGAD) and the Karballah Foundation for Liberation.[91]

In Germany, the center for Hizballah's European operations, the organization felt so welcomed that in June 2002 it attempted to establish an official headquarters in Berlin.[92] It was only after heavy lobbying from the Christian Democratic Union's representative that Hizballah operations were banned in Germany. In Belgium, due to the presence of the EU and other international organizations in Brussels, Hizballah concentrates its efforts on public relations and propaganda campaigns—fundraising is a secondary activity. In England, activists in the Lebanese community raise funds for Hizballah through the Lebanese Welfare Committee (LWC) and through the "HELP" Foundation. Additional funds are raised individually by Ahmed al-Chipi, a Lebanese man who operates an Islamic center in

London. The money he collects is sent to the Jamaya al-Abrar, a Lebanese charitable organization. The Shiite communities in Switzerland, Italy, and the Netherlands also contribute unknown sums of money to Hizballah.[93]

It is perplexing that the U.S. and other Western intelligence and law enforcement agencies have not identified either the mechanisms through which Hizballah supporters funnel money from the U.S. to Lebanon, or the institutions they use to distribute money to their members. Intelligence sources have traced wire transfers and money orders that have been sent from the U.S. to Lebanon, as well as cash that has been sent by mail and through international delivery companies. As with HAMAS before September 11, the U.S. government seems to regard Hizballah activities in the U.S. more as opportunities for the U.S. to gather intelligence about the group than as the threatening machinations of an active terror organization.

However, in a recent development, the New York–based Alavi Foundation, a major Iranian charity, has been identified as supporting Hizballah. In an affidavit submitted to the court in September 2002, deputy commissioner for intelligence of the New York Police Department David Cohen stated: "The Alavi Foundation is a nonprofit charitable organization ostensibly run by an independent board of directors but totally controlled by the government of Iran. The foundation has assets of about $100,000,000 in the U.S. and an annual income of between $10–15 million. The foundation funds a variety of anti-American causes, including the four Islamic education centers it owns in New York, Maryland, Texas and California. The Maryland center is headed by Mohammad al-Asi, an American convert to Islam who, during the Kuwait crisis, called on Muslims to strike against American interests in the Middle East. Mosques funded by Alavi have organizations which support Hezbollah and Hamas."[94] The Alavi Foundation denies these allegations.

While it is true that Hizballah uses a portion of the money it receives in "charitable donations" to support legitimate programs in Lebanon, such as providing food, health services, and education to impoverished Muslims, it is equally true that large parts of these charitable donations are used to support terrorism by directly funding the procurement of weapons and explosives, the training of terrorists, and payments to the families of "martyrs." For example, as of June 2002 the Iranian revolutionary organization Hay'at Imdad al-Imam al-Khomayni, which is part of Hizballah's welfare system,[95] together with the al-Shahid Association in Lebanon and the al-Mustaz'afin Fund, "transfer[red] phenomenal financial aid to the families of the Hizbullah martyrs, wounded, and handicapped."[96]

Schools run by Hizballah in Lebanon, such as its nine al-Mahdi schools, receive their funding from the Islamic Institution for Education and Teaching, which, in turn, receives its funding from contributions made by Shiite Muslims worldwide. However, even the sponsorship of schools advances Hizballah's terror agenda: the Islamic Institution for Education and Teaching, like Saudi-sponsored educational institutions, runs schools that advocate the importance of *Jihad* and serve as the grounds for recruiting the next generation of Hizballah terrorists.[97]

Hizballah, like other Islamist terror organizations, claims that the money it raises internationally is directed to its "political wing," which it alleges is separate from its "military wing." This distinction enables Hizballah to claim deniability regarding its terrorist activities. However, as terrorism expert Matthew Levitt explains, such a distinction "implies that these Hizballah operatives somehow work independently of the group that recruits, trains, and funds them for terror missions."[98] Levitt goes on to draw a comparison between Hizballah and other terrorist organizations such as HAMAS, saying that "listing only the military wing of Hamas but not the group itself suggests that Hamas is solely a charitable and political organization somehow disconnected from the heinous suicide bombings coordinated, funded, and lauded by its leaders in the West Bank, Gaza, and Damascus. In fact, Hamas social-welfare organizations play a direct role in facilitating Hamas terrorist attacks, including suicide bombings. A November 5, 2001 FBI memorandum . . . provides convincing evidence that Hamas social-welfare organizations (e.g., charity committees and hospitals) form the core of the group's logistical and financial support network, including support for terror attacks."[99]

Levitt concludes: "The very 'wings' of Hamas, Hizballah and others that some are uncomfortable recognizing as terrorist are the ones engaged in terrorist financing. . . . In fact, if authorities are serious about cracking down on terrorist financing, they must focus on the purportedly political or social-welfare 'wings' of terrorist groups— because it is there that the fund raising, laundering and transferring takes place."[100]

FRAUD, THEFT & DRUGS IN THE U.S.
Operation Smoke Screen

In 1996, a group of young Lebanese men began appearing regularly at the JR Tobacco Warehouse in North Carolina, carrying paper bags filled with enough cash to purchase 299 cartons of cigarettes each (the maximum per person allowed by law). An observant security guard at the warehouse called the Federal Bureau of Alcohol, Tobacco, and Firearms, which, together with the FBI, pursued an investigation. In July 2000, the men were arrested for their participation in a cigarette smuggling scheme. Millions of dollars in profits had been funneled to finance Hizballah in Lebanon.[101]

The Charlotte case—codenamed Operation Smoke Screen— resulted in twenty-five arrests, and an additional five suspects are still at large at the time of this writing. The smugglers, led by Muhammad Youssef Hammoud, were further indicted for having provided material support to terrorist groups, specifically "currency, financial services, training, false documentation and identification, communications equipment, explosives, and other physical assets to Hizballah, in order to facilitate its violent attacks."[102] They were convicted under a provision of the 2001 USA PATRIOT Act, which according to Deputy Attorney General Larry D. Thompson states that "it is now a crime for anyone subject to U.S. jurisdiction to provide anything of value—including their own efforts or expertise—to organizations designated as 'foreign terrorist organization.' It does not matter whether the persons providing such support intend their donations to be used for violent purposes, or whether actual terrorism results. If someone subject to U.S. jurisdiction provides, or even attempts to provide, any material support or resources to Hamas, Hizballah, Al Qaeda, the Abu Sayyaf Group or any of the other 34 designated groups, that person can be prosecuted in the U.S. courts."[103]

The evidence linking Hammoud and another conspirator to Hizballah included: "Anti-American and anti-Israeli videos found in Mohamad Hammoud's home; FBI wire taps of Mohamad Hammoud speaking by phone with Sheikh Abbas Harake, Hizballah's military commander in Beirut; a letter found in Mohamad Hammoud's home urging him to donate money to the resistance in Lebanon and suggesting that he had raised money in the past for Hizballah's military operations; [and finally] a photo of Mohamad Hammoud as a teenager at a Hizballah training camp in Lebanon."[104]

The operation had worked by exploiting the 70¢ difference per pack in the tax on cigarettes between North Carolina (5¢) and Michigan (75¢). Hammoud and his men would smuggle carloads and truckloads of cigarettes from North Carolina to Detroit, Michigan, where they would resell them at the higher price. Each carload of contraband cigarettes would yield between $3,000 and $10,000.[105]

In total, over the period of a year and a half, the smuggling ring was able to generate an estimated $7.9 million.[106] Some of the profits were reinvested in businesses owned by Hizballah cell members, and some of the profits were smuggled in cash to Lebanon to support Hizballah's activities. On one occasion, an undercover FBI agent witnessed how Hammoud "put aside for Hizballah several thousand dollars in cash representing the proceeds from trafficking in contraband cigarettes."[107] In addition, profits of $360,000 were converted into cashiers' checks and transferred to Lebanon for Hizballah operations. An additional $1 million in profits from the operation was sent to Lebanon by Hizballah operative Ali Darwish, who had previously been involved in al-Qaeda's diamond smuggling operations in Sierra Leone.[108] The cigarette smuggling profits were also used to purchase equipment for Hizballah, including night vision goggles, global positioning devices, mine detection equipment, radar, nitrogen cutters, blasting equipment, laser range finders, stun guns, naval equipment, sophisticated software, and cellular phones—also sent to Hizballah in Lebanon.[109]

In addition, Hammoud's group had perpetrated check fraud against several U.S. banks, even bribing an employee of First Union National Bank to facilitate the scheme by reactivating the closed account of an individual who had left the U.S.[110] The cell members had also raised money for Hizballah through credit card fraud, through solicitation during meetings at Hammoud's home, and through appeals for donations from members of the Islamic community.[111]

Members of the Charlotte cell would meet every Thursday night for "prayer meetings" at Hammoud's home, where they would discuss Hizballah activities and operations.[112] They would read messages containing directives for the members, which had been transmitted from a Hizballah official in Lebanon to Muhammad Hassan Dbouk, a Canadian colleague. Dbouk, a Hizballah "reconnaissance and intelligence specialist employed by Hizballah-run al-Manar television,"[113] is also believed to have worked for Imad Mugniyah. Dbouk was indicted but fled, and is currently believed to be in Lebanon.[114]

One of the undercover agents who had infiltrated the cell was quoted in the indictment as saying, "The group of individuals is extremely anti–United States. Their meetings invariably include readings from the works of Ayatollah Khomeni."[115] A search of the home of one of the cell members uncovered:

- Hate propaganda
- "A virtual arsenal of weapons" such as shotguns and rifles, and even an AK-47[116]
- Photos of Hammoud posing in front of U.S. landmarks such as the Washington Monument and the White House[117]
- Hammoud's cousin posing with a rocket-propelled grenade launcher[118]

Hammoud, who received military training in Lebanon,[119] is reported to be "close" to Hizballah spiritual leader Fadlallah[120] and, according to one of the FBI agents who infiltrated the group, "is well-connected to Hizballah leaders in Lebanon and, upon returning from his last trip to Lebanon during 1999, [he] bragged about going to Syria with the Hizballah political representative to Iran and Syria."[121] The indictment describes Hammoud as dangerous "because he would likely assist in carrying out any action against the United States interests if he were required to do so by Hizballah."[122]

The arrest of this gang left U.S. investigators uneasy. "Here is a terrorist support cell that sets itself up in America's heartland. They have the ability to move people across borders and give them whole new identities," commented one agent. "They have access to a constant flow of untraced cash, military training, and a network of criminal contacts to get weapons. That's not good news."[123]

According to official estimates, the cell in Charlotte, North Carolina, is only one of many Hizballah cells established throughout the U.S.[124] For example, in July 1998, a Hizballah operative was arrested in Detroit while attempting to purchase over $100,000 worth of thermal imaging gear for Hizballah. In a different case, in September 2001, a Hizballah operative was convicted in Detroit of having shipped weapons and ammunition to Hizballah in Lebanon.[125]

Petty Fraud & Thievery

According to a senior law enforcement official, "The money mechanisms being used to aid terrorism are limited only by your imagination. There is a significant amount of money moved out of the United States attributed to fraud that goes to terrorism."[126]

Traditionally used by organized crime, fraud schemes—which can generate large amounts of money—are now also being exploited by terrorist organizations. According to Congressional testimony in February 1998 by Richard Rohde, a former deputy assistant director with the U.S. Secret Service, these schemes can include:

- Credit card and medical insurance fraud
- Food coupon fraud
- Counterfeiting and selling of merchandise such as designer bags, watches, jewelry, T-shirts, and Nike sports products
- The theft and resale of baby formula
- Counterfeiting resident alien cards and drivers' licenses
- Perpetuating welfare, social security, and marriage fraud (for example, "two of their 'wives' were, in fact, lesbians who lived . . . with each other")[127]
- Telecommunications fraud, such as selling long distance telephone access through fraudulently obtained services, and through cloning the identification of cellular phone subscribers

These schemes not only reap huge profits, but also help terrorists to infiltrate their targeted countries, weakening the countries' economies while furthering the terrorist agenda.[128]

For example, Rohde's testimony describes a scam that benefited several terrorist organizations:

> A group of Middle Easterners organized into "cells" located throughout the United States had applied for and received numerous credit cards. Some members had received in excess of forty credit cards. These cardholders systematically "boosted" the credit limits to the maximum amount available. Once they established their portfolio of unsecured credit card debt, they submitted worthless checks as payment for these accounts in advance of purchases being made. In most cases these checks were in amounts exceeding the card holder's credit limit, and in some instances twice that amount. . . . Before the checks were returned as worthless, the card holders purchased merchandise and/or obtained cash advances . . . in excess of the limit on the accounts, thereby "busting out" the accounts.[129]

The cost to U.S. financial institutions of this kind of fraud in 1998 alone was over $4.5 million dollars. And the total loss from "the misuse of these counterfeit credit cards" was estimated at $17 million.[130]

However, Rohde's 1998 testimony did not identify by name any terrorist organization—despite mountains of evidence. He referred only to "a group of Middle Easterners." The government, it seems, was reluctant to name any terrorist organization involved. However, in new testimony given on terrorist cells in the U.S. since the September 11 attacks, terrorist organizations have been identified by name.

Money obtained by Hizballah operatives through this kind of crime and fraud is sent from the U.S. to Lebanon through a variety of methods:

- The *hawala* system
- Wire transfers of sums less than $10,000
- Cash carried by individuals in money belts or suitcases

- Cash mailed through courier companies such as Federal Express, DHL Worldwide Express, and United Parcel Service.

In 2002, the U.S. Treasury Department's Operation Green Quest "seized $16 million in currency and monetary instruments such as cashier's checks that were being sent out of the country illegally. Although some of the money is related to the drug trade and other criminal activity, officials traced much of it to bank accounts in Lebanon and elsewhere that were directly controlled by Hezbollah."[131]

That same year, another federal operation, the Drug Enforcement Agency's "Operation Mountain Express," broke up another of Hizballah's illegal fundraising ventures in the United States—the nationwide methamphetamine ring discussed in chapter 1.

Jihad by Drugs

In the mid-1980s Hizballah's use of the illicit drug trade as a funding source and a weapon against the West was sanctioned by an official *fatwa* (religious edict) issued by Hizballah: "We are making these drugs for Satan America and the Jews. If we cannot kill them with guns, so we will kill them with drugs."[132]

According to South American and Israeli intelligence sources, Hizballah generates at least tens of millions of dollars in profits annually (the exact amount is unknown)[133] from the illegal drug trade, which it practices worldwide. Although a 2002 U.S. special research report claims that Hizballah's role in the drug trade in Lebanon "is not clear" and that it does not seem "to be of major dimensions," the report acknowledges the credibility of Israel's claim that Hizballah's involvement in the drug trade is significant, admitting that the production and trade of heroin and cocaine in Lebanon occurs under the control of the Syrian military and Hizballah.[134] Israeli sources also note that the revenues of the illegal drug trade in Lebanon "also significantly contribute to the economies of Syria, Lebanon, and to the Hizballah as an organization (which needs large sums of money for its political-social activities in the Shiite community)."[135]

HIZBALLAH'S MAJOR DRUG TRAFFICKING CENTERS

Hizballah's involvement in the illegal drug trade "is centered on a transnational triangle of illicit activity conducted from areas of Lebanon, the Balkans, and the 'tri-border region' of Argentina, Brazil and Paraguay."[136] As a U.S. defense analyst explains: "All three regions have unstable, often corrupt, government structures with weak economic platforms. Their porous borders and largely unsupervised waterways and airfields are highly conducive to the conducting of illicit operations that go undetected."[137]

Lebanon

For centuries, Lebanon's Beka'a Valley has been a center for the illicit cultivation and production of drugs. When Hizballah established itself in the Beka'a in the early 1980s, it appropriated and increased the area's already ongoing production of hashish and heroin; in the 1990s, it added cocaine and methamphetamine production.[138]

Morphine base, from which heroin is produced, is channeled from Pakistan, Afghanistan, Iran, Turkey, and Syria to Lebanon, where it is refined into heroin by Hizballah in laboratories in the Beka'a Valley and Syria. Cocaine base, from which powder cocaine is produced, is sent to Lebanon from Latin America (Colombia, Bolivia, Peru, Brazil, and Paraguay); it is also refined in laboratories in the Beka'a Valley. The distribution of Hizballah's cocaine and heroin to the Middle East, the Gulf States, other Arab countries, and Europe is carried out by international drug trafficking organizations.[139]

Before the September 11 attacks on the U.S., the U.S. Department of State's *International Narcotics Control Strategy Report* stated that "there is no significant illicit drug refining in Lebanon," and that "Lebanon is not a major transit country for illicit drug traffickers." However, since September 11, U.S. intelligence sources have admitted that this assessment was not accurate. They explained that, since most of the Lebanese drugs do not reach the U.S., "we haven't paid too much attention."[140]

In addition to the production and trade of heroin and cocaine, Hizballah facilitates—for a fee—the traffic of other drug smuggling networks. Hizballah cooperates, for example, with the "Abadan drug ring," a long-established Iranian drug trafficking network, allowing them to use the Hizballah-controlled drug routes in Lebanon to transport heroin and opium from Iran and Afghanistan to Europe and North Africa.[141]

The Balkans

Imad Mugniyah, Hizballah's "external security apparatus" head, has "long viewed the Balkans as the gateway to an Islamic conquest of Europe and utilized Albania and Kosovo as 'the main base for Islamic armed action in Europe.'"[142] According to a U.S. defense analyst, "The 'Balkan Road' [which runs through Albania, Kosovo, and Macedonia] is considered the doorway to Europe and North America, and accounts for over 80 percent and 40 percent, respectively, of the continent's heroin trade."[143] The Balkan Road serves both Hizballah and al-Qaeda, and is guarded primarily by the Kosovo Protection Corps (KPC), formerly known as the Kosovo Liberation Army, as well as by the Macedonian National Liberation Army—both militant Islamist groups. The KPC's share of the profits has been estimated by *Jane's Intelligence Review* to be in the "high tens of millions."[144]

The Tri-Border Region

The lawless tri-border region of South America, where Argentina, Brazil, and Paraguay intersect, is a center not just for al-Qaeda's drug trafficking activities (see chapter 2), but for Hizballah's as well. In the mid-1980s, Hizballah clerics and members of other Islamist organizations began proselytizing, planting operatives from the Middle East, and recruiting new members from among the tri-border region's residents.[145] The jungles in the region were soon filled with terrorist training camps, which continue to this day to turn out well-trained operatives.[146] Lately, Hizballah is reported to have increased its activities in the area: in the Panamanian town Darien, which borders with Colombia, in Lago Agrio in northern Ecuador, also near the Colombian border, and in Cuba.[147] In addition, Brazilian, Colombian, and Argentinean intelligence sources report that special weekend camps, run by Hizballah, train children and teenagers in the use of weapons and combat techniques, as well as indoctrinating them with Ayatollah Khomeini's anti-American and anti-Jewish ideologies.[148]

Former State Department coordinator for counterterrorism Ambassador Philip Wilcox stated in 1995 that Hizballah cells in the tri-border region were actively involved in narcotics trafficking, smuggling, and terrorist activities. He further testified that Hizballah had developed cells in Venezuela and Colombia, conducted fundraising and recruiting operations, and received guidance and logistical support from Iranian diplomats in the region.[149] The chief minister of Brazil's Institutional Security Office, General Alberto Cardoso, similarly explained that "smuggling, drug trafficking and money laundering in the Triborder region . . . make the area a more favorable place for using laundered money to finance illegal activities, including terrorism."[150]

In addition to drug trafficking, Hizballah operatives in the region are involved in other illicit activities and are making fortunes—for themselves and for the organization—in areas such as:

- Piracy of compact discs and DVDs
- Forgery of passports, drivers' licenses, and other forms of identification
- Counterfeiting currencies
- Trafficking in humans
- Laundering money
- Smuggling weapons and stolen vehicles[151]
- Conducting elaborate import/export schemes with traders from India and Hong Kong[152]

As in other areas, they also extort "donations" for Hizballah from Arab residents of the region under the threat of physical harm or death.[153]

Hizballah's involvement in the illegal drug trade in the tri-border region includes money laundering, drugs-for-arms deals, and straightforward drug trafficking. Hizballah operatives have developed strong relationships with major narco-terrorist and drug trafficking organizations from Colombia, Peru, and Bolivia, including the Revolutionary Armed Forces of Colombia (FARC), the National Liberation Army (ELN) in Colombia, and the Sendero Luminoso (Shining Path) in Peru.

Brazilian authorities have estimated in recent years that criminals in the tri-border region have been laundering approximately $6 billion annually. According to Paraguayan interior minister Julio César Fanego, from 1999 to 2001 Hizballah received anywhere from $50 to $500 million from this region alone.[154] And Brazilian security agencies estimate that, in the year 2000 alone, at least $261 million was sent from Islamist organizations operating in the tri-border region to the Middle East. Most of it went to Hizballah.[155] Thus the tri-border area seems to have become, after Iran, Hizballah's most significant source of funding.[156]

HIZBALLAH OPERATIVES IN THE TRI-BORDER REGION

Ali Khalil Mehri

In February 2000, Paraguayan authorities arrested a newly natural-ized thirty-two-year-old Lebanese businessman in Ciudad del Este on the edge of the tri-border region. Ali Khalil Mehri had made mil-lions of dollars selling pirated software—funds that he then funneled to Hizballah in Lebanon. In a search of Mehri's properties, the au-thorities found not only videotapes of homicide bombers and terror-ists belonging to Hizballah, but also fundraising forms for the Hizballah-affiliated al-Shahid Association in Lebanon and receipts for over $700,000 that had been transferred to Canada, Chile, Lebanon, and the U.S.[157]

After his arrest, Mehri was identified by British intelligence as also having been a fundraiser for al-Qaeda. Despite this allegation, it was two more years before U.S. authorities publicly acknowledged that al-Qaeda had been operating through, and cooperating with, other Muslim fundamentalist organizations around the world.[158]

Mehri bribed his way out of the Paraguayan prison in June 2000 by paying off Paraguayan politicians. He was last reported to have been seen in Damascus.[159]

Assad Muhammad Barakat

After September 11, intense pressure from the U.S. prompted Paraguayan law enforcement to heighten its scrutiny of Hizballah ac-tivities in the tri-border region. That same September, Paraguayan police raided the Apollo import/export trading company, a whole-sale electronics store located in the Page Shopping Gallery, a run-down shopping center in Ciudad del Este. The owner, Assad Muhammad Barakat, was in Sao Paolo, Brazil, on business and es-caped arrest, but the police succeeded in arresting two of his employees. In addition, the police seized boxes "containing financial statements detailing $250,000 in monthly transfers to the Middle East and descriptions of at least 30 recent attacks in Israel and the Israeli-occupied territories."[160] The Paraguayan police also seized Hizballah hate propaganda, including:

- Training videos for homicide bombing and other terrorist activities
- More than sixty hours worth of videotapes and CD-ROMs showing attacks with explosives
- Motivational speeches by Hizballah's leader, Hassan Nasrallah[161]
- A personal letter from Nasrallah thanking Barakat for his financial contributions, specifically those to the al-Shahid Association[162]

The search also uncovered evidence that Barakat and an associate, Kalil Saleh, had sent $505,200 to Hizballah bank accounts in Canada, Chile, and the U.S., and $524,000 to Lebanon.[163] The head of the Paraguayan police anti-terrorist unit said, "We believe [Barakat] sent some $50 million to Hizballah since 1995."[164]

In a media interview from Sao Paulo, Barakat later admitted that the training material had been sent six years earlier from Lebanon, but downplayed the content, saying such videos are "something very common in the community."[165] However, police established that Barakat had used these materials to recruit new members.[166]

The Paraguayan police further identified Barakat as "the Hizballah military chief in the Tri-Border Region," who had also served as the group's major fundraiser in the area. He raised money through counterfeiting and money laundering operations, and also by blackmailing Lebanese immigrants in the region.[167] Barakat is even reported to have used death threats to force Lebanese expatriates to contribute to Hizballah.[168]

After subsequent U.S. pressure, Barakat was finally arrested in Brazil; his extradition to Paraguay is now pending.[169] Brazil's Supreme Tribunal ruled in favor of his extradition in December 2002; at the time of this writing, Barakat is still incarcerated in Brazil, fighting the court's decision. However, the Brazilian Justice Ministry's spokesperson said there is "a very strong probability" that Barakat's extradition to Paraguay will take place.[170]

After Barakat's arrest, Argentinean police revealed that they, too, had tracked him for many years. They claimed that he had distributed $60 million in Colombian-printed counterfeit U.S. dollars, and that he had participated in the 1994 bombing of the Jewish Community Center in Buenos Aires—but that the Argentineans had "lacked the evidence" to indict Barakaat.

Sobhi Mahmoud Fayad

As a result of the raid on Barakat's offices, in November 2001 Paraguayan police arrested another key Hizballah operative in the tri-border region, Sobhi Mahmoud Fayad. At the time of his arrest, police found in his possession documents that revealed he had been sending funds to Lebanon and Canada.[171] Fayad, whose brother is a high-ranking Hizballah official in Lebanon, had been coordinating Hizballah's fundraising operations together with Barakat.[172] A letter seized by police shows that, in the year 2000 alone, Fayad had moved more than $3.5 million to the al-Shahid Association, the same Hizballah organization to which Mehri and Barakat had sent money.[173] Sobhi currently awaits trial on charges of tax evasion and associating with a criminal organization.[174]

These arrests did little to impede Hizballah's narco-terrorist activities in the tri-border region, however. In May 2003, Assad Muhammad Barakat's cousin was arrested in Paraguay with 2.3 kilograms of cocaine destined for Syria. The revenues from the sale of this drug were to benefit Hizballah.[175]

OTHER DRUG TRAFFICKING CONNECTIONS

Uruguay

In September 2001, after seizing nearly 200 kilos of cocaine, the Uruguayan Federal Police linked the Uruguayan "Arab Mafia" and the Brazilian "Lebanese Mafia" to drug trafficking. A confidential report issued by the Uruguayan Federal Police stated that "the money obtained from the sale of the product would be used to finance international terrorism."[176]

Venezuela

Venezuela and its neighboring island, Aruba, have long had a well-established drug trafficking, drug smuggling, and money laundering network, which was created in the early seventies by the Cosa Nostra's Cuntrera-Caruana family.[177] In the 1990s, the Aruba-based Mansur family, of Lebanese descent, took over the network, adding cigarette smuggling to their operations. According to U.S. court documents from March 2001, "Much of the proceeds garnered by the Mansur brothers went to Hizballah."[178]

Colombia

The Colombian free-trade-zone city, Maicao, which borders Venezuela, has a large Shiite community, and is a known "vacation spot" for Islamist groups. According to an U.S. intelligence source, "Cells of the radical group Hizballah control 70% of the local commerce." In addition, "the merchants from there make contributions equivalent to 10% and up to 30% of their profits. Those responsible for the fund send the money via banks in Maracaibo, Venezuela and Panama. Sometimes a part of it is carried personally by emissaries from those cells."[179]

According to Colombian law enforcement, Maicao is known for its "black market for weapons and money laundering."[180] Moreover, the

Hizballah cells in Maicao also launder money for drug traffickers and other criminals in Colombia, and use the money to fund Hizballah's international terrorist activities.[181]

THE "SECONDARY" THREAT

The globalization of narco-terrorism, and particularly of the Islamist narco-terror network, which includes Hizballah, has been common knowledge to international law enforcement and intelligence services for decades. But the special report prepared by the Library of Congress for the U.S. Defense Department on "Narcotic-Funded Terrorist/Extremist Groups" in May 2002 states: "There are *indications* [emphasis added] that Hizballah is involved in narcotics trafficking and perhaps even in drug production . . . but such activity appears to be quite secondary to the struggle against Israel."

However, volumes of evidence concerning Hizballah's narcotic activities suggest that this is not quite a secondary activity, nor is it directed only against Israel. Hizballah's quiet and effective implementation of its *fatwa,* calling for the use of drugs as a weapon against the West, is likely to continue to fill its coffers with enough money to threaten not only the national security of the U.S., but also that of other countries in the West.

Remarkably, despite all this, despite U.S. Deputy Secretary of State Richard Armitage's statement that Hizballah may well be the A-team of international terrorism,[182] and despite the designation of Hizballah as one of the U.S. Designated Foreign Terrorist Organizations, the most recent *Patterns of Global Terrorism* report from the U.S. State Department characterizes Hizballah and other Syrian- and Iranian-sponsored terror organizations simply as "Palestinian rejectionist groups."[183]

"If we really want to win the war against terrorism, we need to continue and expand our commitment to cutting off all sources of terrorism financing, including drug trafficking."

Orrin Hatch, Chairman,
Senate Committee on the Judiciary,
May 20, 2003

CHAPTER FIVE

Other Narco-Terrorists

Political violence/terrorism and the narcotics trade are not new to human history; neither is the overlap between the two. It existed as far back as medieval Syria and Persia, where the legendary (but by no means mythical) "Assassins"—in reality, the Nizari branch of the Muslim Ismaili sect[1]—used hashish to embolden themselves to commit political murders. In its modern form, however, narco-terrorism has become global in nature. In the last five decades, it has grown from modest beginnings into a geopolitical reality that threatens not just the U.S., but Western civilization itself.

In September 1984, then–secretary of state George P. Schultz warned: "Money from drug smuggling supports terrorists. Terrorists provide assistance to drug traffickers. Organized crime works hand in hand with these other outlaws for their own profit. And what may be most disturbing is the mounting evidence that some governments are involved, too, for their own diverse reasons."[2] Almost a decade later, in June 1992, an article in the *Atlantic Monthly* called attention to the need for "major changes in the way the United States confronts terrorism," stating, "A number of reports suggest a growing threat from terrorist groups that have ties with and receive support from drug traffickers—not only in Latin America but also South East

Asia, the Middle East and Northern Ireland." The article continues:
"Terrorist groups with ties to drug traffickers are the ones most likely
to be the first to commit major acts of terrorist violence in the main-
land U.S. . . . . They command the infrastructure and transportation
network that could be used as easily for smuggling in the imple-
ments of terrorism, as for smuggling in drugs."[3] And a decade later
still, in February 2003, Secretary of State Colin Powell told the Senate
Foreign Relations Committee that "around the world we are combat-
ing the unholy alliance of drug traffickers and terrorists who threaten
the internal stability of countries."[4]

WESTERN DENIAL

Clearly, the drug trade has become a major funding source for most
terrorist organizations—and especially for the Islamists. As noted
earlier, for example, Hizballah not only uses the illicit drug trade as a
funding source; it also sanctions the use of drugs as a weapon in an
official *fatwa* (religious edict) issued in the mid-1980s: "We are making these drugs for Satan America and the Jews. If we cannot kill
them with guns, so we will kill them with drugs."[5] Despite such evidence, the narco-terrorist threat is still widely discounted and largely
ignored within a good portion of Western governments and media
establishments. Many still see it as merely one more conspiracy the-
ory that litters the ideological landscape.

Perhaps this is because narco-terrorism is not yet seen as an immediate threat or a "clear and present danger" in the same league as
the proliferation of nuclear, biological, and chemical weapons. Furthermore, comfortable and tolerant societies find it difficult to accept that they are vulnerable to other societies that might wish to do
them harm. It took the attacks of September 11 for the U.S. to admit
this fact to itself. Our societies would perhaps consider it paranoid to
further suggest that these adversaries would use not only terrorism

but also narcotics in their war against us. The U.S. and most of its Western allies insist that narco-terrorism is confined to a few of the most vicious terrorist organizations and, sometimes, rogue states. But, in fact, the U.S. has been under attack by international drug cartels for decades. It is a war the United States has spent many billions of dollars fighting all over the world, with a constantly changing strategy and very little to show for it.

The Colombian drug cartels, together with their fellow traffickers in Mexico, Venezuela, Panama, Ecuador, Costa Rica, Argentina, Brazil, Belize, and Jamaica, are moving their products into the U.S., Europe, and markets all over the world. They cooperate with international terrorists groups such as al-Qaeda, Hizballah, and the IRA, and with international criminal organizations such as the Russian Mafiya, the Chinese Triads, and the Italian Mafia. In addition to raising unlimited funds through the illicit drug trade, all of these narco-terrorists also exchange drugs for arms and other essentials such as false identification papers, counterfeit currency, and safe houses. The drugs-for-arms partnership provides illegal weapons that end up in the hands of Islamist terrorists from the Philippines, the West Bank and Gaza, Spain, Russia, Bosnia, India, Pakistan, the U.K., and the U.S., to name just a few locations. Money is washed "clean" not only in the Caribbean, the Channel Islands, Hong Kong, Nauru, the Philippines, and other offshore banking havens, but also in financial centers such as New York, London, Frankfurt, Paris, and Zurich.

The use of drugs to fund terror activities is exemplified in the story relayed by a former East German official, Alexander Schalck-Golodkowsky, who defected to the West in December 1989. A thick dossier he brought with him documented a well-oiled machine that had dealt in cocaine and illegal arms sales for twenty years. Described in meticulous detail are the activities of the East German security services, on orders from the former East German Communist leader, Erich Honecker, in the trade of arms and drugs with terrorists from all over the world. Some of the profits found their way to Mr. Honecker's South American bank accounts. Most of the money went to fund terrorist activities against the West.

Earlier chapters have described the activities and resources of the world's most prominent narco-terrorist groups. Below are profiles of five more groups that employ drug trafficking as a weapon and a fundraising tool: Colombia's Revolutionary Armed Forces, National Liberation Army, and United Self-Defense Forces, the Philippines' Abu Sayyaf Group, and Sri Lanka's Liberation Tigers of Tamil Eelam.

THE REVOLUTIONARY ARMED FORCES OF COLOMBIA (FARC), THE NATIONAL LIBERATION ARMY (ELN) & THE UNITED SELF-DEFENSE FORCES (AUC)

Colombia, Latin America's oldest democracy, has become the region's narco-terrorist superstate. Despite its legal traditions, Colombia has the most violent history in the region, with scores of wars in its past. The War of the Thousand Days in the late nineteenth century claimed more than one hundred thousand lives. The next full-scale conflict, which occurred in the decade after World War II, is known simply as *La Violencia;* it cost two hundred thousand lives.[6] At *La Violencia*'s height in the late 1940s, warring factions were murdering each other at the rate of two thousand per month.[7]

The turmoil generated by *La Violencia* never truly ended; it merely transformed. The killing continued, albeit at a slower rate. That period of relative tranquility ended after Fidel Castro came to power in Cuba. With Castro's help, new guerrilla armies sprang up in the 1960s to undermine Colombia's government.[8] The Colombian drug cartels are relatively new compared to the guerrillas, but their violence has been far more effective in undermining the Colombian state. Moreover, the traffickers' lawlessness has inspired others in Colombia to use illegal aggression, including members of the Security Force, who are mandated to uphold the law.

The climate of insecurity has also led to the rise of "self-defense" groups, which battle independently against guerrillas, drug traffickers, and common criminals. Not surprisingly, these vigilantes commit their share of atrocities as well. The AUC, a paramilitary umbrella organization for some thirteen "self-defense" groups supported by local businessmen, ranchers, and communities, claims to be "a regional and counter-insurgent force." Ironically, it too engages in the drug trafficking business.[9]

Since the current war began in 1964, "more than 200,000 people have been killed . . . and about 3,000 people are kidnapped per year by the rebels and drug gangs."[10] The spiraling violence has worked to the advantage of the narco-traffickers; the government has not been able to guarantee either law or order, and has thereby been even further discredited.

Colombia's main terrorist groups, the FARC and the ELN, have been listed in the U.S. Department of State's *Patterns of Global Terrorism* for decades.[11] They have waged war against the Colombian government since the early 1960s, and have survived longer than any other such group in Latin America. Since the mid-1960s, the ELN, which is pro-Cuban, and the FARC, which was the armed wing of the pro-Soviet Colombian Communist Party (PCC), have acted independently from one another, with only small amounts of aid from Havana, according to Colombian government sources.[12]

The ELN commander, Fabio Vasquez, and FARC's commander, Manuel Marulanda Velez, have always been devoted followers of Fidel Castro. Both groups have called for comprehensive agrarian reforms, and have claimed to represent the oppressed people of Colombia.[13] In their first decade, the ELN and the FARC followed the Che Guevara school of "rural guerilla warfare," which "propounded the notion that the Colombian proletariat was utterly unable to fight a war in the cities—only in the very last stage of revolution could it even have a role."[14] Their involvement in the drug trade began only in the early 1980s, after Colombia's drug cartels had already established a flourishing market.[15]

The amalgamation of drug trafficking and terrorism in Colombia began as a marriage of political convenience. Drug trafficking organizations would pay the guerrilla groups to provide them with security, and to transport and store their cocaine and heroin. The economic incentive for the leftist guerrillas was clear: drug money provided them with the resources to carry out their revolution. In exchange, the drug traffickers received guerrilla protection—as well as assassins to carry out acts of intimidation. While the initial motives of the drug traffickers and the guerrillas were different, their common goal was to destabilize and undermine the government. But, since at least 1987, the DEA has reported on the FARC's and the ELN's growing involvement in the cultivation of coca and opium; the refining of these drugs; the establishing of their prices; and the transporting of the drugs within Colombia.[16] According to a U.S. General Accounting Office report of 2000, the FARC and the ELN are responsible for the country's expanding heroin and cocaine production.[17] And the DEA's Rogelio Guevara reported in December 2002 that the FARC and the ELN generate about 70 percent of their operating funds from drug trafficking.[18] The so-called "Marxist" rebels have long since abandoned their "social" agenda for the lucrative drug trade.[19] This change from service providers to drug lords allows them now to exchange drugs for weapons and to offer services such as money laundering, necessary for international terrorist groups not only in Latin America but throughout the world, including the IRA, al-Qaeda, and Hizballah.[20]

The unwillingness of the Colombian and U.S. governments to acknowledge that this metamorphosis occurred has enabled the narco-terrorists to thrive. The FARC and the ELN together have an estimated twenty-five thousand fighters. They regularly threaten to—and do—retaliate against neighboring countries ready to help U.S. efforts to combat drug trafficking. With Cuba's political and strategic support, and with the huge revenues they generate from the illegal drug trade, the two groups have managed to occupy more than 50 percent of Colombia's territory.[21]

Not surprisingly, these pseudo-Marxist groups deny their involvement in the drug trade. What was surprising was that former Colombian president Andres Pastrana chose to support their claim, stating in an interview in 2000 that "there is no evidence that the FARC are drug traffickers." Said Pastrana, "The FARC have always said they are interested in eradicating illegal crops."[22] In fact, President Pastrana *gave* large parts of the country to the narco-terrorists as a "gesture of goodwill," and cajoled them into "peace" talks.[23] Similarly, in 1999 then–U.S. drug czar Barry McCaffrey, though noting the linkage between the drug traffickers and the guerrillas, claimed that only "two-thirds of their units . . . are in some way associated with the drug trade."[24] Pastrana's refusal to dispel the myth of a distinction between the terrorists and the drug traffickers, coupled with McCaffrey's decision to turn a blind eye to the terrorists' involvement in narcotics, did not help to restore Colombia's crumbling civil society.

In Geneva in the summer of 2000, "peace talks" with the ELN were faltering,[25] while Colombia's biggest narco-terrorist force, the FARC, was continuing its assaults on the nation's police and military officers. (The Colombian media reported daily on the dozens of law enforcement officers killed and kidnapped while trying to stop the terrorists and drug cartels from growing and processing opium and cocaine.) The narco-terrorists continue to earn millions of dollars per week, to use their profits to buy arms to fight the government, and to buy off law enforcement officers and politicians—all still under the guise of furthering their "Marxist" agenda.[26]

The sporadic negotiations between the Colombian government

and narco-terrorist groups ended in May 2002, when Colombians elected Alvaro Uribe to replace Andres Pastrana as president. In truth, the talks had never been significant; the rebels had no real agenda other than a vague demand for "real socialist justice and reform." Yet these narco-terrorists are the first to violate the rights of the Colombian people who suffer under their "protection." At the same time the narco-terrorists continue to profit from drugs and to use the proceeds to expand their political power through violent means. For example, Colombia's kidnapping rate is second to none: three thousand victims—eight per day—for the year 2001 alone.[27] On April 15, 2003, President Uribe rejected the FARC's proposal to establish demilitarized zones. Uribe instead declared war on the FARC— the "bunch of bandits."[28]

Despite Uribe's efforts, Colombia is still the most visible and most publicized illegal-drug battleground, on which narco-terrorists are pitted against the ineffectual drug enforcement policies of the United States. Decades after Colombia's leftist guerrillas adopted narco-terrorism as their main path for achieving their political agenda—and long after they traded in that agenda for their roles as drug warlords—they continue to benefit from a strange case of willful blindness prevalent among many U.S. policymakers—a blindness that became most apparent during the second Clinton administration.

In 2000, drug czar McCaffrey testified before Congress that the problems in Colombia had reached "emergency" proportions. Although the Clinton administration and Capitol Hill agreed with his general assessment, they were unable to contend with the situation. Along with the European Union, Clinton's administration encouraged the "land for peace" initiative[29]—handing over almost half the country to the FARC in order to bring it to the negotiating table. In the summer of 1999, New York Stock Exchange chairman Richard Grasso visited FARC's headquarters in San Vincente, at the invitation of President Pastrana, "to meet with the guerilla leadership and put [in] a good word for peace and the free market."[30] And the EU went as far as to invite FARC and ELN terrorists to Europe and even send them diplomatic delegations, thus conferring upon them both legitimacy and political power.[31]

But the more governments attempted to appease the terrorists, the bolder the terrorists became.[32] (In the Middle East, similar offers of conciliation from the EU and the Clinton administration to Palestinian terrorists groups, including financial aid and another "land for peace" initiative, had the same result.) Not only did negotiating with the narco-terrorists lead Colombia to social anarchy and economic devastation; it also enabled the spread of narco-terrorism into neighboring countries—which, in turn, encouraged Islamist radicals to exploit the weakness of these governments, all of which only further destabilized the region.

Even before September 11, U.S. officials had identified the FARC, as "the most dangerous international terrorist group based in the Western Hemisphere."[33] However, it was only in late June 2002—and over French and Swedish objections—that the EU added FARC to its terrorist list—yet still omitting the ELN. And it was only after September 11, and Colombia's election of President Uribe in May 2002, that the Bush administration stepped up its efforts to aid Colombia in its war on narco-terrorism. Despite some success in arresting FARC members and negotiating with AUC terrorists, the war rages on, spilling over to neighboring countries such as Brazil, Venezuela, Panama, and Ecuador.[34]

From 1999 to 2002, the U.S. poured over $2 billion into Colombia's war on drugs, with no results to show for it. About 70 percent of the heroin used on the U.S. East Coast originates in Colombia, and, according to congressman Dan Burton in hearings of the House Government Reform Committee in December 2002, "This heroin is the purest, most addictive and deadly heroin produced anywhere in the world." He added, "With a single dose costing less than $4, and having purity levels as high as 93 percent, this is a problem that demands the attention of Congress."[35] The hearings revealed that the U.S. State Department and other federal agencies had cut back on cocaine and heroin eradication in Colombia. Addressing a State Department official about this issue, Congressman Benjamin Gilman from New York stated, "I think you have made some wrong decisions that have resulted in the massive increase in the exportation of heroin into the U.S."[36] Despite evidence that Colombia's narco-terrorists are cooperating with Hizballah, HAMAS, al-Qaeda, and the IRA, the U.S. has allocated only about $300 million in aid to Colombia for the year 2003 (62 percent is military aid, and the rest is economic support).[37]

Stopping mass murders and other human rights atrocities has been reason enough for countless U.S. and UN military and peace-keeping campaigns. Yet such conditions in Colombia were not deemed serious enough to justify putting an end to the Latin American drug war, even though, over past decades, it has cost tens of thousands of lives, corrupted democratic institutions throughout the region, subverted economic markets, and destabilized financial systems throughout the Americas. This not only has posed a growing threat to the social stability of the region, but also, over the last decade, has helped to finance and facilitate growing numbers of international terror cells—especially Islamist terror cells—operating in Latin America.

The FARC's International Connections

On April 24, 2002, the U.S. House of Representatives Committee on International Relations published the findings of its investigation into the Irish Republican Army's activities in Colombia. Their report clearly demonstrated the IRA's longstanding connection to the FARC, mentioned at least fifteen IRA terrorists who had been traveling in and out of Colombia since 1998, and estimated that the IRA had received at least $2 million in drug proceeds for having trained members of the FARC.[38]

The IRA/FARC connection was first made public on August 11, 2001, after the arrest in Bogota of two IRA experts in explosives and urban warfare and a representative of Sinn Fein (the IRA's "political wing") who had been stationed in Cuba on the payroll of the Cuban Communist party. The three had traces of explosives on their clothes and on their luggage, but claimed they were in Colombia to advise the FARC on its "peace talks" with the government. Their false travel documents raised further doubts about their peaceful intentions.[39]

During President Alvero Uribe's inauguration, a mortar attack carried out by the FARC killed twenty-one people and injured sixty. Further attacks resulted in the deaths of more than one hundred people. Colombian law enforcement sources confirmed that the bombing techniques used by FARC were identical to those of the IRA.[40]

The IRA is not the only terrorist organization that cooperates with Colombia's narco-terrorists. Al-Qaeda, Hizballah, HAMAS, and Islamic Jihad factions, for example, are also engaged in illegal arms smuggling, drug trafficking, and money laundering in Colombia.

Al-Qaeda's involvement in developing the Colombian heroin trade began in the mid- to late 1990s. According to Colombia's former police chief, General José Cadena: "The ones who brought this problem [to Colombia] were Afghanis and Pakistanis. They entered with tourist visas through Peru, Ecuador and Bolivia, and here they worked giving instructions for planting . . . poppy."[41] Al-Qaeda did not limit its activities in Colombia to giving instructions on how to produce heroin. In 1998, an Egyptian Islamic Jihad member, Muhammad Abed Abd al-Aal, was arrested in Colombia for his involvement in drug trafficking, arms smuggling, and money laundering with the FARC, and for having raised money for al-Qaeda. He was deported to Ecuador, where he disappeared.[42]

On December 22, 1999, the Colombian government suspended the construction of an Iranian-sponsored meatpacking plant and slaughterhouse in Colombia's demilitarized zone, an area run by the FARC. According to reports, Colombian officials suspected that "Iranian interest in that immediate region may be linked with the narcotics trade and the FARC."[43] In early 2001, U.S. intelligence alerted the Brazilian, Paraguayan, and Argentine governments that the FARC had been trafficking drugs and weapons together with Islamist groups in the tri-border region. "It is very probable," said U.S. investigators, "that there is an alliance between the Taliban regime and bin Laden, who are taking part in this illegal trade, with the Colombian traffickers, to stimulate the production of heroin."[44]

Connections with Colombia's narco-terrorists extend throughout the world. Intelligence sources have established that the FARC and the ELN have strong ties to Venezuelan President Hugo Chavez,[45] the Mexican mafia, and the "Russian, Ukrainian, Croatian, and Jordanian mafias, among others, which supply weapons and communications systems."[46] FARC is known to have ties to armed groups in at least eighteen other countries.[47]

ABU SAYYAF GROUP (ASG)

The radical Philippine Islamist group Abu Sayyaf ("Bearer of the Sword")[48] was founded in the late 1980s by Abdurajak Abubakar Janjalani, who had been seeking "complete religious and political independence for the predominantly Muslim island of Mindanao."[49] He was born in the Philippines in 1953, and, with a Saudi government grant, went to study Islamic jurisprudence and Arabic in Mecca in 1981. While abroad, he received military training in Libya and Syria and fought in Afghanistan against the Soviet invasion, where he met Osama bin Laden. Upon his return to the Philippines, he promoted Islamic fundamentalism and created the ASG.

In 1991, after the ASG split from the Moro Islamic Liberation Front (MILF), the original Muslim secessionist group in the Philippines,[50] Osama bin Laden's brother-in-law, Muhammad Jamal Khalifa, who headed the Philippine office of the Saudi charity International Islamic Relief Organization, became an advisor to Janjalani, and oversaw the expansion of the ASG. According to a former Muslim rebel, Gerry Salapuddin, who is now deputy speaker of Congress in the Philippines, without Khalifa, Abu Sayyaf would not have existed.[51] In addition to funding from al-Qaeda and the IIRO, the ASG has received financial support from another Saudi charity, the Muslim World League, as well as millions of dollars from Libyan leader Muammar Qaddafi.[52]

The ASG's links with al-Qaeda extend beyond financial aid. Abubakar Janjalani provided refuge to Ramzi Yousef, the 1993 World Trade Center bomber. While in the Philippines, Ramzi, who had fought together with Janjalani in Afghanistan, provided explosives training to ASG members and direct links to al-Qaeda.

In the late 1990s, through his connections with al-Qaeda and bin Laden, Janjalani broadened Abu Sayyaf's networking with other terrorist organizations, increasing its ability to mount larger, more effective, and more successful terrorist attacks. For example, Abu Sayyaf obtains weapons from the Pakistan-based Islamist group Harakat ul-Mujahideen.[53] The weapons are manufactured in Pakistan but delivered by yet another terrorist organization, the LTTE of Sri Lanka. Abu Sayyaf has separate links with the Southeast Asian terrorist group Jemaah Islamiyah,[54] Kumpulan Mujahideen Malaysia (KMM), and al-Qaeda. Al-Qaeda provided the training; the others continue to share intelligence with Abu Sayyaf, help select targets, and assist with other such matters.[55] Other ASG-linked organizations include, but are not limited to: Egyptian Islamic Jihad, Chechen Islamists, the Islamic Movement of Uzbekistan, Algeria's Armed Islamic Group, the Islamic Army of Aden, HAMAS, and Palestinian Islamic Jihad.[56]

Abu Sayyaf also received funding from Iraq under Saddam Hussein. This support was confirmed in March 2003, in a statement by Hamsiraji Sali, the local commander of the Abu Sayyaf Group in Basilan, who boasted that he received at least $20,000 a year from Iraq. "It's so we would have something to spend on chemicals for bomb-making and for the movement of our people."[57]

Abubakar Janjalani was killed in 1998 in a clash with the Philippine police. His brother Khaddafy Janjalani—who was not a scholar of Islam, but rather an explosives expert—succeeded him, and steered the ASG into criminal activity. According to a 2002 U.S. Congressional report, the Abu Sayyaf organization finances its operations through robbery, piracy, kidnapping, and drug trafficking.[58] Philippine intelligence has detailed ASG's growing involvement in the cultivation of marijuana on the islands of Jolo and Basilan, and in the production and sale of methamphetamine hydrochloride in cooperation with the Hong Kong Triad 14-K (a Chinese drug ring), which also provides the ASG with arms.[59]

Abu Sayyaf is one of the most overtly criminal of Islamist terrorist groups; it does not hide the fact that it has raised millions of dollars from illegal acts. Intelligence sources believe that Abu Sayyaf holds more than $25 million in bank accounts—most of that money extorted from relatives of kidnapped hostages—and is better equipped than the Filipino military.[60]

THE LIBERATION TIGERS OF TAMIL EELAM (LTTE)

The Liberation Tigers of Tamil Eelam (LTTE) is another terror organization that finances itself through drug trafficking.[61] It was established in 1976 as a nationalist separatist movement to create an independent state for the Tamil ethnic minority of northern Sri Lanka,[62] but by the year 1983 it had begun its terror activities. Like other nationalist terror organizations, the LTTE was originally sponsored by the Soviet Union, much of its weaponry originated in the former Soviet satellites,[63] and many of the LTTE's operatives were trained by the PLO.[64]

In 1995, the LTTE expanded its operations into South Africa. There it registered as a "closed corporation," which enabled it to establish training camps. International law enforcement sources monitored how the LTTE enlisted and trained recruits from all over Africa and India in their South African camps.[65] The LTTE also made connections with other terrorist groups such as HAMAS, Hizballah, the Kurdistan Workers Party (PKK),[66] and al-Qaeda, all of which operated—and still operate—out of South Africa.[67] As mentioned above, the Tamil Tigers have transferred weapons from al-Qaeda and its affiliates in Pakistan to the Abu Sayyaf group in the Philippines. Alliances with Islamist groups are especially noteworthy because the Tamil are predominantly Hindu—thus, they point at the growing trend of cooperation between terrorist groups despite differences in their political and ideological agendas.

The LTTE, which counts at least twenty thousand fighters among its ranks,[68] has killed more than sixty-five thousand people and displaced at least 1.6 million during twenty years of fighting against the government of Sri Lanka.[69] The LTTE is noted for its use of homicide bombings, which are carried out by its élite Black Tigers group. Intelligence sources have reported that in the summer of 2000, when the PA and Yassir Arafat planned attacks against Israel, they approached the Tamil Tigers and asked if the Black Tigers would help them out by providing suicide bombers in Israel; the Tigers refused.[70]

The LTTE raises funds both legally—from Tamil communities in Asia, Europe, and North America—and illegally, mostly through piracy and drug trafficking.[71] In the 1980s and '90s, LTTE members were arrested in Sri Lanka, India, Australia, Britain, France, Germany, Switzerland, Canada, and the United States on charges of drug trafficking.[72]

International law enforcement investigations throughout the nineties uncovered close collaboration between the authorities in Burma and the LTTE. "The LTTE reportedly has close ties to drug trafficking networks in Burma," stated the assistant secretary of state for international narcotics and law enforcement affairs, Rand Beers, in hearings before the Senate Judiciary Committee in March 2002. "And Tamil expatriates may carry drugs in exchange for training from Burma, Pakistan and Afghanistan," he added.[73] Indeed, the Tamil Tigers have been allowed to train in Southern Burma in return for supplying couriers for Burmese heroin. In November 1996, the Indian authorities seized $71 million worth of heroin that had been smuggled by LTTE members into India.[74] According to a narcotics officer based in Bangkok, "The Tamil drug smuggling network has become an integral part of Burmese drug trafficking around the world."[75]

The LTTE is also noted for the capabilities of its Sea Tigers naval forces. Most of the Sea Tigers' assets were obtained through piracy and naval military operations. However, some of the LTTE vessels were allegedly purchased with money obtained from Tamil diaspora communities,[76] and are still registered with Lloyds of London.

Progressing peace talks with the Sri Lankan government seemed to have stopped most of the LTTE terror activities. But, on February 7, 2003, with the fifth round of peace talks underway, LTTE arms smugglers blew themselves up off Sri Lanka's coast in a boat carrying antiaircraft gun and ammunition.[77] By April 2003, the LTTE had declared its "displeasure" with the ongoing peace talks, and new clashes had erupted between the Tamil and Muslims.[78]

U.S. EFFORTS AGAINST NARCO-TERRORISM

On December 14, 2001, President Bush launched a new anti–drug use campaign, stating that using drugs "supports gangs here at home. And abroad, it's so important for Americans to know that the traffic in drugs finances the work of terror, sustaining terrorists, that terrorists use drug profits to fund their cells to commit acts of murder." He appealed to America's youth to stop using drugs, because "if you quit drugs, you join the fight against terror in America."[79]

Unfortunately, the president's effort to make the public aware of the connection between drugs and terrorism has done little to reduce illegal drug consumption in the U.S. The evidence points to an *increase* in domestic consumption,[80] as well as to an increase in the international drug trade.

Although the administration has identified most of the rogue countries and terrorist organizations that make up the axis of evil, it has failed to include in the same list the countries that produce and grow illicit drugs, and the organizations that sell them, profit from them, and then use these profits to finance the murders of Americans and others. Moreover, the new Department of Homeland Security has reassigned six thousand customs agents, who had been employed to trace illegal drugs and money laundering, and has left their positions vacant. Despite DEA Chief of Operations Steven Casteel's acknowledgment that "drugs are a weapon of mass destruction that can be used against Western societies and help bring them down," the DEA, instead of expanding its efforts to trace the movement of illegal drugs and their profits internationally, is merely focusing on demand reduction and domestic treatment.[81]

If more efforts were made by the U.S. and the EU to expand their lists of terrorists with "global reach" to include all narco-terrorist organizations—including the Islamist Hizballah, all Palestinian terror organizations, the IRA, and the ELN—the West might be in an improved position to win the war on terror. As a specialist in international affairs with the Congressional Research Service stated before the Senate Judiciary Committee in May 2003, "By according recognition and policy focus to the combined threat of drug trafficking and terrorism, we may be better able to devise cohesive strategies to deal with these threats in an effective and holistic manner."[82]

"Fighting corruption is fighting terrorism."

Vaclav Havel, Prague, 2001

CHAPTER 6

Prospects for Change

"We will starve terrorists of funding," President George W. Bush promised in the weeks following the September 11 attacks.[1]

The previous chapters have demonstrated the importance of following through on this pledge—but they have also shown the difficulty in fulfilling it. Since the objective of terrorism is to gain power through violence, and since money is the essential tool to that end, the ongoing violence perpetrated by such groups as al-Qaeda, the Palestinian Authority's al-Aqsa Martyrs Brigades, Hizballah, and Colombia's FARC constitute the proof that much work is yet to be done.

This final chapter examines the ways that the United States, and the world, can more effectively identify, acknowledge, and eliminate the financial resources that empower international terror.

CHALLENGING STATE SPONSORSHIP

Although the Bush administration cannot fight the war on terror on all fronts simultaneously, it can better demonstrate its political will by treating *all* terror-supporting entities equally. The U.S. went to war with al-Qaeda, the Taliban, and Saddam Hussein's Iraq, yet it is negotiating with Syria and the Palestinian Authority, both of which harbor, finance, train, and use Hizballah, HAMAS, al-Aqsa Martyrs Brigades, and Islamic Jihad terrorists to further their political agendas. The U.S. is even in the process of *rewarding* Palestinian terrorists with statehood.

Calling on antiterror mechanisms already in place, the U.S. can use its voice and its vote in international financial organizations to prevent any financial aid to countries that support terrorism. It can also take more action to censure countries that are known to fund or otherwise support terrorism—countries such as Saudi Arabia, Iran, Syria, Sudan, Indonesia, Libya, and North Korea. In addition to freezing assets where appropriate, the U.S. could take action not only against the states themselves, but also against other entities that do business with these countries, whether directly or indirectly (through affiliates and fronts). Such businesses generate immense amounts of money for countries such as France, Germany, Russia, and China, and for politicians and private and public companies in these and other "allied" nations—and within the U.S. itself. They also enable terrorists to exploit U.S. inattention and increase their power.

For example, after years of U.S. disregard for the Palestinian Authority's corruption, incitement, and association with terrorism, the Bush administration finally called for the replacement of Arafat and the PA's leadership in the summer of 2002. But, in May 2003, Arafat, the godfather of modern terrorism, and a "new" but still corrupt PA cabinet are in power, planning and carrying out more terror attacks with money not only from Muslim and Arab sponsors of terror, but also from UNRWA, from the European Union,[2] and more recently even from the U.S.—all banking on yet more promises for reform.[3]

Similarly, Saudi Arabia's hypocrisy was exposed in public[4] on May 12, 2003, when, after the U.S. repeatedly asked Saudi authorities to provide security for American and other Western sites but received no cooperation, al-Qaeda launched a terror attack in Riyadh that killed at least thirty-four people, including at least eight Americans.[5] Saudi Arabia, one of the most repressive police states in the world, claimed that it couldn't have foiled the attack.[6] Strangely, even after this attack, the U.S. administration lacks the political will to condemn the Saudis; instead, they continue to defend the kingdom— and even to praise it for its well-publicized statements regarding new measures to control financial support for terrorists.[7]

This policy of nonconfrontation has endured for years, even in the face of irrefutable evidence presented to the Pentagon's Defense Policy Board in July 2002 "that Saudi Arabia was an enemy of the United States . . . [and] that the Saudis were active 'at every level of the terror chain,'"[8] and even when another report on Saudi Arabia's funding of terrorism submitted in December 2002 to the UN Security Council asserted the same.[9] Even though the kingdom spends more than $87 billion funding a *Wahabist,* anti-Western agenda,[10] and even though it funds Islamist terrorist groups around the world,[11] the U.S. chooses not to challenge the House of Saud. Until it does, the kingdom's sponsorship of terror will continue.

In addition, the U.S. has refused for decades to crack down on IRA fundraising in the U.S. It even failed to denounce Gerry Adams, head of the IRA's political wing, Sinn Fein, for his refusal to testify before the U.S. House of Representatives International Relations Committee about his direct involvement with the FARC in Colombia.[12] The U.S. also failed to censure Indonesia, whose government refused for a long time to close down the bank accounts of al-Qaeda operatives and affiliated organizations, or even to acknowledge their presence within its borders.[13] Instead, Indonesia is now a candidate for special grants from the U.S. administration's new aid program, the Millennium Challenge Account.[14]

In December 2002, HAMAS operatives in Richardson, Texas, were indicted for illegal dealings with terror sponsor Libya.[15] However, when Attorney General John Ashcroft announced the indictments, he stated only that "today's charges against a senior leader of Hamas are the latest in an aggressive campaign to identify, disrupt and destroy the sources of funding that make terrorism possible." He did not mention either Libya's role or the fact that its leader, Colonel Muammar Qaddafi, had pursued international terrorism for more than thirty years.[16]

Countries with strong terror ties demonstrate occasional cooperation with the U.S., as in the arrest of Khalid Sheikh Muhammad in Pakistan in March 2003, Saudi Arabia's new anti-money-laundering laws, or Syria's promises to stop the activities of terror organizations it harbors. But the U.S. should not be content with promises, halfhearted reforms, or sporadic assistance. Although it may be politically inconvenient to criticize "friendly" states, the U.S. should identify all countries that sponsor terrorism, and hold them as responsible for the violence they enable as any terror organization that graces the official list of the State Department. In addition, it is equally important for the United States to acknowledge that states such as Pakistan, Syria, and Cuba[17] are involved in the illicit drug trade—the primary source of terrorist funding.[18]

The U.S. has, to date, won some battles against international terrorism, perhaps most directly against the al-Qaeda network. But as long as the U.S. remains unwilling, for whatever reason, to identify its real enemies in the war on terror, it can never achieve a true long-term victory.

THE TOOLS TO FIGHT TERROR FINANCING

Internationally, the United Nations has already put into place mechanisms designed to aid the dismantling of terrorists' financial networks. The International Convention for the Suppression of the Financing of Terrorism, adopted by the UN General Assembly in December 1999, calls for "all States to take steps to prevent and counteract, *through appropriate domestic measures* [emphasis added], the financing of terrorists and terrorist organizations, whether such financing is direct or indirect through organizations which also have or claim to have charitable, social or cultural goals or which are also engaged in unlawful activities such as illicit arms trafficking, drug dealing and racketeering."[19] The convention further calls on each member country to enact domestic laws that will criminalize the activities of terrorists, and requires member states to "ensure that criminal acts covered by the Convention will not be considered justifiable for any political, philosophical, ideological, racial, ethnic or religious considerations."[20] By April 2002, "132 countries had signed the Convention, and 26 countries had completed the ratification process and become States Parties."[21]

Although this convention has been in place since 1999, it evidently has had little or no effect upon the behavior of its signatories, or upon the flow of money to terrorist organizations. Similarly, the Organisation for Economic Cooperation and Development's Convention against Transnational Bribery,[22] the Organization of American States' Convention Against Corruption,[23] and UN proposals for an anticorruption convention[24] have done little to diminish bribery and corruption, which also facilitate terrorism. The same can be said for the 1988 UN Convention against the Illicit Traffic in Narcotic Drugs and Psychotropic Substances; since this convention's adoption, drug trafficking and drug money laundering, instead of decreasing, have increased exponentially.

As with other international agreements, most countries that have ratified these conventions do not feel the need to comply with them, and no mechanisms exist to enforce compliance. The International Monetary Fund and the World Bank, for example, only see to it that the money they provide to a country arrives in its central bank. Because they fear being accused of violating the state's sovereignty, they are not willing to monitor how the money is allocated and disbursed once it arrives. Thus, the chief purpose of such international conventions seems to be illusory—to create the impression that steps are being taken to remedy a situation, while in reality nothing is accomplished.

International cooperation may be difficult to ensure, but without it very little can be accomplished to stop the flow of money to terrorist groups. The pursuit of terror funds must extend beyond national borders because terror networks themselves know no borders; as terrorism expert Matthew Levitt points out, "The global nature of today's terrorist threat stems not only from the targets of the terrorists' attacks (from Djerba, Tunisia to Bali, Indonesia, and everywhere in between), but from the global marketplace, in particular the cross-border opportunities created by the global financial and communications markets."[25] Recognizing this fact, the Council on Foreign Relations published a report in 2002 recommending that the international community "establish a specialized international organization dedicated solely to investigating terrorist financing."[26] However, since most conventions ratified by international bodies have yet to be complied with, the creation of yet another international body does not seem to be the appropriate remedy. Until international mechanisms are created that can *enforce* compliance with laws against terrorism, money laundering, and drug trafficking—by imposing sanctions or other penalties—all similar international efforts will continue to ring hollow.

A step in the right direction would be the universal adoption of a standardized code that criminalizes terrorist financing and money laundering, as well as bribery and corruption. As long as each state is free to operate under its own definitions of what constitutes terrorist financing, money laundering, and so on, depending on its own political considerations, no real advances can be made. The implementation and enforcement of universal standards might also prevent global terrorists from exploiting the gaps in permissiveness that currently exist between various countries. (Matthew Levitt, for example, describes how, until recently, terrorists would purchase prepaid international cell phones in Switzerland—because in that country no identification was required of the buyer.)[27]

THE WAR ON NARCO-TERROR

In his State of the Union Address in January 2003, President George W. Bush stated that "the ideology of power and domination has appeared again, and seeks to gain the ultimate weapons of terror."[28] He cautioned that "the gravest danger in the war on terror . . . facing America and the world, is outlaw regimes that seek and possesses nuclear, chemical, and biological weapons. These regimes could use such weapons for blackmail, terror, and mass murder. They could also give or sell those weapons to terrorist allies, who would use them without the least hesitation."[29]

However, President Bush failed to mention another devastating weapon that is plentifully available, that has killed thousands of Americans each year and disrupted the lives of millions, and that has cost the economy hundreds of billions of dollars annually—illegal drugs.[30] The government's failure to identify and to take action against narco-terrorism—the flooding of the U.S. and the West with illicit drugs by terrorist organizations and states—is particularly troubling since similar failures in the past are precisely what helped the narco-terrorists to become such a successful, independent, and global threat.

Since the late 1970s, drug money has become an increasingly significant feature in the economies of many countries. The expansion of the drug trade has turned drug money into one of the world's most powerful items. During the Reagan administration, a new procedure, the "Narcotics Certification Process," was implemented to "evaluate countries that have [been] designated as a major illicit drug-producing or drug-transit countries."[31] By law, economic sanctions should be imposed on countries that produce and traffic in drugs, and that have been declared uncooperative with U.S. efforts to counter the drug trade. However, for the years 2002 and 2003, there has been no change in the list of twenty-three countries identified by the U.S. State Department[32]—despite monstrous amounts of evidence linking international narco-terrorist networks to a large number of countries that both facilitate and benefit from the shipment of drugs, the laundering of money, and the harboring of narco-terrorists. Apparently, the failure to mention all the countries involved stems from what the U.S. considers "other priorities"—in direct conflict with its alleged national security priority, the war on terror.

The war on terrorism will be fought with little or no chance of victory as long as the U.S. fails to identify *all* narco-terrorist organizations and the states that sponsor and harbor them. The narco-terrorist, looking at the accumulating evidence of misdirected U.S. and Western efforts, will find reasons to believe that he is winning this war of attrition—all he needs to do is outlast the ineffective attempts to defeat him. If the U.S. hopes to mount a genuine challenge, a good start might be to honestly acknowledge and penalize not only the states and organizations that cultivate, produce, and traffic in drugs, but also those countries that launder narco-terrorists' money. To minimize the heroin and cocaine trade, instead of spraying herbicides that have no real effect on the growing poppy and coca plantations,[33] the U.S. should employ new technologies that permanently destroy coca and poppy plants; they are available, cost-effective, and have been tested and shown to work in an environmentally responsible way.[34]

As the DEA's Steven Casteel stated, illicit drugs are "weapon[s] of mass destruction that can be used against Western societies and help bring them down. . . . We've been under attack in this country for a long time, and it didn't start on Sept. 11."[35] Therefore, in addition to the creation of new policies in the U.S. and elsewhere to destroy illicit drug production, to confront drug trafficking organizations, and to address the problem of domestic consumption, the U.S. and the West should acknowledge that illicit drugs are an effective weapon of mass destruction. Terrorist organizations and other subversive groups have seen firsthand—and have benefited directly from—the failure of democratic governments to seriously address the problem of the illicit drug business. They have simply become emboldened to spread and intensify their businesses. It is time to stop classifying drug trafficking as merely a criminal enterprise; it is ultimately a political problem and should be dealt with as a national security priority.

An acid test of the U.S. commitment to combat narco-terrorism would be the reordering of U.S. diplomatic priorities; the implementation *and enforcement* of international conventions by signatory countries; and a clampdown not only on money that is suspected of funding terrorism, but also on drug-money-laundering operations, in banks and other financial institutions throughout the world. A failure to take these steps can only help to ensure that countries and terrorist organizations alike will continue to use illicit drugs as both economic and political weapons.

CONFRONTING CORRUPTION

Terrorism, like organized crime and drug trafficking, can flourish only when abetted by government corruption. Without corruption, the House of Saud and the *mullahs* of Iran could not have sustained their power; Yasser Arafat and Hugo Chavez—like Saddam Hussein until recently—could not have remained in their positions; and the Colombian FARC and ELN could never have gained their stranglehold on more than 50 percent of that country's territory.

The most prevalent forms of corruption in government are:

- *Illegitimacy* of governments and methods of succession.

- *Nepotism*, including obstacles to free competition through favoritism or patronage of family or tribe, as occurs in Asia, the Middle East, Africa, and Latin America, and parts of Europe.
- *Cronyism*, including the appointment of friends to political positions. Practiced in many areas of the world, including China, Japan, Russia, Egypt, Syria, Indonesia, and the U.S.
- *Kleptocracy*, including the sale of state assets—at less than market value—to favored customers. This has been prevalent not only in régimes examined earlier, such as the Palestinian Authority and Saddam Hussein's Iraq, but also in many transitional economies with incomplete or flawed privatization programs, such as Russia and the Balkans.
- *Narcocracy*, the subversion of political and economic structures with the huge profits from illegal drug traffic, as in Colombia, Peru, Afghanistan, and Burma.
- *Government for hire*, in which officials may be bribed or intimidated to influence government policy and judicial decisions, and to obtain favored treatment from government agencies. It is practiced both in developing countries like Brazil and South Africa, and in industrialized nations such as France and Germany.[36]

Years of silence, indifference, and willful blindness by the West have greatly exacerbated the problem of corruption, mostly in Muslim, developing, and Third World countries. In 1996, this fact compelled James Wolfensohn, the president of the World Bank, to publicly announce the launch of "a war against corruption" because corruption "is a cancer."[37] However, despite many international conventions and multinational and international agreements, corruption appears to be on the rise. In the words of Horst Köhler, managing director of the International Monetary Fund (IMF), "Fighting corruption is as difficult as it is essential."[38]

Considering corruption's destabilizing effects on national and international security, the U.S. and most international organizations, including the IMF, the World Bank, the Organization for Economic Cooperation and Development, the Organization of American States, the Organization for Security and Cooperation in Europe, the European Bank for Reconstruction and Development, the European Union, the African and Asian Development Banks, and the United Nations, have explicitly recognized the need to take more effective international action against corruption. All of these organizations currently fund programs to combat corruption and poverty through the promotion of good governance. However, as former U.S. secretary of treasury Paul O'Neill stated in June 2001, "The World Bank Group alone has lent $470 billion since its inception and $225 billion in just the last decade. Visit some of the poorest nations in the world and you will see that we have little to show for it."[39] In fact, the World Bank's internal records for the year 2000 showed a 70 percent failure rate of its overall programs in the poorest countries.[40] According to a World Bank senior advisor, during the last decade in thirty-six poor countries that were given ten or more loans each with conditions attached by the IMF and the World Bank, the growth rate of income per person remained at zero.[41] (Shortly after the World Bank advisor revealed these statistics, the bank sent him on a "sabbatical.")[42]

In the United States, the USA PATRIOT Act may prove an effective tool for deterring and controlling money-laundering operations in banks and financial institutions. Uniform implementation is a must, however. No exceptions should be made, not even for individuals such as former Bolivian president Jaime Paz Zamora. Paz Zamora's U.S. visa was revoked in 1994[43] because he received campaign contributions from known drug traffickers. A strict implementation of the PATRIOT Act would have prevented him from regaining his right to enter the U.S.[44]

However, financial regulations alone cannot address the larger problem of corruption that is a way of life in the countries from which terrorism originates.

Political Reform in the Islamic World

Terrorism stems from cultural violence rooted in a perversely callous attitude toward human life and a general disregard for the worth of individual rights. These conditions are all too prevalent in Islamic and Arab countries that were bypassed by the twentieth century's waves of democratization. Islamic and Arab peoples, on the whole, have seen few if any improvements in political, religious, and educational freedoms; civil society; rule of law; or human rights, accountability, and transparency—trends that have improved both lives and cultural attitudes in other parts of the world.

Freedom House's "Survey of Freedom" for 2000–2001 confirms that "the democracy gap between the Islamic world and the rest of the world is dramatic."[45] And according to the eminent scholar of Islam Bernard Lewis:

> To a Western observer, schooled in the theory and practice of Western freedom, it is precisely the lack of freedom—freedom of the mind from constraint and indoctrination, to question and inquire and speak; freedom of the economy from corrupt and pervasive mismanagement; freedom of women from male oppression; freedom of citizens from tyranny—that underlies so many of the troubles of the Muslim world.[46]

Freedom House's survey notes that the combination of extremist ideas and Islamist terrorism now prevents political freedom and democracy from taking hold in the Islamic world.[47] Even a 2002 report cosponsored by the United Nations Development Program and the Arab Fund for Economic and Social Development stresses:

how far the Arab states still need to go . . . to tackle the human and economic scourge of joblessness, which afflicts our countries as a group more seriously than any other developing region. And [the report] clearly outlines the challenges for Arab states in terms of strengthening personal freedoms and boosting broad-based citizen participation in political and economic affairs.[48]

Régime Change

One way to overcome corrupt institutions and institute such political and humanitarian reforms is through the wholesale removal of oppressive régimes. However, a régime change without a proper transitional process to guide the state into a working democracy can open the door to social anarchy—and even worse corruption.

For example, in Indonesia, the country with the largest Muslim population in the world, President Suharto's corruption (he stole an estimated $80 billion from his country over the course of his thirty-two-year reign)[49] led to his removal from power. But the West had permitted Suharto's corruption to go unchecked for more than thirty years, and no provisions had been set in place for a stable régime change that could withstand a new onslaught of corruption from successive governments. In the year 2000, $22 billion—45.6 percent of Indonesia's national budget—was found to be totally missing.[50] (However, even this did not prevent the Consultative Group on Indonesia [CGI], led by the IMF, from approving a $4.8 billion loan to cover part of Indonesia's $7.1 billion budget deficit that year.)[51] As corruption ran wild following Suharto's departure, the way was paved for the emergence of radical Islamic elements, who like other Islamists had initially promised to fight corruption but soon became corrupt and criminal themselves. Radical Islam took advantage of the new freedoms to establish footholds throughout the fourteen thousand islands in the archipelago that make up that country.

In Afghanistan, although the removal of the Taliban from power by the U.S. in 2001 led to the election of a new government and to reforms such as the reinstatement of rights and opportunities for women, corruption is pervasive, and opium cultivation and heroin production are reaching new heights[52]—all this while U.S. and international forces are on the ground, and aid agencies are purportedly helping to implement reform.

There is still hope that reform in a post–Saddam Hussein Iraq will fare better than it did in Afghanistan and Indonesia. The arrival of the new U.S. presidential envoy to Iraq, the seasoned counterterrorism expert Paul Bremer, on May 6, 2003, as the senior coalition official in Iraq,[53] is an indication that the U.S. is taking the rebuilding of Iraq seriously.[54] The Iraqi people, although traumatized by decades of tyranny, have not been radicalized by religion (though the Shiite majority, supported by Iran, has begun flexing its muscles). The loud anti-American propaganda and the complaints about looting and lack of services by the Iraqis—who never dreamed of complaining about anything while Saddam Hussein was in power, and who suffered massive human rights abuses—could be attributed to both remnants of Hussein's Baath party and radical Islamists. However, this could also be the first sign that the Iraqi people have discovered the freedom to express themselves—which is a good sign, because neither the U.S. nor its coalition will be able to create a more democratic political system in Iraq without the active participation and support of the Iraqi people.

Millennium Challenge Account (MCA)

If endemic corruption facilitates both terrorism and the means to finance it, leading military campaigns to liberate a country from the tyrannous leaders such as the Taliban or Saddam Hussein could be in vain unless corruption is attacked as well. Recognizing that good-governance and anticorruption programs and existing attempts at "reform" have been unsuccessful, and that governments have failed to meet their people's most basic needs, President George W. Bush stated in March 2002 that "these failed states can become havens for terror."[55] To remedy this situation, the president announced that, as part of his new Millennium Challenge Account, the United States would increase by 50 percent its core assistance to developing countries over the next three years—adding $5 billion annually. These funds, according to President Bush, will support "nations that encourage economic freedom, root out corruption, and respect the rights of their people."[56] They are also intended to encourage initiatives to improve the economies and standards of living in qualified developing countries, by rewarding sound policies that support economic growth and reduce poverty. Qualified countries will be assessed by sixteen performance indicators that will be used to evaluate strong commitment toward:

- Good governance. Rooting out corruption, upholding human rights, and adherence to the rule of law are essential conditions for successful development.
- The health and education of their people. Investment in education, health care, and immunization provide for healthy and educated citizens who become agents of development.
- Sound economic policies that foster enterprise and entrepreneurship. More open markets, sustainable budget policies, and strong support for individual entrepreneurship unleash the enterprise and creativity for lasting growth and prosperity.[57]

AN INTERNATIONAL INTEGRITY STANDARD

President Bush's new Millennium Challenge Account could become a powerful weapon in the war on terror, but obstacles to its success—

and the success of any anticorruption initiative—still remain. The failure to effectively combat corruption can perhaps be attributed mainly to the following factors:

- There is no accepted definition of corruption
- No objective, uniform standard exists to identify the prevalence of corruption, to measure the vulnerability of countries to its various forms, or to serve as a basis for an anticorruption program

Since there is no firm agreement on what constitutes corruption, the surveys, indices, and analyses that have been developed to assess this predicament tend to be based mostly on individual perceptions and anecdotal information. Moreover, there is also no way to gauge objectively the success of reform programs. Thus, it is not surprising that existing programs have failed to control—let alone eliminate—the problem.

The solution might be to develop a truly authoritative model based on basic, internationally recognized anticorruption principles that would set forth a detailed and universally accepted set of anticorruption standards.[58] The development of an International Integrity Standard could provide an essential policy tool for objective, practical, and measurable systemic reform. The International Integrity Standard could offer methods for assessing the robustness of countries' economic, legal, and political systems, and their ability to resist corruption. Such an audit would provide, for the first time, an objective assessment of a country's seriousness both in managing its affairs and in fighting corruption.

The International Integrity Standard would help to:

- Determine whether countries are eligible for loans or any other financial assistance
- Monitor the implementation and success of reform programs

- Develop preventive measures to make business more reliable and honest, and make funding for countries strictly
  contingent upon their adherence to these measures

The U.S. could use the International Integrity Standard to better
determine whether countries qualify for U.S. assistance from the
new Millennium Challenge Account. It could also employ the standard to evaluate the performance of international organizations,
such as the UN and the World Bank, that also provide aid and grants
to countries to carry out reforms. (For example, the UN's "Office of
the Iraq Programme" abused funds of the oil-for-food program, en-
riching Saddam Hussein, the countries participating in the program,
and the UN's own treasury, instead of providing food and medicine
to the Iraqi people.)[59] And finally, the U.S. and international organizations such as the World Bank, the IMF, and the UN could rely on
the standard to monitor the states to which their grants are being
made.

Audits of these organizations could focus on the following:

- If the international organization provides funds to countries
  and officials, does it publicly disclose its standards and procedures for allocation and disbursement?
- Has the recipient country publicly disclosed its standards,
  procedures, and contractual arrangements for obtaining pri-
  vate-sector funding and bank loans?
- Has the recipient country publicly disclosed the accounting
  and auditing arrangements for the use of international and
  bilateral donor funds?
- Has the international organization or other donor agency introduced codes of conduct for its officials that incorporate
  the standard definition of bribery set forth by the UN?
- Have recipient countries introduced and implemented basic
  antibribery and anticorruption legislation?

• Do methods exist to safeguard the appropriate channeling of aid funds by the donor and the recipient country?

This system could form the benchmark against which the anticorruption programs of *all* countries could be tested. This, in turn, would help to level at least some of the disparities among countries and provide incentives to reform in order both to receive aid and to attract investment—because, if a donor were required to divide aid among several different recipient countries, those that rated the highest on the International Integrity Standard would be eligible to receive the most aid. In turn, their success in fighting corruption will help restore the legitimacy of their governments and benefit their populations.

The Conflict Securities Advisory Group (CSAG), a Washington, D.C.–based company, has developed a different method to prevent the funding of countries with ties to terrorism—the Global Security Monitor (GSM). The GSM's database enables investors to examine the international connections of the companies in which they invest, to find out if their money helps fund terrorism. The GSM has already identified more than three hundred international companies, mostly in Europe and Asia, that continue to trade with the countries labeled as terrorist by the U.S. government: Iran, Iraq, Syria, Cuba, Libya, and North Korea. According to the CSAG, such identification encourages investors to move their funds into more socially responsible and risk-averse investments.[60]

However, more countries aid and abet terrorism than are officially identified on the U.S. government's list; indeed, some are considered to be the U.S. allies in the war on terror. For instance, Pakistan, Saudi Arabia, Burma, and Egypt produce and traffic in illicit drugs, launder drug money, and/or actively support the terror agenda. Others have traded, and continue to trade, with rogue countries such as Saddam Hussein's Iraq, Syria, North Korea, and Iran. For example, France, Germany, Russia, and China became Iraq's major traders and suppliers of weapons and restricted technology. While making billions of dollars, they helped Saddam Hussein to remain in power and terrorize the world for decades.[61] In addition to helping the Iraqi dictator, France, which seeks to position itself as a major player in the Middle East, also turns a blind eye to fundraising for HAMAS—and, according to U.S. officials, hinders the EU from taking measures against its activities.[62] For that reason, a truly successful antiterrorism standard would have to rely on a more objective assessment than the politically motivated terror lists currently maintained by the U.S. government.

THE FUNDING OF EVIL

To truly stem terrorist financing, political will and leadership are a must. Only then could the International Integrity Standard model— or one equally objective—be developed, implemented, and enforced. Moreover, the U.S. needs to be more truthful about who our enemies are, so that the evil nexus can be defeated and its sources of funding severed. It's either them or us. As U.K. Foreign Minister Jack Straw stated:

> Small evils went unchecked, tyrants became emboldened, then greater evils were unleashed. At each stage good men said wait; the evil is not big enough to challenge: then before their eyes, the evil became too big to challenge.[63]

In saving ourselves, we will also be saving many millions of innocent people who are suffering under illegitimate and oppressive governments. Unless a comprehensive reform process such as this gets underway, our fate may be the same as that of the radicalized Islamist foot soldiers who threaten to inflict their way of life upon us. As Bernard Lewis states, "If the people of the Middle East continue on their present path, the suicide bomber may become a metaphor for the whole region."[64] Unless we take all the steps necessary to comprehensively combat terror, including the adoption of an outright, aggressive campaign to cut off all sources of terrorist funding— and name states and groups that are not only providing funding but also safe haven—the metaphor of the suicide bomber may soon apply to us all.

Understanding the ideology, strategies, and instruments of terrorists' success can help us to better identify how al-Qaeda and other terrorist organizations operate financially. This understanding also helps identify the necessary steps to stop them. More importantly, it can give us the tools to ensure that history will not repeat itself.

"Terrorism is not an enemy. It is a method. It is the most sinister, brutal, inhumane method of our age. But it is nonetheless just that: a method. You cannot, and you do not, make war on a method. War is made on an identified—and identifiable—enemy."

Andrew C. McCarthy,
National Review Online, May 13, 2004

"A war on terror is insufficient reason for a democracy to lie down with a dictator . . . democracy should deal with dictatorships primarily to bring them down. For with them gone—and only with them gone—their crop of horrors will wither and die."

Ambassador Mark Palmer,
Breaking the Real Axis of Evil, 2003

Epilogue

Thirty-two months after al-Qaeda attacked the World Trade Center and the Pentagon, Attorney General John Ashcroft and FBI Director Robert Mueller warned that al-Qaeda is not done yet: "Disturbing intelligence indicates al-Qaeda's specific intention to hit the United States hard."[1] This warning came on the heels of the news that, around the world, at least eighteen thousand al-Qaeda members are ready to launch operations.[2] Indeed, in early August 2004, Secretary of Homeland Security Tom Ridge announced that authorities "have new and unusually specific information about where al-Qaeda would like to attack . . . [the] financial services sector in New York City, Northern New Jersey and Washington, DC."[3]

Recent, successful terror attacks—on U.S. allies around the world, and particularly against U.S. forces in Iraq—have helped advance al-Qaeda's virulent anti-American propaganda campaign and brought new recruits into their ranks. Moreover, a report from the International Institute for Strategic Studies (IISS) in London found that, although two thousand al-Qaeda operatives had been killed or captured since September 2001,[4] al-Qaeda was able to rebound because its "financial network has survived largely intact."[5]

Despite these latest developments, the U.S. government assures us that its operations to stop al-Qaeda's finances around the world have been successful. By the end of April 2004, the U.S. government had:

- Designated 361 individuals and entities as financing terrorism[6]
- Prosecuted 58 people for providing "material support" to al-Qaeda and other terror organizations[7]
- Blocked fourteen hundred accounts and frozen $136.7 million[8]

At the same time, according to a Treasury Department official, "the international community has frozen and seized approximately $200 million of terrorist-related funds."[9]

However, even if $200 million has been seized in the U.S. and elsewhere, it is merely a drop in the billion-dollar bucket for the financial networks of al-Qaeda and other Islamist terror organizations. Neither the U.S. government nor the international community has done much to truly stop the money flow,[10] besides making occasional public statements about how important a job it is. It seems that, because of political and public relations considerations, governments would prefer to arrest individual terrorists[11] rather than destroy global terror's financial infrastructure. After all, exposing the many legitimate fronts throughout the international business and banking community that funnel money to terrorist organizations could not only result in major political conflicts, but also disturb the global economy.

For a particularly striking example, consider the kingdom of Saudi Arabia. The U.S. economy benefits from Saudi oil reserves and the kingdom's recent increase in oil production, and the stability of the régime in Saudi Arabia ensures that the oil continues to flow. Thus, the U.S. and Saudi governments assure us that the Saudis are on our side in the war on terrorism, even though:

- In 2003 a former Treasury Department official referred to Saudi Arabia as "an 'epicenter' of terrorist financing."[12]
- The Saudi Embassy in Washington, D.C., reportedly transferred tens of millions of dollars through Riggs Bank, money suspected to have gone to terrorists.[13] (The Saudi Embassy not only denied that these transfers occurred, but also stated that the FBI assured the embassy that "there were no concerns" in the agency that these accounts were involved in terror financing.)[14]
- Members of the Saudi National Guard facilitated al-Qaeda's attack in May 2003 on a housing compound in Riyadh, which killed thirty-five people and injured two hundred.[15]
- Saudi special forces facilitated the escape of three al-Qaeda terrorists who attacked the Oasis Compound in Khobar, killing twenty-two foreigners, on May 30, 2004.[16]
- Saudi clerics and the government-funded and government-controlled media continue their incitement against the U.S., Israel, and the West.

Despite all this, the U.S. still considers Saudi Arabia an American ally, and frequently challenges those who offer arguments to the contrary. For example, in June 2004 the U.S. administration disputed a Council on Foreign Relations report that criticized Saudi Arabia's stated attempts to control terror financing.[17]

This dismissive attitude is apparent even in the findings of the independent commission created by the United States Congress to investigate the September 11 terror attacks. According to the National Commission on Terrorist Attacks upon the United States, better known as the 9/11 Commission, "Saudi Arabia has long been considered the primary source of al Qaeda funding, but we have found no evidence that the Saudi government as an institution or senior Saudi officials individually funded the organization."[18] The commission clearly attempts to divorce the Saudi régime from its support of al-Qaeda and its nurturing since its founding of what a senior U.S. intelligence official has called "an Islamic ideology, whose goals . . . can be met only by annihilating all non-Muslims."[19]

The commission's "findings" contradict volumes of documents accumulated by several United States government agencies, which attest to the Saudi government's sponsorship and control of charitable organizations that funded al-Qaeda and other Islamist militants. For example, it was Prince Turki al-Faisal, the former head of Saudi Intelligence for twenty-four years, who is reported to have given Osama bin Laden $200 million in 1998 to move to Afghanistan.[20] And it was the interior minister, Prince Nayef, who oversaw and sponsored "most of the major [Saudi] charities," according to David Aufhauser, a former Treasury Department official.[21] Moreover, "Prince Salman, a full brother of King Fahd, controls the International Islamic Relief Organization (IIRO) distributions 'with an iron hand.'"[22] On one occasion, in October 2003, the IIRO provided directly, mostly through the Amman-based Arab Bank, at least $280,000 to fourteen HAMAS charities in the West Bank and Gaza.[23]

All along, the Saudis have been denying, in English, that they support terrorism. However, in April 2002 an Arabic-language Saudi daily, *Al-Jazira*, carried the following announcement by the regional director of the central area for the largest Saudi bank,[24] the National Commercial Bank (NCB). Muhammad Mashehour al-Kaf wrote: "The NCB is willing to support the telethon for the Palestinian *intifada*. The bank, with the coordination of the Saudi Committee in Support of al-Quds Intifada, eased the procedures to receive donations designated for the *intifada*."[25] (Just as a reminder, by then it was known all over the world that the major "weapon" in the hands of the Palestinian terrorists was the *shahid* [homicide bomber], and that the funds were the "insurance policy" to encourage potential *shahids* to volunteer, assuring them that their future widows and orphans would be handsomely rewarded.) Al-Kaf further detailed the new and more efficient procedures for making donations through the NCB's branches:

- "NCB's branches in Riyadh, Jeddah, Qasim, Mecca, Medina, and Khobar stayed open until midnight
- "A toll-free phone number . . . was allocated for the donors
- "A special bank account was opened in NCB branches . . . for donations in support of the al-Quds Intifada"[26]

In April 2004, in another instance of apparent double-dealing, Saudi Defense Minister Prince Sultan bin Abd al-Aziz, who was named as a defendant in a lawsuit on behalf of victims of the September 11 attacks, defended himself by admitting that he gave about four million dollars over the last sixteen years to the IIRO and WAMY—Saudi charities that funded terrorism. Sultan's lawyers argued that, as the head of the "special committee" of the Council of Ministers, he gave this money to further "the national and foreign policy of Saudi Arabia." Therefore, the donations were, in their words, "clearly an official act," thus outside U.S. jurisdiction.[27]

How could the 9/11 Commission be ignorant of such admissions? By ignoring volumes of evidence, as well as the testimonies of government officials under oath before Congress, the commission made a mockery of its role, in turn raising questions about the validity of the Treasury and State Departments' terrorist lists. And the statement by 9/11 Commission member Richard Ben-Veniste that "we are hopeful that now that the Saudis in particular have seen the results of these years of support of this kind of a movement, that they will now move to change what has been in place for so long"[28] sounds more like wishful thinking than a proper response.

Evidently, Saudi oil is thicker than our blood. To change these backward priorities, the ground rules of the U.S.-Saudi relationship must be radically overhauled. Stability in the kingdom and in the region is

dependent upon the Saudis' willingness and ability to make critical social and economic reforms, to change the kingdom's education system
and textbooks, and to remove radical clerics and repressive laws.
These changes can be made without compromising the government's
religious legitimacy, and Washington should help to formulate and
pursue a reasonable policy toward these ends. The United States
should also monitor the implementation of these reforms.

We are told that Saudi Arabia is now cooperating with U.S. law
enforcement in order to destroy al-Qaeda's financial infrastructure.
In August 2003 it even passed new anti-money-laundering laws,
which were overseen by the Financial Action Task Force (FATF), an
international body with thirty-three member nations that promotes international compliance with anti-money-laundering and
counterterrorist guidelines.[29] However, the kingdom did not stop
the funding of other Islamist organizations, such as the Palestinian
Authority, to the tune of $7.7 million per month.[30]

In early June 2004, under U.S. pressure and following the al-Qaeda
attack in Khobar, the Saudi government froze some (but not all) of
the assets of the al-Haramain Islamic Foundation for funding al-
Qaeda and other Islamist terror organizations,[31] and declared the establishment of a new Saudi National Commission for Relief and
Charity Work Abroad. The Saudi government vowed that this new
commission would be responsible for overseeing all Saudi contributions that support charity outside of the kingdom, and ensure that
the money did not fall into the hands of terrorists.[32] However, even
when the Saudi government has identified a charitable organization
as supporting terrorism and reportedly shut it down, none of its officials have been arrested, reprimanded, or brought to justice in any
manner. In addition, the Saudis have not stopped the funding of
such organizations as WAMY, whose youth camp manual lists songs
to be taught such as "'Youth of the True' [which] urges kids to 'un-
sheathe the swords' of militant Islam to conquer the world of infidels

for Allah and to become 'sacrificing soldiers' prepared to die in holy war."[33] Even if these new attempts at reform do yield positive results, they should not be seen as a reason to exempt the funders of terrorism from responsibility.

U.S. government entities such as the 9/11 Commission do not limit their complacency to their findings about Saudi Arabia. When the commission reports, in the elusive language with which Washington insiders are so skilled, that "it does not appear that any government other than the Taliban financially supported al Qaeda before 9/11,"[34] it removes responsibility not only from the leaders of Saudi Arabia, but also from the governments of countries such as Sudan, Somalia, and Yemen, to name just a few. It also contradicts numerous testimonies of U.S. government officials before Congress, as well as published reports and investigations in many countries about Muslim and Arab régimes that have supported al-Qaeda either financially or in kind. Since Saudi Arabia, Sudan, Libya, Syria, and Yemen are totalitarian police states, and al-Qaeda has doubtlessly recruited, raised funds, and trained terrorists in these countries, their activities could not have gone unnoticed. These nations' support of al-Qaeda and other Islamist organizations has been well documented; they should be held responsible and sanctioned by the international community, as retired generals Thomas McInerney and Paul Vallely suggest in their "blueprint for victory in the war on terror."[35]

The commission also reports that "the 9/11 plotters eventually spent somewhere between $400,000 and $500,000 to plan and conduct their attack," but, disturbingly, "the origin of the funds remains unknown."[36] The commission does go on to say that "we have a general idea of how al Qaeda financed itself during the period leading up to 9/11,"[37] but, since the commission's major source of information regarding al-Qaeda's financing was former al-Qaeda leader Khalid Sheikh Muhammad, one wonders whether his "revelations" constitute disinformation rather than information, especially in view of the many documented reports the government, Congress, and even the public have seen.

Meanwhile, although U.S. law enforcement has raided and shut down some Muslim charities that funded terrorism, many remain open either under their original name or under cover of a new name, despite being listed on U.S. terrorist lists. These charities include: the Islamic Union for Palestine (IAP); the Texas-based Islamic Association for Palestine; the Muslim World League; the United Association for Studies and Research (UASR);[38] the Muslim American Union and the Muslim American Society (MAS);[39] the Muslim Student Union; the Islamic Circle of North America (ICNA);[40] the Lebanese Palestinian Fund; the U.K.-based INTERPAL;[41] and one of the biggest Saudi charities, the World Assembly of Muslim Youth (WAMY).[42]

The U.S.'s efforts to punish offending financial institutions has also been halfhearted. Take the case of the Union Bank of Switzerland (UBS), Switzerland's largest bank. After the fall of Saddam Hussein, in April 2004, $650 million in new U.S. currency was found hidden around Baghdad. An investigation revealed that the money had found its way to the Iraqi central bank through illegal transfers from, among others, UBS.[43] The Federal Reserve levied an unprecedented fine of $100 million on UBS, yet the bank's management was not implicated in the affair. According to the Swiss Federal Banking Commission's investigation, only "a handful" of low-level employees of the bank were involved—some were dismissed, others left the bank, and "none took bribes or received extra income from the transactions."[44] Why did they do it, then? Anyone familiar with banking operations in Switzerland will be hard-pressed to believe that a handful of low-level employees could conspire to divert illegal funds from Switzerland over a period of several years, without the knowledge of, and implicit instructions from, the bank's management. How could the U.S. swallow such a fable?

The liberation of Iraq also exposed corruption within the UN's Oil for Food program, which was established to provide food and medical necessities to the Iraqi people. The program was instead an "Oil for Fraud" program; according to the U.S. General Accounting Office (GAO), Saddam skimmed revenues from the Oil for Food program, netting nearly $10 billion for himself and his associates.[45] According to a list reportedly discovered in Iraq's Oil Ministry, at least three hundred entities and individuals benefited from the program's corruption, including:

- Benon Savan, the UN administrator of the program[46]
- Ministries in countries such as Russia, Jordan, and Ukraine
- Organizations such as the PLO, the Russian Communist Party, the Hungarian Interest Party, the Indian Congress Party, and the Bulgarian Socialist Party
- Companies such as Russia's Rosneft, Sibneft, LUKoil, and Gasprom; South Africa's Omni Oil; Switzerland's Elcon; and Turkey's Delta Petroleum[47]

Many politicians and business moguls in at least fifty countries were also alleged beneficiaries, as were relatives and friends of political leaders. The list even includes Cotecna, a Swiss consulting firm that employed Kojo Annan, son of UN Secretary General Kofi Annan.[48] Most of those named denied their involvement, while the GAO, the U.S. Congress, and even the UN have begun investigations to determine who partook of the loot.[49]

Saddam Hussein's Iraq also played a major role in the trafficking of illegal drugs. A senior Iraqi official who defected to the West in 1996 revealed not only that a sophisticated heroin trafficking operation from Moscow through Baghdad had helped fund some of Iraq's military programs, but also that this heroin trafficking had helped pour millions of dollars into the pockets of Saddam Hussein, his family, and his régime.[50] U.S. intelligence failures regarding Iraq extend to the fact that, to date, nothing has ever been said publicly about the dictator's major narco-terrorist activities.

North Korea, another dictatorship and member of President Bush's "axis of evil," commenced heroin production and trafficking on a large scale in the early 1990s after the collapse of its major sponsors, the Soviet Union and the Communist bloc.[51] It was only after the September 11 attacks on the U.S., however, that public information about North Korea's "heroin-for-nukes" business got some attention.[52] In August 1992, according to U.S. intelligence sources, Kim Jong-il ordered the Central Party's Thirty-ninth Office to oversee opium cultivation and heroin production and traffic to fund the North Korean nuclear program. Those who sold more than $1 million worth of heroin were awarded with the title "Hero of White Bellflower."[53] Since the late 1990s, North Korea is reported to have produced at least 44 tons of heroin annually, which it smuggles along with tons of methamphetamines[54] and counterfeit currency through its diplomatic missions around the world. While North Korea's revenues from legitimate exports was estimated by South Korea's central bank to be approximately $650 million for 2001, U.S. military officials in South Korea estimate that its profits from the illegal drug trade are as high as $1 billion per year.[55]

On April 20, 2003, in the middle of the international crisis regarding North Korea's development of nuclear weapons, as Secretary of Defense Rumsfeld called for "régime change" in Pyongyang, Australian special forces raided a North Korean ship off New South Wales containing "110 pounds of heroin, worth an estimated $48 million."[56] North Korea has also forged alliances with international crime syndicates, such as the Chinese Triads, the Japanese Yakuza, the Russian Mafyia, and Taiwanese criminal gangs, to distribute both the heroin and the counterfeit currency it produces—activities that are said to generate at least $100 million in hard currency per year.[57] (To generate more money, enabling North Korea to advance its nuclear weapons program, the country also sells illegal arms, especially missiles and related technology. Secret shipments of missiles are sent from North Korea to Iran, Syria, Egypt, Yemen, Libya, Pakistan, and Vietnam—which generated at least $560 million in the year 2001 alone.)[58]

Previous chapters have already detailed how drug trafficking, along with the diamond trade,[59] is also a major source of financing for terror groups such as al-Qaeda. Yet, again, the 9/11 Commission saw "no reliable evidence that Bin Ladin was involved in or made his money through drug trafficking. Similarly, we have seen no persuasive evidence that al Qaeda funded itself by trading in African conflict diamonds."[60] This statement is all the more puzzling because already in October 2001, DEA administrator Asa Hutchinson announced that "the degree to which profits from the drug trade are directed to finance terrorist activities . . . is of paramount concern to the DEA." He even observed that "these [drug trafficking] groups today are a merger of international organized crime and terror,"[61] while the chairman of the Subcommittee on Criminal Justice, Drug Policy, and Human Resources, Mark Souder, described the partnerships between drug traffickers and terrorists as "dark synergies."[62] In June 2004 the Council on Foreign Relations' Independent Task Force on Terrorist Financing reported that the UN Monitoring Group "also found that 'al-Qaeda continues to receive funds it needs from charities . . . [and] the drug trade.'"[63]

As mentioned earlier, the drug trade not only puts hundreds of millions of dollars in the coffers of global terrorists, but also constitutes a serious threat to Western societies in and of itself. The assistant secretary of state for international narcotics and law enforcement affairs, Robert B. Charles, draws a chilling comparison to the losses we suffered from terrorists on September 11: "Drugs are a very big national security issue. We lost 21,000 kids in this country last year to drugs—that's seven Twin Towers."[64] According to the 2002 policy booklet of the Office of National Drug Control Policy, the U.S. spends at least $160 billion a year fighting narcotics—including the costs of law enforcement, environmental impact, and treatment for addiction.[65] By comparison, the administration has requested only $40.2 billion for the Department of Homeland Security for the 2005 fiscal year.[66]

The U.S. commitment includes $310 million for the eradication of Afghanistan's opium poppies, which fuel the opium and heroin trade that helped finance al-Qaeda's war chest. (Afghan president Hamid Karzai outlawed the plant's cultivation when he took office in 2002.)[67] However, since the G8 nations designated the U.K. to lead the counternarcotic efforts in Afghanistan, it is the U.K. that decides how to spend U.S. taxpayers' money. The U.K.'s financial contribution to this effort for the period of 2002 to 2005 totals $127.5 million, while the U.S. contribution for 2004 alone is $123 million.[68] Britain's three-year eradication policy dictates that the procedure be done "by hand." Furthermore, the British have entrusted Afghan provincial governors with the eradication process, even though provincial governors, many of whom are powerful warlords, have been engaged in the drug trade for decades.

According to the International Monetary Fund, the revenues from the opium and heroin trade accounted for at least half of Afghanistan's gross domestic product in 2003.[69] In fact, according to an annual report by the UN Office on Drugs and Crime, opium production in Afghanistan *increased* at least 6 percent from 2002 to 2003, and at least 1.7 million Afghans were engaged in the opium trade.[70] And Secretary Charles projected that Afghanistan's 2004 opium poppy harvest would soar to a world record of 120,000 hectares,[71] providing 80 percent of the world's heroin supply. Thus it becomes clear that the U.K.-led counternarcotics efforts in Afghanistan are failing miserably. If there is not a significant strategic and tactical change, the next three years of the U.K.'s proposed campaign could possibly result in even higher yields of opium poppies.

Afghanistan does not have three years to wait for the U.K.-led by-hand drug eradication program to take effect. By then, the narco-economy will be hopelessly entrenched, strengthening the power of tribal warlords. It will wreak havoc against the rule of law and help further finance the Islamists' global terrorism. "This is a source of income for the warlords and regional factions to pay their soldiers," says Interior Minister Ali Ahmad Jalili. "The terrorists are funding their operations through the illicit drug trade, so they are all interlinked."[72]

The use of mycoherbicides offers a better solution. Mycoherbicides are naturally occurring fungi—not chemicals, but living organisms that attack and kill a specific plant. They are used to control such illicit pest-plants as the coca shrub, the opium poppy, and other noxious weeds. Unlike chemical controls, mycoherbicides assail only the targeted plant.[73] They survive in the soil, thus preventing the future growth of that plant. Biochemists say mycoherbicides will not cause a plant to become extinct; rather, they will greatly reduce yield and render cultivation uneconomical. The use of mycoherbicides to destroy coca plants was signed into law in the U.S. on July 13, 2000.[74] However, giving in to pressure from the international drug legalization lobby and drug producing countries, the U.S. government chose not to implement it.

The use of mycoherbicides in Afghanistan and South America will mitigate the production of heroin and cocaine and cut off the terrorists' major money supply. It will also help prevent Afghanistan from reverting to a haven for terrorists and their leaders. The procedure can free up billions of dollars we are currently using to fight the results of opium and cocaine addiction, making those monies available to help fight terrorism directly and to fund an array of social and governmental reforms in Afghanistan and elsewhere. Ultimately, eradicating narcotics means eliminating the cost of fighting them. This is true not only in Afghanistan, but throughout the world.

As for the larger struggle against terror financing, political correctness and willful blindness are behind the U.S.'s negligence to identify its real enemy—militant Islam. Instead, when the G8 Summit convened in Sea Island, Georgia, on June 8, 2004, it acknowledged that the lack of democracy and transparency in Arab and Muslim countries is a breeding ground for terrorism, and adopted several plans for reform: the "Partnership for Progress and a Common Future," the "G8 Plan of Support for Reform," and the "Democracy Assistance Dialogue" that will channel aid from the Organization for Economic Cooperation and Development (OECD) countries to governments, peoples, and societies to promote democracy and reform.[75] The plans originated with President George W. Bush's initiative to "promote 'freedom, democracy and economic growth' throughout the Middle East,"[76] and tens of billions of dollars will be allocated to support them. However, the recipients will be selected and spending will be overseen by the same international lending organizations that did not prevent recipient nations from siphoning billions of dollars of aid in the past, facilitating the growing corruption and widening gap between the rich and poor in these countries. Thus, little is expected to change. In addition, these plans were already watered down due to strong opposition from most Arab, Muslim, and European countries, which view the promotion of democracy and transparency as American interventionism. Several countries even declined President Bush's invitation to participate in the summit: Egypt, the second-largest recipient—after Iraq—of U.S. aid,[77] Morocco, and Saudi Arabia.[78]

Overall, the political statements made during the G8 Summit sounded all too familiar, especially the one regarding "Middle East peace," Yasser Arafat, and his Palestinian Authority. In a typical but deplorable example of willful blindness, the G8 declared its support for giving more aid to the Palestinian Authority,[79] despite growing international recognition that Arafat's régime was deeply involved in corruption and terror. In fact, on July 13, 2004—just weeks after the G8 released its statement—the vocally pro-Palestinian UN Mideast envoy Terje Roed-Larsen stated that "the Palestinian Authority, despite consistent promises by its leadership, has made no progress on its core obligation to take immediate action on the ground to end violence and combat terror, and to reform and reorganize the Palestinian Authority." He cautioned that "the Palestinian Authority is in deep distress, and is in real danger of collapse."[80] And yet between June 2003 and April 2004 the PA had received at least $290 million to prevent the collapse of this corrupt and murderous régime.[81]

Meanwhile, the European Community's Anti-Fraud Office's (OLAF) report about the PA's abuse of EU money to fund terrorism was delayed so that investigators could review overwhelming amounts of new evidence.[82] But it seemed that no amount of evidence, whether in the form of documents, public statements by the Palestinians, or thousands of Israelis murdered by Palestinian terrorists, was enough for the world community to stop the funding of the culture of death nurtured by the Palestinian Authority, led by Arafat. In hearings in November 2003 regarding the PA's misuse of EU money, a member of the European Parliament for the Social Democratic Party of Austria made a statement that stunningly illustrates the depth of international complacency. Hannes Swoboda argued that "there is no proof that any terrorist acts they committed were ordered by the PA—they may have been acting alone. Only if the DNA of the suicide bombers will match the DNA of those who received euros will we accept it as evidence."[83]

Such an attitude was not unique to the Europeans, and in the face of this ostrich mentality the situation in the Palestinian territories only worsened:

- Palestinian terrorism persisted under Arafat's control and direction
- The Central Council of Fatah (Arafat's party) admitted that the al-Aqsa Martyrs Brigades—responsible for many murderous attacks on Israelis—was part of their organization, and al-Aqsa Martyrs Brigades members openly stated that "the leadership in Ramallah [Arafat] told us that we must now sit quiet and that because of pressure from the international community they would not be able to continue paying us our salaries"[84]
- The Palestinians, with Egypt's help,[85] continued smuggling weapons through tunnels into Gaza[86]
- Even the Palestinian Legislative Council protested the PA's epidemic corruption by dismissing the Palestinian Monetary Authority governor[87]
- Former Palestinian prime minister Mahmoud Abbas told *Newsweek* magazine that he resigned because Arafat had been threatening his life[88]

By July 18, 2004, the situation had gotten so bad that the man Arafat chose to replace Abbas as prime minister, Ahmed Qurie, also resigned, but ten days later he retracted under Arafat's pressure.[89] Arafat, yet again, promised instant reforms, while thousands of disenfranchised and disillusioned Palestinians took to the streets to demonstrate against the PA's and Arafat's corruption.[90]

Following the death of Yasser Arafat in November 2004, the United States does indeed have the ideal opportunity to help establish a viable, democratic Palestinian state, as President Bush has suggested. But this effort will only have a chance to succeed when the Palestinian leadership no longer calls for the destruction of Israel, and when the U.S. no longer attempts to appease the Muslim/Arab world and the European Union by forcing a premature "peace in the Middle East."[91]

If President Bush is serious about the war on terror, he should follow his doctrine of not negotiating with terrorists and withstand, as
he seem to be doing, British prime minister Tony Blair's efforts to
hastily "solve" the Palestinian problem. The president should not fall
into the Arab/European trap of prematurely creating an independent
Palestinian state—"prematurely" because what Arafat left behind is
not a functioning, viable democratic society but an utterly corrupt
terrorist entity. A change of leadership alone is not enough to undo
decades of hate indoctrination; it will take several generations to re-
verse the culture of death, destruction, and corruption that Arafat
has so successfully established with the generous help of the Arab
League and the European Union.

In the aftermath of the demise of the Soviet Union, when political
corruption seemed to be getting out of hand, James D. Wolfensohn,
the president of the World Bank, declared a "war" against corruption.
He warned that "the international community simply must deal with
the cancer of corruption, because it is a major barrier to sustainable
and equitable development."[92] By September 2003, after Arab governments received billions of dollars in aid from the World Bank, the
UN, the EU, USAID, and other international organizations, Wolfensohn was asked at a press conference in Dubai, "What's your opinion
about the Arabian governments' efforts regarding war on corruption
and transparency in the Arab world?" His response, "Which governments?"[93] said it all.

In his book *Breaking the Real Axis of Evil*, Ambassador Mark
Palmer offers an Action Agenda explaining how to rid the world of
its remaining dictators and how to replace the oppressive, corrupt
régimes of today, which breed hatred and death, with democracies.
He makes the case that without external help, especially the help of
the U.S., none of these urgently needed changes are possible.[94] The
same help is needed in other areas of the terrorist fight; according
to the head of compliance for the American Bankers Association,

"Terrorist financing cannot be detected by [the] banks [alone]. It's virtually impossible without intelligence from the government."[95]

Unless serious efforts are put into stopping all terrorist financing, the war will continue, and the West is unlikely to survive the multi-pronged terror attacks aimed at it. For, as Senator Chuck Grassley warned in March 2004, "the terrorists aren't waiting for us to get our enforcement act together. While we struggle over how to restructure our agencies, they're squirreling away money to fund their attacks. Shutting down terrorism financing must be an urgent and high priority."[96]

Clearly, terrorism is difficult to control and even more difficult to stop. However, terrorism is a manmade hazard—not a natural disaster. While our governments and politicians warn us constantly about the dangers of terrorism and the difficulty of stopping such activities, they deliberately shy away from identifying our enemy: fascist fundamentalist Islam. In the words of Andrew C. McCarthy, a former federal prosecutor and terrorism expert: "For the success of our struggle, we need to be clear that the enemy here is militant Islam. If we are to appreciate the risks to our way of life, and our responsibilities in dealing with them, we need to understand that we are fighting a religious, political and social belief system—not a method of attack, but a comprehensive ideology that calls for a comprehensive response."[97]

Instead, our governments tell us they are doing all they can to prevent terror attacks—even though, as we have seen, they are not. So now they condition us to believe that terrorism is inevitable. We know it is not. Terrorism is not a tornado or an earthquake that is beyond human control. Terrorism is manmade tactic and it can, and should, be controlled. One of the most effective ways to do so is to launch a genuine all-out effort, using our best intelligence and most advanced technology to cut off the funds for terror, while implementing a massive worldwide campaign to discredit and dissolve the hostile Islamist ideology that spawned this menace in the first place.

APPENDIX A
MAPS & CHARTS

The following maps and charts are not official, but were designed to show the threat the Islamist terrorists and their collaborators—criminal organizations and rogue governments—pose to freedom, to the U.S., and to democratic counties everywhere.

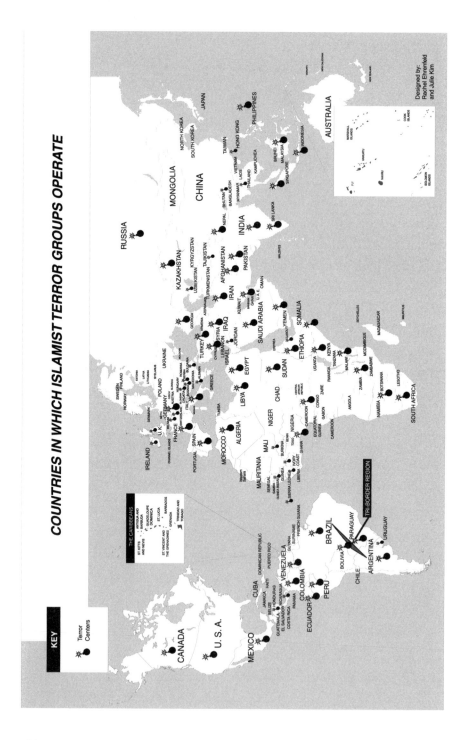

COUNTRIES IN WHICH ISLAMIST TERROR GROUPS OPERATE

214

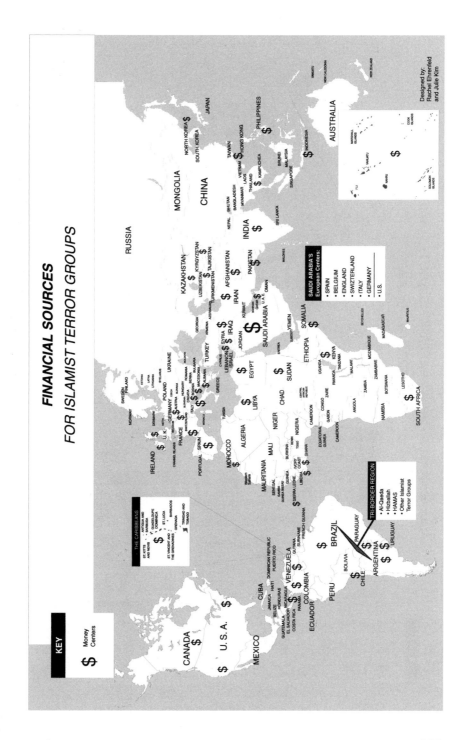

FINANCIAL SOURCES
FOR ISLAMIST TERROR GROUPS

KEY
$ Money
  Centers

SAUDI ARABIA'S
European Centers:
• SPAIN
• BELGIUM
• ENGLAND
• SWITZERLAND
• ITALY
• GERMANY
• U.S.

TRI-BORDER REGION
• Al-Qaeda
• Hizballah
• HAMAS
• Other Islamist
  Terror Groups

Designed by:
Rachel Ehrenfeld
and Julie Kim

215

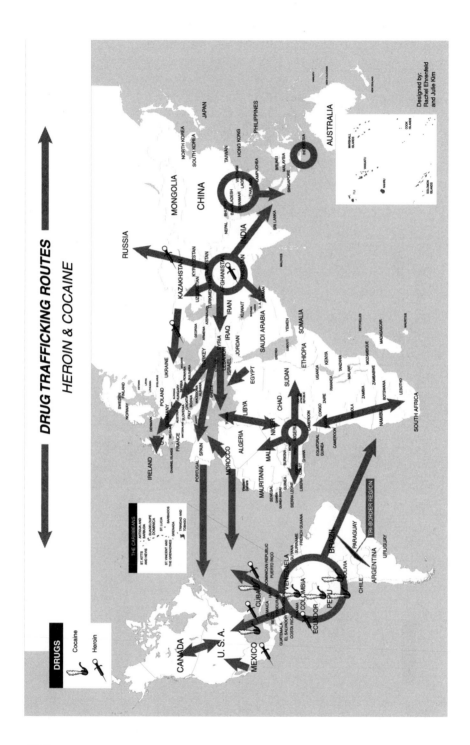

DRUG TRAFFICKING ROUTES
HEROIN & COCAINE

Designed by:
Rachel Ehrenfeld
and Julie Kim

216

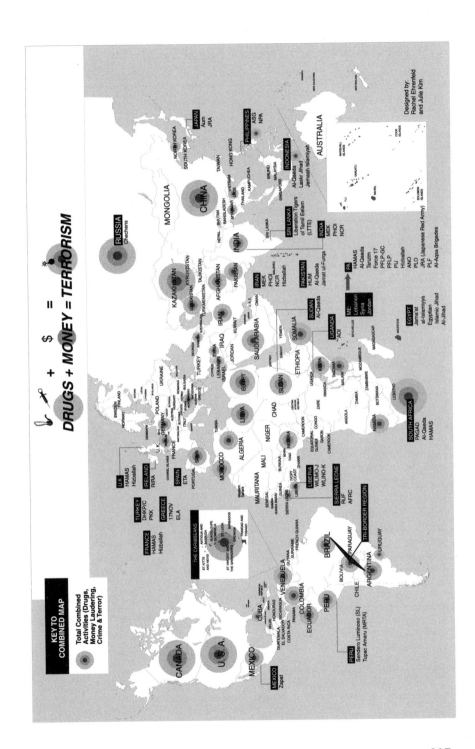

DRUGS + MONEY = TERRORISM

KEY TO
COMBINED MAP

Total Combined
Activities (Drugs,
Money Laundering,
Crime & Terror)

Designed by:
Rachel Ehrenfeld
and Julie Kim

CONNECTIONS AMONG TERROR GROUPS

	Abu Sayyaf	al-Aqsa	ETA	Jama'at	HAMAS	Hizballah	IMU	al-Jihad	PKK	Lashkar-i-Taiba	LTTE	ELN	PIJ	PLF	PFLP	PFLP-GC	IRA	FARC	PLO	Salafist Group	Shining Path	Jemaah	Kosovo Lib. Army	AL-QAEDA
Abu Sayyaf	O			X							X								X			X		X
al-Aqsa		O			X	X							X	X	X	X	X		X					X
ETA			O									X			X	X	X		X					X
Jama'at	X			O	X														X					X
HAMAS		X		X	O	X		X					X	X	X	X	X		X				X	X
Hizballah		X			X	O	X	X	X			X	X	X	X	X		X	X		X		X	X
IMU						X	O																	X
al-Jihad					X	X		O					X	X	X	X			X					X
PKK						X			O														X	X
Lashkar-i-Taiba										O												X		X
LTTE	X										O								X					X
ELN			X			X						O							X					X
PIJ		X			X	X		X					O	X	X	X			X					X
PLF		X			X	X		X					X	O	X	X			X					X
PFLP		X			X	X		X					X	X	O	X			X					X
PFLP-GC		X			X	X		X					X	X	X	O			X					X
IRA		X	X	X													O	X	X					X
FARC		X		X													X	O	X		X			X
PLO	X	X	X	X	X	X		X			X	X	X	X	X	X	X	X	O			X	X	X
Salafist Group																				O				X
Shining Path						X												X			O			X
Jemaah	X									X									X			O		X
Kosovo Lib. Army					X	X			X										X				O	X
AL-QAEDA	X	X	X	X	X	X	X	X	X	X	X	X	X	X	X	X	X	X	X	X	X	X	X	O

APPENDIX B
PALESTINIAN AUTHORITY DOCUMENTS

Document 1: *A memo from a Fatah activist to Yasser Arafat, requesting payment for Fatah/Tanzim terrorists. Arafat approved this request in his own handwriting.*[1]

[Letterhead: PA Office of the President]

To the Fighting President
Brother Abu Amar, may the Lord protect you,
Greetings,

I hereby request you to allocate financial aid in the sum of $2,500 for the following brethren:

1. *Raed al-Karmi [former commander of the Tanzim in Tulkarm]*
2. *Ziad Muhammad Daas [commander of a group within Fatah/Tanzim in Tulkarm that masterminded the attack on a bat mitzvah party in Hadera, Israel]*
3. *Amar Qadan [senior activist of Force 17 in Ramallah; involved in the activities of its operational cell]*

Thank you,
Your son, Hussein al-Sheikh [senior Fatah activist in the West Bank]

[Yasser Arafat's handwriting:]
Treasury/Ramallah
Allocate $600 to each of them.
Yasser Arafat [signature]
(9/19/2001)

Document 2: "Urgent," "Top Secret" memo to Yasser Arafat, asking for permission to secretly purchase Kalashnikov rifles for Palestinian Authority police and Preventive Security, a smuggling operation that violates PA agreements with Israel. Again, a note in Arafat's handwriting gives approval.[2]

[Letterhead: PA Office of the President]

Urgent
Top Secret

To the Honorable President,
Greetings of the homeland,

There is a deal of Kalashnikov-type arms offered for sale in a secret location through brokers. It involves a quantity of 250 Kalashnikovs. The price quoted for the entire quantity is 2,600 Jordanian dinars [for each rifle]. This is the minimum price. To date, nothing has been purchased. It is of note that HAMAS and the other organizations want to buy any quantity at a price of 4,000 dinars per rifle.

Please your instructions to purchase the quantity [stated above] for the police and Preventive Security.

Sincerely,
Head of Preventive Security   *Police Chief Superintendent*
Muhammad Dahlan   *Razi al-Jebali*
[Signature]   *[Signature]*
12/15/2001

[*Yasser Arafat's handwriting:*]
To Shubaki [at the time of writing, head of the Financial Directorate of Preventive Security]: it is approved.

Documents 3 & 4: *Banking records showing that the PA misused funds to pay for expenses not listed in its official budget. The English text in the upper-left-hand corner of the photocopied check clearly indicates that money was drawn from the "Ministry of Finance—Salaries" account, and the accompanying letter shows that this check was used not to pay PA salaries but to finance Fatah activities.*[3]

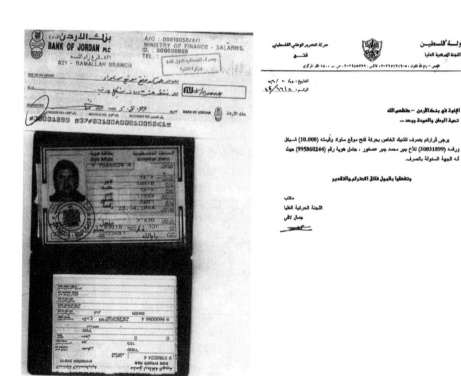

[Letterhead: Fatah Supreme Movement Council]

Date: August 15, 1999
Ref. 42/1618

To: The brothers at al-Urdan Bank, May Allah protect you
Greetings of the homeland and the return,

We request that you cash the check payable to the Fatah movement,
Saluad local branch, for the sum of NIS 10,000 numbered 30031899, to
the brother Jaber Muhammad Asfur, I.D. number 995860244, as he is
the plenipotentiary for the payment.

Sincerely in appreciation,
The Office of the Supreme Movement Council
Jamal Lafi
[Signature]

Documents 5: *Letter indicating that Fuad Shubaki, the PA's former chief financial officer, was behind the appointment of his successor, Mahmoud Awdallah, and that Shubaki continued to perform PA functions for the Central Financial Directorate—even though he'd been imprisoned by the PA for his role in the* Karine-A *arms smuggling operation.*[4]

[Letterhead: PA Preventive Security, Gaza Strip]

Date: July 14, 2002

To: Assistant Head [Preventive Security] for Activity Affairs
Subject: Appointment of Amid [Brigadier General] Mahmoud Awdal-
*   lah as head of the Military Financial Directorate*

Two days ago, on Monday, July 12, 2002, Brigadier General Mahmoud
Awdallah, who was appointed by the president [Yasser Arafat] to be
in charge of the Financial Directorate, arrived.

*   Brigadier General Awdallah is residing in the home of Jihad al-*
Haj, which is located opposite the Jabalya municipality.

*   Yesterday, Tuesday, Awdallah went to the office of Liwa [Major*
General] [Abd al-Razek] al-Majaida [head of the General Security Di-
rectorate and commander of the National Security Forces in the Gaza
Strip], who phoned the president [Arafat] to inform him that Awdal-
lah had arrived. The president asked General al-Majaida to imple-
ment the decision [of Awdallah's appointment].

*   Haj Matlaq [head of the Palestinian General Security Organization*

and Administration Directorate], issued yesterday, Tuesday, a decision based on the decision of the president, ordering the appointment of Brigadier General Mahmoud Awdallah to be in charge of the Financial Directorate.

Through our contacts, it was learned that Brigadier General Fuad Shubaki is behind this appointment. When the decision was about to be nearly cancelled, the president repeatedly insisted on the appointment of Mahmoud Awdallah as head of the Financial Directorate.

Brigadier General Shubaki conducts many affairs in the Central Financial Directorate via his cell phone. He has very close ties with Brigadier General Mahmoud Awdallah. Hindi Shubaki, AKA Abu al-Walid [Fuad Shubaki's brother and a member of the Revolutionary Council], and the al-Shubaki family attended the last reception.

Head of the Palestinian Authority   *Head of Local Activity*
[Security] Apparatus Section   *Department*
[Signature]   *[Signature]*

NOTES

Preface to the Expanded Edition

1. Kendall Freeman to Rachel Ehrenfeld and Bonus Books, January 23, 2004, sent via e-mail by Antonio Suarez-Martinez.

2. Ibid.

3. Sarah Lyall, "Are Saudis Using British Libel Law to Deter Critics?" *New York Times,* May 22, 2004.

4. For just one example among many, see this testimony by a former U.S. deputy assistant secretary of state for international law enforcement, which alleges wealthy Saudis' support for Islamist terror organizations such as al-Qaeda and HAMAS: Jonathan Winer, prepared statment in "Terrorism Financing: Origination, Organization, and Prevention," hearing before the Senate Committee on Governmental Affairs, 108th Cong., 1st sess., July 31, 2003, serial 108-245 (Washington, D.C.: U.S. Government Printing Office, 2003), 110–30.

5. "Litigation," Bin Mahfouz Information official Web site, *www.binmahfouz.info/faqs_4.html.*

6. Statement made by bin Mahfouz's lawyers in a telephone conversation with the author's lawyer in London, June 2004.

7. "World's Richest People 2004," Forbes.com, February 26, 2004.

8. "New Heights for Saudi's Banks," *The Banker,* March 3, 2004.

9. "The Events of September 11th 2001 and Their Aftermath," Bin Mahfouz Information official Web site, *www.binmahfouz.info/faqs_2.html.*

10. David Aufhauser, General Counsel, U.S. Department of the Treasury, to M. Claude Nicati, Deputy Attorney General, Switzerland, November 29, 2001.

11. Robert M. Morganthau, news release, Office of the District Attorney, County of New York, July 1, 1992, quoted in *The Matter of Khalid bin Mahfouz, Haroon Rashid Kahlon, and National Commercial Bank, Saudi Arabia,* docket nos. 92-074-CMP-I1, 92-074-CMP-I2, and 92-074-B-FB (Board of Governors of the Federal Reserve System, July 8, 1992).

12. The BCC Group was the holding company for BCCI, First American Bank, and Sun Trust Bank. *State of New York v. Khalid bin Mahfouz and Haroon Kahlon,* case no. 92 Civ. 5096 (Supreme Court of the State of New York, County of New York, July 1, 1992), 2.

13. Morganthau, news release.

14. Mark Potts and Robert J. McCartney, "BCCI Is Indicted on Fraud Charges," *Washington Post,* July 30, 1991.

15. Nathan Vardi, "Sins of the Father?" *Forbes*, March 18, 2002, *www.forbes.com/global/2002/0318/047.html*; Christopher Byron, "Terrorists, Dollars and a Tangled Web," MSNBC.com, September 24, 2002.

16. *The Matter of Khalid bin Mahfouz*, 7, ¶6.

17. "U.S. Lists Targets for Freezing of Assets," Associated Press, October 13, 2001.

18. Aufhauser to Nicati.

19. "The Events of September 11th 2001 and Their Aftermath," Bin Mahfouz Information official Web site.

20. David Pallister and Jamie Wilson, "Disaster Response Muslim Relief Groups Caught in Crossfire," *Guardian Unlimited*, September 26, 2001, *society.guardian.co.uk/disasterresponse/story/0,1321,558348,00.html*.

21. Aufhauser to Nicati.

22. National Commission on Terrorist Attacks upon the United States, *The 9/11 Commission Report* (Washington, D.C.: U.S. Government Printing Office, 2004). However, the list came under attack in a U.K. court before the 9/11 Commission issued its report, and therefore may have limited authority in the U.K.

23. National Commission on Terrorist Attacks, *The 9/11 Commission Report*, 66.

24. "Government's Evidentiary Proffer Supporting the Admissibility of Co-conspirator Statements," *United States v. Enaam Arnaout*, case no. 02-CR-892 (N.D.Ill., January 6, 2003). *See also* "Al Qaeda Financing Documents Turn Up in Bosnia Raid," Associated Press, February 19, 2003; "Bosnia, 1 degree of separation from Al-Qaeda," Centre for Peace in the Balkans, July 2003, *www.balkanpeace.org/our/our15.shtml*.

25. Glenn R. Simpson, "Al Qaeda List Points to Saudi Elite," *Wall Street Journal*, March 18, 2003.

26. Anonymous source.

Preface to the First Edition

1. Rachel Ehrenfeld, "Evil's Unwitting Helper," *Wall Street Journal Europe*, September 12, 2001.

2. Abd al-Aziz al-Rantisi, "Iraq Will Triumph, by Allah's Will," HAMAS official Web site, trans. in "Hamas Spokesman: Iraq Must Establish a Suicide Army," *MEMRI Special Dispatch* 457 (January 9, 2003). Bracketed interpolations in original.

Chapter 1

1. Paul Beckett, "Sept. 11 Attacks Cost $303,672; Plot Papers Lacking, FBI Says," *Wall Street Journal*, May 15, 2002.

2. "Al Qaeda Spends Less Than 10% on Operations," *MENL*, January 20, 2003.

3. Rachel Ehrenfeld, *Evil Money* (New York: HarperBusiness, 1992), 159–210; Yossef Bodansky, *Bin Laden: The Man Who Declared War on America* (Rocklin, Calif.: Forum, 1999), 315; Asa Hutchinson, "Narco-Terror: The International Connection Between Drugs and Terror," speech presented at the Heritage Foundation, Washington, D.C., April 2, 2002.

4. Quoted in "Al Qaeda Spends Less than 10% on Operations."

5. "Al Qaeda Spends Less than 10% on Operations."

6. John Ashcroft, prepared remarks to the DEA/Drug Enforcement Rollout, Washington, D.C., March 19, 2002.

7. The U.S. Department of State's *Patterns of Global Terrorism 2002* listed the following groups: Abu Sayyaf, ETA, Hizballah, IMU, KPP, LTTE, ENL, PIJ, al-Qaeda, FARC, Shining Path, and AUC. U.S. Department of State, *Patterns of Global Terrorism 2002*, April 2003, *www.state.gov/documents/organization/20177.pdf,* iii–xiii, 155–56.

8. Rebecca Carr, "Authorities Say Terrorists Planned Drugs-for-Guns Plots," Cox News Service, November 7, 2002.

9. Ibid.

10. Ehrenfeld, *Evil Money,* xvi.

11. The State Department Bureau of International Narcotics Matters (INL) estimates the production of 1 kilo of cocaine costs about $3,000. The wholesale price for the same kilo is $20,000, and the street dealers pay $250,000 for the uncut cocaine. The State Department figures for the street value of cocaine in the year 2000 was $10 billion per metric ton. Cocaine production takes as long as the leaves grow, and in Latin America they grow fast; in Colombia, Peru, and Bolivia, the cultivation is practically limitless. The estimate is that at least 800 metric tons of cocaine are produced in Colombia annually. Opium is cultivated twice a year in Asia and the Middle East, and at least three to four times in Mexico and Colombia. Four hundred to 500 metric tons of heroin are produced in Afghanistan; approximately 180 are produced in Burma; and 7 metric tons in Mexico. According to an interview with John Walters, the White House drug czar, Colombia produced at least 16 metric tons of heroin in 2001, but only 12 metric tons in 2002. Frances Robles, "Poppy Crops Down: U.S. Expects Weaker Heroin," *Miami Herald,* May 10, 2003. The production of heroin is more expensive than cocaine. In 2000, the estimate was about $4,000 to $5,000 to produce a kilo. That kilo sold for $250 to $300,000 on the street. The 500 metric tons of heroin produced in Afghanistan in the year 2000 are said to have generated at least $30 billion on the street.

12. George W. Bush, remarks upon signing Drug-Free Communities Act Reauthorization Bill, Omni Shoreham Hotel, Washington, D.C., December 14, 2001.

13. David Pryce-Jones, quoted in U.S. House of Representatives, Task Force on Terrorism and Unconventional Warfare, "BCCI: An Introduction," (September 4, 1991, internal congressional publication), 3.

14. United Nations Development Programme and the Arab Fund for Economic and Social Development, *Arab Human Development Report 2002 (AHDR)* (New York: United Nations Publications, June 2002).

15. Bernard Lewis, *The Crisis of Islam* (New York: Modern Library, 2003), 31; Bernard J. Shapiro, "Is Peace Possible with Islam?" *www.americanfriends.org/nuclear/peace Islam_N313.html;* Chuck Morse, "Islam and the State of Israel," *www.chuckmorse. com/islam_and_state_of_israel.html.*

16. Yigal Carmon, "Securing the Future from the Threat of Terrorism," paper presented at a meeting in Washington, D.C., 1991. In addition to Mr. Rabin, Carmon also advised former Israeli premieres Shimon Peres and Binyamin Netenyahu.

17. Carl von Clausewitz, *Principles of War,* trans. and ed. Hans W. Gatzke (Harrisburg, Pa.: Military Service Publishing, 1942).

18. Kenneth R.Timmerman, "Proof That Saddam Bankrolls Terrorism," *Insight,* November 26, 2002.

19. David Blair, "Saddam's Friend Galloway Keeps Odd Company in Baghdad," *Daily Telegraph,* May 6, 2002, *www.telegraph.co.uk/news/main.jhtml?xml=/news/2002/05/06/ wirq06.xml;* Peter Collins, "Corruption at CNN," *Washington Times,* April 15, 2003.

20. Natan Sharansky, "Democracy for Peace," address to AEI World Forum, Beaver Creek, Colorado, June 20, 2002.

21. World Islamic Front, "Jihad Against Jews and Crusaders," *al-Quds al-Arabi*, February 23, 1998, trans. available at *www.fas.org/irp/world/para/docs/980223-fatwa.htm*.

22. Abu Aiman al-Hilali, quoted in "'Targeting Citizens in Western Countries is Legitimate,'" IDF Spokesperson, December 4, 2002.

23. *Sovetskaya Voyenna Entsiklopedia*, vol. 7 (Moscow: Voyenizdat, 1979), 493; S. Pope, "Diversion: An Unrecognized Element of Intelligence?" *Defense Analysis* 3, no. 2 (1987): 133–51. *See also* Victor Suvorov, "Spetsnaz: The Soviet Union's Special Forces," *International Defense Review*, September 1983, 1210.

24. *Sovetskaya Voyenna Entsiklopedia*, vol. 7, 493; Pope, "Diversion," 133–51. *See also* Suvorov, "Spetsnaz," 1210. In addition, see Russian texts of the *Soviet Military Encyclopedia Dictionary* of 1986 wherein the definition of special reconnaissance remains the same. Information was also verified by consulting with experts on Soviet strategy, among them Dr. Leon Goure from SAIC, MaLean, Virginia, December 1989.

25. Raphael Israeli, ed., *PLO in Lebanon: Selected Documents* (London: Weidenfeld and Nicholson, 1983), 33–168.

26. *Sovetskaya Voyenna Entsiklopedia*, vol. 7, 493; Pope, "Diversion," 133–51. *See also* Suvorov, "Spetsnaz," 1210.

27. According to U.S. intelligence sources, Afghani and Lebanese heroin growers and producers were instrumental in Colombia's heroin production—instructing them how to grow and how to refine heroin.

28. Antonio Farach, testimony in "The Cuban Government's Involvement in Facilitating International Drug Traffic," joint hearing before the Senate Committee on the Judiciary, Subcommittee on Security and Terrorism and the Senate Foreign Relations Committee and the Drug Enforcement Caucus, Subcommittee on Western Hemisphere Affairs, 98th Cong., 1st sess., April 30, 1983, serial J-98-36 (Washington, D.C.: U.S. Government Printing Office, 1983), 48.

29. Fourth Fatah Conference, "Fatah Political Platform," May 1980, quoted in Israeli, ed., *PLO in Lebanon*, 18.

30. J. Laffin, *Holy War: Islam Fights* (London: Grafton Books, 1988), 13–14.

31. Awdah Awdah, *Al-Ra'y*, October 5, 1990, quoted in Yossef Bodansky, *Target America* (New York: SPI. Books, 1993), 369–70.

32. U.S. Drug Enforcement Administration (DEA), "Afghanistan Country Brief: Drug Situation Report, September 2001," *www.usdoj.gov/dea/pubs/intel/intel0901.html*.

33. "Afghan Drug Crop Increasing," *Corruption Watch* 2, no. 38 (October 25. 2002): *www.rferl.org/corruptionwatch/2002/10/38-251002.asp*.

34. Ibid.

35. Iraq's involvement in international drug trafficking was revealed to the author by a former high-ranking Iraqi official in January 2003.

36. The different routes of illicit drug trafficking around the world, including the movement of heroin from Afghanistan to its destined markets, are detailed in: Library of Congress, Federal Research Division, "A Global Overview of Narcotics-Funded Terrorist and Other Extremist Groups" (May 2002, draft); Joseph Molyneux, "The Worldwide Terror Network: Operations and Financing" (December 2002, unpublished paper).

37. Library of Congress, "A Global Overview of Narcotics-Funded Terrorist and Other Extremist Groups," 11–70.

38. State Department unofficial estimates.

39. "More Than 100 Arrested in Nationwide Methamphetamine Investigation," DEA,

January 10, 2002, *www.usdoj.gov/dea/major/me3.html;* "Drug Money for Hezbollah?" CBSNEWS.com, September 1, 2002.

40. Rowan Bosworth-Davis and Graham Saltmarsh, *Money Laundering* (London: Chapman and Hall, 1994), 113.

41. NATO Parliamentary Assembly, General Report. "The Economic Consequences of September 11, 2001 and the Economic Dimension of Anti-terrorism," AV 187 EC(02)7, Section 5(35).

42. The term *offshore center* usually refers to: (1) a jurisdiction that has a relatively large number of financial institutions engaged primarily in business with nonresidents; (2) a financial system with external assets and liabilities out of proportion to domestic financial intermediation designed to finance domestic economies; and, most popularly, (3) a center that provides some or all of the following services: low or zero taxation, moderate or light financial regulation, banking secrecy, and anonymity. See International Monetary Fund, Monetary and Exchange Affairs Department, *Offshore Financial Centers IMF Background Paper,* June 23, 2000, *www.imf.org/external/ np/mae/oshore/2000/eng/back.htm#II.*

43. For example, local lawyers in offshore centers like the Bahamas or the Cayman Islands who register the corporation.

44. U.S. Departments of the Treasury and Justice, *2002 National Money Laundering Strategy, www.treas.gov/press/releases/docs/monlaund.pdf,* 33.

45. U.S. Senate Committee on Government Affairs, 1985, quoted in Bosworth-Davis and Saltmarsh, *Money Laundering,* 53.

46. Departments of the Treasury and Justice, *National Money Laundering Strategy,* 22.

47. Ibid, 47.

48. Funds provided by international organizations such as the United Nations and the European Union sometimes, as in the Palestinian territories, pay for the members of terrorist organizations—EU funds to the Palestinian Authority paid for members of the al-Aqsa Martyrs Brigade.

49. *Uniting and Strengthening America by Providing Appropriate Tools Required to Intercept and Obstruct Terrorism (USA PATRIOT Act) Act of 2001,* U.S. Public Law 107-56, October 26, 2001. "The USA PATRIOT Act contains sweeping provisions to our anti-money laundering and anti-terrorist financing regime that dramatically enhanced Treasury's ability to combat the financing of terrorism and money laundering. These provisions reflect the important principles of (1) enhancing transparency in financial transactions; (2) protecting the international gateways to the U.S. financial system; and (3) increasing the vigilance of all our financial institutions that are themselves the gatekeepers of the financial system." *Contributions by the Department of the Treasury to the Financial War on Terrorism: Fact Sheet,* U.S. Department of the Treasury, September 2002, *www.ustreas.gov/press/releases/reports/2002910184556291211.pdf,* 10.

50. "Green Quest: Finding the Missing Piece of the Terrorist Puzzle," U.S. Department of the Treasury, Customs Service, *www.customs.ustreas.gov/xp/cgov/enforcement/ investigative_priorities/greenquest.xml.* OGQ was announced on October 25, 2001. The agencies involved are: the U.S. Customs Service; the IRS; the Secret Service; the Bureau of Alcohol, Tobacco, and Firearms; the Office of Foreign Assets Control; the Financial Crimes Enforcement Network; the FBI; the Postal Inspection Service; the Naval Criminal Investigative Service; and the Department of Justice.

51. Departments of the Treasury and Justice, *National Money Laundering Strategy,* 4.

52. "U.S. Treasury Department Announces New Executive Office for Terrorist Financing

and Financial Crimes," U.S. Department of the Treasury, March 3, 2003, *www. ustreas.gov/press/releases/js77.htm.*

53. Department of State, *Patterns of Global Terrorism 2002.* However, Secretary of State Colin Powell, in his press conference to release this report, stated that "since 9/11, more than $134 million of terrorist assets have been frozen." See *www.state.gov/ secretary/rm/2003/20067.htm.*

54. "Lebanon Refuses to Back U.S. Stance on Hezbollah," IslamOnline.net, November 7, 2001.

55. Pam Belluck with Eric Lichtblau, "Federal Agents Raid a Software Company Outside Boston, Seeking Links to al Qaeda," *New York Times,* December 7, 2002.

56. Mark Hosenball, "High-Tech Terror Ties?" *Newsweek* Web exclusive, December 6, 2002, *www.msnbc.com/news/844098.asp.*

57. It is not surprising that bin Laden was welcomed in Sudan, for it was here that state-sponsored *Jihad* over two decades caused the deaths of at least two million people and displaced another four million. The slogan of the ruling party was "*Jihad,* victory, and martyrdom." With government sanction, *jihaddists* there "have physically attacked non-Muslims, looted their belongings and killed their males . . . then enslaved tens of thousands of females and children." Daniel Pipes, "What Is *Jihad,*" *New York Post,* December 31, 2002.

58. John Willman, "Trail of Terrorist Dollars That Spans the World," *Financial Times,* November 29, 2001.

59. Yael Shahar, *Tracing bin Laden's Money: Easier Said Than Done,* International Policy Institute for Counter-Terrorism, September 21, 2001, *www.ict.org.il/articles/ articledet.cfm?articleid=387.*

60. John Mintz, "Fifteen Freighters Believed to be Linked to al Qaeda," *Washington Post,* December 30, 2002.

61. Farah, Douglas, "Al Qaeda Gold Moved to Sudan," *Washington Post,* September 3, 2002.

62. Bin Laden videotape, broadcast on al-Jazeera TV, Doha, Qatar, December 27, 2001, trans. in "Bin Laden Calls Sept. 11 Attacks 'Blessed Terror,'" CNN.com, December 27, 2001.

63. Kimberlery Thachuk, "Terrorism's Financial Lifeline: Can It Be Severed?" *Strategic Forum* 191 (May 2002).

64. The bank's prior history in money laundering goes back to its $80 million investment in the Bank of Credit and Commerce International (BCCI). It was also involved in other illegal financial activities, including a $242 million money laundering operation through gold trading with a rogue billionaire from Mali. The United States District Court for the District of Columbia, Civil Action, Case Number 1:02CV01616(JR), Third Amended Complaint, September 2002, 248/49. (This source is cited subsequently as "Civil Action.")

65. Willman, "Trail of Terrorist Dollars."

66. Civil Action, 251.

67. U.S. Department of the Treasury, Office of Foreign Assets Control, *Specially Designated Nationals and Blocked Persons, www.treas.gov/offices/enforcement/ofac/ sdn/t11sdn.pdf.*

68. PLO documents captured by the IDF, dated April 12, May 6, and June 5, 2002. These are only samples of the voluminous PA paper trail documenting the PA's many meth-

ods and sources of funding terrorism that were captured by the IDF. For more information, see the archive at the IDF Web site, *www.idf.il*.

69. Matthew Levitt, "The Political Economy of Middle East Terrorism," *Middle East Review of International Affairs (MERIA) Journal* 6, no. 4 (December 2002).

70. This was an attack on a bat mitzvah celebration in Hadera. "Senior Fatah Militant in Lebanon Directed and Financed Serious Terror Attacks in Territories and Israel," Israeli Prime Minister's Media Adviser, May 26, 2002, *www.imra.org.il/story. php3?id=12156*.

71. Civil Action, 352.

72. Lucy Komisar, "Shareholders in the Bank of Terror?" Salon.com, March 15, 2002; Mark Hosenball, "Terror's Cash Flow," *Newsweek*, March 25, 2002; Levitt, "Political Economy of Middle East Terrorism."

73. Komisar, "Shareholders in the Bank of Terror?"

74. "Recent Office of Foreign Assets Control Actions," U.S. Department of the Treasury, November 7, 2001, *www.treas.gov/offices/enforcement/ofac*.

75. *Contributions by the Department of the Treasury to the Financial War on Terrorism*, 12.

76. Civil Action, 258–90.

77. The practice is not unique to Islamist terror groups. It took the Colombian narco-terror organization, the Revolutionary Armed Forces of Colombia (FARC), about a decade to take over large parts of the country. Funded by tremendous revenues from the illegal trade in cocaine and heroin, FARC fought violently and bribed its way to replace legitimately elected but corrupt governments, all the while providing basic needs to the impoverished population.

78. Levitt, "Political Economy of Middle East Terrorism," 56.

79. Ibid., 51.

80. Kevin Dowling, "The Ties That Bind: Barclays, a bin Laden Relative, Carlyle and the BCCI Boys," *Online Journal*, November 3, 2001. Following the bombings, former secretary of state Madeline Albright identified bin Mahfouz as having deposited tens of millions of dollars into terrorist accounts in London and New York.

81. Civil Action, 258–90.

82. Marc Perelman, "Argentina Set to Indict Iran Agents," *Forward*, October 4, 2002.

83. "Iraq's Sponsorship of Terrorism," U.S. Government's International Broadcasting Bureau, June 4, 2002, *www.ibb.gov/editorials/09925.htm*.

84. Bodansky, *Bin Laden*, 92–94, 200 (Pakistan as a center for Islamist terrorism, 26–27, the sponsor of foreign *Jihad*, 340).

85. Rachel Ehrenfeld and Peter Samuel, "Drugs, the DEA and Damascus," *AIReview*, August 25–September 7, 1987, 4–5.

86. The U.S. Department of State's 2002 report of nations designated as sponsoring terrorism lists Cuba, Iran, Iraq, Libya, North Korea, Syria, and Sudan. "Seven Nations Cited as Sponsors of Terror in State Department Report," U.S. Department of State, April 30, 2003, *usinfo.state.gov/cgi-bin/washfile/display.pl?p=/products/washfile/ latest&f=03043023.plt&t=/products/washfile/newsitem.shtml*.

87. Israel Defense Forces, Military Intelligence, *Iran and Syria as Strategic Support for Palestinian Terrorism (Based on Interrogations of Arrested Palestinian Terrorists and Captured Palestinian Authority Documents)* (doc. no. TR6-548-02, 2002), 8.

88. Claudia Rosett, "The Oil-for-U.N.-Jobs Program," *Wall Street Journal*, September 26, 2002.

89. David Harrison, "Secret Documents Show German Spies Offered Help to Saddam in Run-Up to War, As Russian Spies Funneled Information on Bush's Likely Justification to Invade," *Sunday Telegraph*, April 21, 2003; "German Businessman Who Sold Arms to Iraq Sentenced to Five Years Jail," Agence France-Presse, January 31, 2003.

90. "Iraq's Oil-for-Food Program in Limbo," Middle East Online, April 22, 2003, *www.middle-east-online.com/english/?id=5241;* Sol W. Sander, "Cleaning the U.N. Trough," *Washington Times*, April 22, 2003.

91. George Galloway to Attorney General Lord Goldsmith, April 24, 2003, quoted in Owen Bowcott, Richard Norton-Taylor, and Jamie Wilson, "Charity Commission Launches Galloway Inquiry," *Guardian*, April 25, 2003, *society.guardian.co.uk/ Print/0,3858,4654868,00.html.* Elision in original.

92. "Letter from Iraqi Intelligence Chief, 3 January 2000" and "Letter from Tariq Aziz, 5 February 2000," in "The Documents: Contacts, Money, Oil and the Need for Anonymity," *Daily Telegraph*, April 22, 2003, *www.telegraph.co.uk/news/main. jhtml?xml=/news/2003/04/22/ndocs22.xml.*

93. Ibid.

94. A. La Guardia, "'Terror Link' Saudi Prince to be Envoy in Britain," *Daily Telegraph*, December 5, 2002.

95. Jean-Charles Brisard, "Terrorism Financing: Roots and Trends of Saudi Terrorism Financing" (report prepared for the president of the UN Security Council, December 19, 2002), 18. Brisard, the French investigator who authored this report, lost a libel case brought against him in London by Khalid bin Mahfouz, based on allegations made against the Saudi billionaire in Brisard's report. However, Brisard told the author that the judgement was by default, since he didn't have the financial means to defend himself against the Saudi billionaire.

96. US intelligence sources.

97. *Madrasas* are schools at which Muslim boys are taught only the Koran—and, in those supported by terror groups, terror ideologies.

98. Donald Rumsfeld on *Larry King Live*, CNN, December 18, 2002.

99. *Ain-al-Yaqeen*, March 1, 2002, quoted in "Ayn-al-Yaqeen: The Saudi Royal Family Spent Billions of Riyals to 'Spread Islam to Every Corner of the Earth,'" *MEMRI Special Dispatch* 360 (March 27, 2002).

100. Allan Gerson and Ron Motley, "Is Saudi Arabia Tough Enough on Terrorism?" *New York Times*, December 30, 2002.

101. Dore Gold, *Hatred's Kingdom* (Washington D.C.: Regnary Publishing, 2003), 211–28.

102. R. James Woolsey, prepared remarks at Center for the Study of Popular Culture Restoration Weekend, Palm Beach, Fla., November 16, 2002, available in "World War IV," FrontPageMagazine.com, November 22, 2002, *www.frontpagemag.com/Articles/ ReadArticle.asp?ID=4718.*

103. Daniel Pipes, "Not Friend or Foe," *New York Post*, May 14, 2002.

104. Ibid.

105. *Ain-al-Yaqeen*, March 1, 2002, quoted in "Ayn-al-Yaqeen: The Saudi Royal Family Spent Billions."

106. Ibid.

107. Ibid.

108. Ihsan Bagby, Paul M. Perl, and Bryan T. Froehle, *The Mosque in America: A National Portrait* (Washington, D.C.: Council on American-Islamic Relations, 2001), 2, 57.

109. Ibid, 34–35.

110. Susan Katz Keating, "The Wahhabi Fifth Column," *FrontPageMagazine.com*, December 30, 2002.

111. Bodansky, *Bin Laden*, 300–301.

112. An anonymous independent observer of the 2002 Turkish election.

113. Michael Isikoff and Evan Thomas, "The Saudi Money Trail," *Newsweek*, December 2, 2002; "Saudi Money Linked to Two 9/11 Hijackers," *Agence France-Fresse*, November 23, 2002.

114. "US Warns of New Terror Threat in Jeddah," ABS-CBN News, May 16, 2003.

115. Stephen Schwartz, "The Real Saudi Arabia," *Wall Street Journal*, May 15, 2003.

116. Gerson and Motley, "Is Saudi Arabia Tough Enough on Terrorism?"

117. Bodansky, *Bin Laden*, 207.

118. Ibid., 207–10.

119. "What Started the al-Aqsa Intifada in September 2000?" Palestine Facts, *www.palestinefacts.org/pf_1991to_now_alaqsa_start.php*.

120. Council on Foreign Relations, "Q&A: What Are Post-Saddam Peace Prospects in the Mideast?" February 4, 2003, *www.nytimes.com/cfr/international/mustreads020403.html*.

121. Civil Action, 343.

122. George W Bush, *The National Security Strategy of the United States of America*, Washington, D.C., September 2002.

123. The number of countries afflicted with various degrees of systemic corruption has been identified by the author, using a more encompassing definition than that of the World Bank. The total sum of loans was calculated based on each country's respective loan over this period.

124. R. Sandbrook, *The Politics of Africa's Economic Stagnation* (Cambridge, U.K.: Cambridge University Press, 1986), 95.

125. Tom Masland and Jeffery Bartholet, "Tracking Abacha's Billions," *Newsweek*, March 13, 2000.

Chapter 2

1. U.S. expert on biological warfare, interview by author, December 2002.

2. "Glanders *(Burkholderia mallei):* General Information," Centers for Disease Control, Division of Bacterial and Mycotic Diseases, *www.cdc.gov/ncidod/dbmd/diseaseinfo/glanders_g.htm*.

3. Yossef Bodansky, *Bin Laden: The Man Who Declared War on America* (Rocklin, Calif.: Forum, 1999), 2.

4. "A Private Terrorist; Osama bin Laden: Folk Hero, Pariah, Terrorist Kingpin," ABC-NEWS.com, March 6, 2003, *abcnews.go.com/sections/world/DailyNews/binladen_profile.html*.

5. Paul Harris and Martin Bright, "Saudi Envoy in UK Linked to 9/11," *Observer*, March 2, 2003.

6. Bodansky, *Bin Laden*, 13–14.

7. Ibid., 12.

8. Boaz Ganor, "The Changing Threat of International Terrorism," International Policy Institute for Counter-Terrorism, December 20, 2002, *www.ict.org.il/articles/ articledet.cfm?articleid=455.*

9. Rohan Gunaratna, Columbia University expert, quoted in Mark Baker, "World: 11 September—Does al-Qaeda Represent a Different Type of Terrorism?" part 2, Radio Free Europe Radio Liberty, September 2002, *www.rferl.org/nca/features/2002/09/ 02092002142833.asp.*

10. Judith Miller, "Holy Warriors: Killing for the Glory of God, in a Land Far from Home," *New York Times*, January 16, 2001.

11. Roger Hardy, "Analysis: Al-Qaeda's Origins and Links," BBC News, November 22, 2001, *news.bbc.co.uk/1/hi/world/south_asia/1670089.stm.* To read more about the international spread of al-Qaeda or the "Afghans," see Bodansky, *Bin Laden,* 373–406. About terror cells in the U.S., see Lisa Mayer, "Terror Trails Followed in Eight U.S. Cities," MSNBC News, March 10, 2003, *www.msnbc.com/news/883435.asp?0cv=CB10.*

12. Paul Wolfowitz, quoted in Linda D. Kozaryn, "Wolfowitz: Al Qaeda Is an Infections Disease with No One-Shot Cure," American Forces Press Service, June 26, 2002.

13. The Saudi royal family directly controls the government in the Saudi Kingdom, and it is either involved with or indirectly controls most large-scale businesses in Saudi Arabia.

14. Library of Congress, Federal Research Division, "A Global Overview of Narcotics-Funded Terrorist and Other Extremist Groups" (May 2002, draft).

15. Laurent Murawiec, "Taking Saudi Out of Arabia," presentation to the Defense Policy Board, briefing in Defense Secretary Rumsfeld's private conference room, July 10, 2002.

16. These contributions represent "about 20% of the Saudi GNP." Jean-Charles Brisard, "Terrorism Financing: Roots and Trends of Saudi Terrorism Financing" (December 19, 2002, report prepared for the president of the UN Security Council), 3. Brisard, the French investigator who authored this report, lost a libel case brought against him in London by Khalid bin Mahfouz, based on allegations made against the Saudi billionaire in Brisard's report. However, Brisard told the author that the judgement was by default, since he didn't have the financial means to defend himself against the Saudi billionaire.

17. David Armstrong, "An Investigation of Saudi Charitable Efforts," presentation at the World Anticrime and Antiterrorism Forum, Washington Forum, September 24, 2002.

18. Jeff Gerth and Judith Miller, "Saudi Arabia Is Called Slow in Helping Stem the Flow of Cash to Militants," *New York Times,* November 27, 2002.

19. Paraphrased in Alex Alexiev, "A Failing Ally: Lessons from Pakistan" (Center for Security Policy, Washington. D.C., March 2003, draft); this draft is the expanded version of Alex Alexiev, "The Pakistani Time Bomb" *Commentary* 115, no. 3 (March 2003).

20. The United States District Court for the District of Columbia, Civil Action, Case Number 1:02CV01616(JR), Third Amended Complaint, September 2002, 313. (This source is cited subsequently as "Civil Action.")

21. Jennifer Harper, "Saudi Arabia Lacks Commercial Appeal," *Washington Times,* April 30, 2002.

22. Gerth and Miller, "Saudi Arabia Is Called Slow in Helping Stem the Flow of Cash to Militants."

23. Prince Sultan is one of the "Sudairi seven," the seven sons of Abd al-Aziz bin Abd al-Rahman al-Saud, who founded the modern Saudi Kingdom.

24. Civil Action, 313–14.

25. Civil Action, 287.

26. "Islamic and Non-Islamic Organizations," Islamic Knowledge Islam Information Page, *www.islamic-knowledge.com/Organizations.htm.*

27. Adnan Basha, quoted in Civil Action, 282.

28. Adnan Basha, paraphrased in David B. Ottaway and Dan Morgan, "Muslim Charities Under Scrutiny: Saudi-Funded Groups Deny Ties to Terror but Cite Vulnerability," *Washington Post,* September 29, 2001.

29. Civil Action, 282.

30. Ibid., 283.

31. *Rose al-Yusuf,* paraphrased in Civil Action, 283.

32. Embassy of Israel, "Arafat: Where Did the Saudi Aid Money Go?" app. E in *Saudi Committee for Support of Intifada al Quds,* May 10, 2002, *www.embassyofisrael.org/articals/2002/May/2002051008.html.*

33. Steven Emerson, testimony in "PATRIOT Act Oversight: Investigating Patterns of Terrorist Financing," hearing before the House Committee on Financial Services, Subcommittee on Oversight and Investigations, 107th Cong., 2nd sess., February 12, 2002, serial 107-53 (Washington, D.C.: U.S. Government Printing Office, 2002). 126–277.

34. Civil Action, 281.

35. Lucy Komisar, "Funding Terror: Investigating the Role of Saudi Banks," *In These Times,* December 20, 2002, *www.inthesetimes.com/comments.php?id=4_0_2_0_M.*

36. Civil Action, 289.

37. Douglas Farah, and John Mintz, "U.S. Trails Va. Muslim Money, Ties," *Washington Post,* October 7, 2002.

38. Civil Action, 289.

39. Farah and Mintz, "U.S. Trails Va. Muslim Money, Ties."

40. Ibid.

41. "Green Quest: Finding the Missing Piece of the Terrorist Puzzle," U.S. Department of the Treasury, Customs Service, *www.customs.ustreas.gov/xp/cgov/enforcement/investigative_priorities/greenquest.xml.*

42. Quoted in Farah and Mintz, "U.S. Trails Va. Muslim Money, Ties."

43. Civil Action, 321.

44. Ibid., 325.

45. Matthew Levitt, "The Political Economy of Middle East Terrorism," *Middle East Review of International Affairs (MERIA) Journal* 6, no. 4 (December 2002).

46. George Robertson, quoted in Civil Action, 322.

47. Civil Action, 321–25.

48. Muhammad Rashid, trans. in "Al-Rashid Trust," South Asia Terrorism Portal, *www.satp.org/satporgtp/countries/pakistan/terroristoutfits/Al-Rashid_Trust.htm.*

49. "Al-Rashid Trust," South Asia Terrorism Portal.

50. ART runs the largest mosque in Pakistan: Arabia-Islamia on the Karakoram Highway in Mansehra.

51. "Madrassa students often graduate functionally illiterate with virtually no job skills, but thoroughly indoctrinated for a career in extremism and *jihad*. Nor is Islamic indoctrination the only training they receive. A third of the radical seminaries provide military training as well, according to one of the few limited government studies on the subject. Predictably, the vast majority of recruits for Pakistani terrorist organizations, as well as the erstwhile Taliban, came from these schools. With approximately 15% of the students coming from foreign countries (estimated at 36,000 in March 2002), virtually all Islamic terrorist groups around the world have benefited and continue to benefit from these willing cadres." Alex Alexiev, "Islamic Extremism and Its Sponsors: Lessons from Pakistan" (Center for Security Policy, Washington. D.C., March 2003, draft).

52. Pepe Excobar, "The Roving Eye: Anatomy of a 'Terrorist' NGO," *Asia Times,* October 26, 2001.

53. Chris Hastings and David Banber, "British Cash and Fighters Still Flow to bin Laden," *Sunday Telegraph,* January 27, 2001.

54. "Al-Rashid Trust," South Asia Terrorism Portal.

55. Ibid.

56. Quoted in B. Raman, "Pakistan and Terrorism: The Evidence," CIFJKINDIA, *www.cifjkindia.org/main/braman_025.html.*

57. "Al-Rashid Trust," South Asia Terrorism Portal.

58. Levitt, "Political Economy of Middle East Terrorism."

59. "Pakistani Judge Convicts Four Men for Pearl Murder," OnlineNewsHour, July 15, 2002, *www.pbs.org/newshour/updates/pearl_07-15-02.html.*

60. Al-Rajhi official Web site, *www.alrajhibank.com.sa*

61. Civil Action, 354.

62. Civil Action, 321.

63. Greg Gordon, "Six Hundred File September 11 Suit," Startribune.com, August 16, 2002.

64. Abdurahman Alamoudi, the secretary of the Success Foundation, contributed $2,000 to McKinney's campaign. The Success Foundation is part of the IIRO, also funded by the al-Rajhi family. McKinney's response to questions about these donations was: "All of our contributions are legal." Investigations revealed that contributions from Arab- and Muslim-Americans totaled "$142,950, one-third of the money McKinney collected from individuals over the last five years." Bob Dart and Stephen Krupin, "McKinney Campaign Donors Named in 9/11 Suit," *Atlanta Journal-Constitution,* August 17, 2002.

65. "Statement of the Attorney General: Indictments," U.S. Department of Justice, February 20, 2003, *www.usdoj.gov/ag/speeches/2003/02202003pressconference.htm.*

66. Lead investigator, interview by author, March 12, 2003.

67. "A businessman who dealt with SAAR," quoted in Douglas Farah and John Mintz, "U.S. Trails Va. Muslim Money, Ties," *Washington Post,* October 7, 2002.

68. Civil Action, 241.

69. On October 3, 2001, Vincent Cannistraro, a former CIA chief of counterterrorism operations and analysis, testified before the House Committee on International Relations that it was "evident that several wealthy Saudis were funneling money to bin

Laden" via the NCB. Vincent Cannistraro, testimony in "Al-Qaeda and the Global Reach of Terrorism," hearing before the House Committee on International Relations, 107th Cong., 1st sess., October 3, 2001, serial 107-50 (Washington, D.C.: U.S. Government Printing Office, 2001), 20. Evidence that NCB continued to transfer money to terror groups was discovered in wire transfers in the al-Aqsa Islamic Bank in Ramallah. The money was sent from the World Assembly of Muslim Youth (WAMY) to a HAMAS organization in the West Bank on February 15, 2001. Copies of the money transfers were provided to the author by the IDF.

70. *The Matter of Khalid bin Mahfouz, Haroon Rashid Kahlon, and National Commercial Bank, Saudi Arabia,* docket nos. 92-074-CMP-I1, 92-074-CMP-I2, and 92-074-B-FB (Board of Governors of the Federal Reserve System, July 8, 1992); William von Raab, quoted in James Ring Adams and Douglas Frantz, *A Full Service Bank: How BCCI Stole Billions Around the World* (New York: Pocket Books, 1992), 238; *The Matter of Khalid bin Mahfouz,* count 4, 40.

71. *The Matter of Khalid bin Mahfouz,* count 4, 40.

72. Nathan Vardi, "Sins of the Father?" *Forbes,* March 18, 2002, *www.forbes.com/global/2002/0318/047.html;* Christopher Byron, "Terrorists, Dollars and a Tangled Web," MSNBC.com, September 24, 2002.

73. Robert M. Morgenthau, July 29, 1991, quoted in Harry W. Albright Jr., *Final Report to the Honorable Joyce Hens Green* (United States District Court for the District of Columbia, December 27, 1999), 2.

74. Civil Action, 244.

75. "Saudi Businessman Remains Incarcerated," Islamic Human Rights Commission, U.K., November 22, 1999.

76. Vardi, "Sins of the Father?"

77. Nathan Vardi, "The Saudi Way," *Forbes,* February 17, 2003, *www.forbes.com/global/2003/0217/021a.html.*

78. Vardi, "Sins of the Father?"

79. *The Matter of Khalid bin Mahfouz,* count 4, 40; Peter Behr, "Lawyers' Warning Preceded Bush's Sale of Harken Stock," *Washington Post,* November 4, 2002. Given the number of reports and investigations that point the finger at bin Mahfouz, one wonders why he has not been placed on the U.S. list of terrorists. Perhaps it really is correct—as bin Mahfouz doubtless would claim—that all those commissions, committees, and investigators just don't have the proof. Just because he paid a $225 million fine does not necessarily mean that he actually did any of the things with BCCI of which he was (perhaps wrongly) accused. He is not above suspicion, but neither is anything yet proved against him.

80. "Fact Sheet: White House on Halting Financial Flows to Terrorists," U.S. Department of State, Office of International Information Programs, November 7, 2001.

81. Ibid.

82. Paul Beckett and Glenn R. Simpson, "Suspect Network Used Major U.S. Banks to Make Wire Transfers," *Wall Street Journal,* November 9, 2001.

83. Greg Cresci, "Western Union Fined over Money Transfers," Reuters, December 20, 2002.

84. "Statement by Treasury Secretary Paul O'Neill," U.S. Department of the Treasury, Office of Public Affairs, November 7, 2001, *www.treas.gov/press/releases/po770.htm.*

85. Khaled Dawoud, "Brotherhood Faces WTC Fallout," *Al-Ahram Weekly Online* 560 (November 15–21, 2001).

86. By the late eighties, the Muslim Brotherhood had gained influence over several major Islamic financial institutions operating in the West, such the Islamic Holding Co., the Jordanian-Islamic Bank, the Dubai Islamic Bank, and the Feisal Islamic Bank in Egypt. Subsequently, by early 1991, the brethren saw, in the establishment of Taqwa Bank of Algeria, the "beginning of '. . . a world bank for fundamentalists' aimed to compete with Western financial institutions." Yossef Bodansky, "Iran's Pincer Movement Gives It a Strong Say in the Gulf and the Red Sea," *Defense and Foreign Affairs' Strategic Policy,* March 1992, quoted and paraphrased in Emerson, testimony in "PATRIOT Act Oversight," 140.

87. DIGOS to Swiss federal prosecutor Carla Del Ponte, quoted in Lucy Komisar, "Shareholders in the Bank of Terror?" Salon.com, March 15, 2002.

88. Civil Action, 367.

89. Quoted in Civil Action, 367.

90. Civil Action, 370.

91. "Statement by Treasury Secretary Paul O'Neill," U.S. Department of the Treasury.

92. Arturu Salinas, "U.S. Drug Czar Says Drug Smuggling Gangs Help Fund Terrorist Groups," Associated Press Worldstream, August 31, 2002.

93. Bodansky, *Bin Laden,* 315. The estimates for the revenues generated from the Afghan heroin trade for the year 2000 vary. According to a State Department official, they range from $8 billion to $30 billion.

94. The author received this information from law enforcement sources who are in a position to know the facts of al-Qaeda's involvement in the trafficking of opium and heroin. These sources wish to remain anonymous.

95. John Pomfret, "Drug Trade Resurgent in Afghanistan," *Washington Post,* October 23, 2001.

96. "Afghan Drug Crop Increasing," *Corruption Watch* 2, no. 38 (October 25, 2002): *www.rferl.org/corruptionwatch/2002/10/38-251002.asp.*

97. James Wolfensohn, paraphrased in Faisal Islam, "World Bank Chief Issues Opium Alert," *Observer,* March 16, 2003.

98. Wolfensohn, quoted in Islam, "World Bank Chief Issues Opium Alert."

99. Figures are unavailable for the year 2001.

100. "Afghan Drug Crop Increasing."

101. Inside source, quoted in Yossef Bodansky, *Bin Laden,* 315.

102. Yossef Bodansky, *Bin Laden,* 315.

103. Jason Burke, "Heroin Fuels bin Laden's War Against the West: Suspected Terrorist Buys Afghan Opium Fields," *Washington Times,* November 30, 1998.

104. Bill Samii, "Further Steps Taken Against Afghan Opium Trade," *Iran Report* 6, no. 7 (February 17, 2003): *www.rferl.org/iran-report/2003/02/7-170203.html.*

105. Rebecca Carr, "Authorities Say Terrorists Planned Drugs-for-Guns Plots," Cox News Service. November 7, 2002

106. "SAMs and the Targeting of Israeli Airliners," Jane's Terrorism Intelligence Centre, November 28, 2002.

107. "Officials: Taliban Regrouping in South Afghanistan," Reuters, January 14, 2003.

108. Carr, "Authorities Say Terrorists Planned Drugs-for-Guns Plots."

109. Bolot Djanuzakov, quoted in Scott Peterson, "Fabled Silk Road Now Paved with Narcotics," *Christian Science Monitor,* January 8, 2001.

110. Peterson, "Fabled Silk Road Now Paved with Narcotics."

111. Rand Beers, testimony in "Narco-Terror: The Worldwide Connection Between Drugs and Terrorism," hearing before the Senate Committee on the Judiciary, Subcommittee on Technology, Terrorism, and Government Information, 107th Cong, 2nd sess., March 13, 2002.

112. Ralf Mutschke, assistant director of Interpol's Criminal Intelligence Directorate, quoted in Ahmed Rashid, "They're Only Sleeping," *New Yorker,* January 14, 2002.

113. Jamie Dettmer, "Al-Qaeda's Links in the Balkans," *Insight,* July 1, 2002.

114. Marcia Christoff Kurop, "Al Qaeda's Balkan Links," *Wall Street Journal Europe,* November 1, 2001.

115. "Macedonian Government Confirms Albanians Buying Arms from Drug Funds," *Nova Makedonija* (Skopje, Macedonia), February 20, 2002.

116. Christian Jennings, "Fear over Islamic Terror Groups Using Macedonia as Base," *Scotsman,* March 4, 2002, 9.

117. Yossef Bodansky, *Bin Laden,* 298.

118. Library of Congress, "A Global Overview of Narcotics-Funded Terrorist and Other Extremist Groups."

119. Ibid.

120. Stan Lehman, "Wanted by Paraguay, Hezbollah Supporter Is Free in Brazilian Town Across the Border," Associated Press Worldstream, December 12, 2001.

121. Germano Oliveira, *O Globo,* September 19, 2001, trans. in Foreign Broadcast Information Service, "Brazil's Former Drug Czar: Bin-Laden Establishing al-Qa'idah Cell on Triborder," LAP200109119000051, September 11, 2001.

122. "International Security Forces Search for Five Afghan fugitives in Paraguay," BBC Monitoring Service, February 5, 2002.

123. U.S. Departments of the Treasury and Justice, *2002 National Money Laundering Strategy, www.treas.gov/press/releases/docs/monlaund.pdf,* 23.

124. U.S. law enforcement official, quoted in Douglas Farah, "Al Qaeda's Gold: Following Trail to Dubai," *Washington Post,* February 18, 2002.

125. Douglas Farah, "Al Qaeda's Gold."

126. Quoted in Douglas Farah, "Al Qaeda Gold Moved to Sudan," *Washington Post,* September 3, 2002.

127. Douglas Farah, "Al Qaeda's Road Paved with Gold," *Washington Post* Foreign Service, February 17, 2002.

128. Rachel Ehrenfeld, *Evil Money* (New York: HarperBusiness, 1992), 163–210.

129. Kimberlery Thachuk, "Terrorism's Financial Lifeline: Can It Be Severed?" *Strategic Forum* 191 (May 2002).

130. Ibid.

131. Quoted in Farah, "Al Qaeda Gold Moved to Sudan."

132. Farah, "Al Qaeda Gold Moved to Sudan."

133. John Sfakianakis, "Antiquated Laundering Ways Prevail," *Al-Ahram Weekly Online* 580 (April 4–10, 2002).

134. Mark Huband, "'Conflict' Diamonds Spur Code of Practice," *Financial Times,* October 20, 2002.

135. Ayman al-Zawahiri, quoted in Douglas Farah, "Report Says Africans Harbored al Qaeda," *Washington Post,* December 29, 2002.

136. Basildon Peta, "War on Terrorism: US Probes Zim Generals," *Financial Gazette* (Zimbabwe), January 10, 2002.

137. Ibid.

138. U.S. law enforcement official, quoted in Farah, "Al Qaeda Cash Tied to Diamond Trade," *Washington Post,* November 2, 2001.

139. Quoted in and trans. from "Diamonds: The Whole Story," *National Geographic* (Hebrew edition), March 2000, 13.

140. Farah, "Report Says Africans Harbored al Qaeda."

141. Ibid.

142. Daniel McGrory, "Al-Qaeda Bought $20m Diamonds to Hide Finances," Times Newspapers, December 30, 2002.

143. Farah, Douglas, "African Gems, al-Qaida Link Established," *Washington Post,* December 29, 2002.

144. When the war ended in Sierra Leone, and forty-eight thousand members of the RUF were disarmed, "hundreds of former RUF, West Side Boys and CDF combatants in Sierra Leone crossed over to fight as mercenaries with either the Liberian government or the Liberians United for Reconciliation and Democracy (LURD)." Human Rights Watch, "Sierra Leone" in *World Report 2003,* January 14, 2003, *www.hrw.org/wr2k3/africa10.html.*

145. Farah, "Report Says Africans Harbored al Qaeda."

146. McGrory, "Al-Qaeda Bought $20m Diamonds to Hide Finances."

147. Farah, "Report Says Africans Harbored al Qaeda."

148. In December 2001, Karavan Construction Company had already been identified by the Albanian government as a front for al-Qaeda money laundering operations. The Albanian government froze Karavan and al-Qadi's assets in eleven Albanian banks, but was only able to trace $3 million in laundered money that passed through accounts al-Qadi shared with other companies based in Saudi Arabia, Algeria, Egypt, and Jordan. "Albania Freezes Saudi Businessman's Assets and Seeks His Arrest; Allegedly Linked to bin Laden," Finanacial Times Information—Global News Wire, February 5, 2002; Alban Bala, "Albania: Officials Crack Down on Terror Suspects," Radio Free Europe Radio Liberty, January 25, 2002, *www.rferl.org/nca/features/2002/01/25012002113045.asp.*

149. Arik Hesseldahl, "Feds Look for Data on Saudi in Ptech Raid," *Forbes,* December 6, 2002, *www.forbes.com/2002/12/06/cx_ah_1206raid.html.*

150. Civil Action, 348–49.

151. Ibid.

152. *Encyclopaedia of the Orient, www.lexicorient.com/e.o/index.htm,* s.v. "Muslim Brotherhood—Saudi Arabia."

153. Civil Action, 349–50.

154. Ibid.

155. Civil Action, 321.

156. Zouaydi gave money to: Muhammad Bahaiah ($105,000); the Global Relief Foundation, a charity based in Bridgeview, Ill ($118,000); the Belgian chapter ($227,000); Mamoun Darkazanli ($16,780). The Global Relief Foundation also raised $5 million in the U.S. in 2001. Matthew A. Levitt, testimony in "Role of Charities and NGOs in Ter-

rorist Financing," hearing before the Senate Committee on Banking, Housing, and Urban Affairs, Subcommittee on International Trade and Finance, 107th Cong., 2nd sess., August 1, 2002.

157. Quoted in Tim Golden and Judith Miller, "Al Qaeda Money Trail Runs from Saudi Arabia to Spain," *New York Times*, September 21, 2002.

158. Quoted in Golden and Miller, "Al Qaeda Money Trail Runs from Saudi Arabia to Spain."

159. Civil Action, 349.

160. Ibid, 294–95.

161. Quoted in James Graff, "Bust in Madrid," *TIME* Europe, July 11, 2002.

162. Civil Action, 255.

163. National High Court, Central Trial Court No. 5, Madrid, Spain, Case Number 35/2002 (ordinary procedure), July 19, 2002, 10–11.

164. Ibid.

165. Golden and Miller, "Al Qaeda Money Trail Runs from Saudi Arabia to Spain."

166. Paraphrased in Antony Barnett and Martin Bright, "Authorities Probe Cleric's Bank Account," *Observer*, November 25, 2001.

167. Al Goodman, "Spanish Authorities Tie Suspects to Key Figures in U.S. Hijackings," CNN.com, November 21, 2001.

168. U.S. intelligence sources, interview by author, March 7, 2003.

169. "The Palestinian Islamic Jihad (Harakat al-Jihad al-Islami al-Filastini) was founded in 1979–80 by Palestinian students in Egypt, who had split from the Palestinian Muslim Brotherhood in the Gaza Strip. The founders were highly influenced by the Islamic revolution in Iran on the one hand, and the radicalization and militancy of Egyptian Islamic student organizations, on the other." "Palestinian Islamic Jihad (PIJ)," International Policy Institute for Counter-Terrorism, *www.ict.org.il/inter_ter/orgdet. cfm?orgid=28.*

170. "Sami al-Arian Fact Sheet," SITE Institute, February 20, 2003, *www.site institute.org/exposing.asp?id=63.*

171. U.S. intelligence sources, interview by author, March 7, 2003.

172. "Feds Bust Alleged Terror Ring," CBSNEWS.com, February 20, 2003.

173. Mayer, "Terror Trails Followed in Eight U.S. Cities."

174. Neil Livingston, quoted in Mike McNamee and Lorraine Woellert with Carol Matlack, "The Cash Squeeze on Terror Inc.: Key Arrests Could Help Choke Off al Qaeda Financing," *Business Week*, March 17, 2003, *www.businessweek.com/magazine/ content/03_11/b3824050.htm.*

175. Eric Lichtblau with William Glaberson, "Millions Raised for Qaeda in Brooklyn, U.S. Says," *New York Times*, March 5, 2003

176. John Ashcroft, testimony in "The Terrorist Threat: Working Together to Protect America," hearing before the Senate Committee on the Judiciary, 108th Cong., 1st sess., March 4, 2003.

177. "The Hunt for al Qaeda," CNN.com, *www.cnn.com/interactive/us/0211/ alqaeda.hunt/frameset.exclude.html.*

178. Damien McElroy, "Al-Qa'eda Fighters Set Up Base in Lebanese Refugee Camp," *Sunday Telegraph*, June 22, 2003.

179. Ein Hilwe resident Zain Farhoud, quoted in McElroy, "Al-Qa'eda Fighters Set Up Base in Lebanese Refugee Camp."

180. "US Warns of New Terror Threat in Jeddah," ABS-CBN News, May 16, 2003.

Chapter 3

1. Groups under the PLO umbrella include the Popular Front for the Liberation of Palestine, Popular Democratic Front for the Liberation of Palestine, General Command, and al-Fatah, the dominant group led by Yasser Arafat.

2. "More Than 100 Arrested in Nationwide Methamphetamine Investigation," DEA, January 10, 2002, *www.usdoj.gov/dea/major/me3.html.*

3. James Adams, *The Financing of Terror* (New York: Simon and Schuster, 1986), 57–58.

4. Avi Davis, "The Tap That's Running Dry," *Pakistan Today*, November 8, 2002, *www.paktoday.com/tap.htm.*

5. Adams, *The Financing of Terror,* 49–50, 93–95, 114, 229–33.

6. "A PLO spokesman officially confirmed this on American television (PBS) on September 27, 1979." Benjamin Netanyahu, ed., *Terrorism: How the West Can Win* (New York: Farrar, Strauss, and Giroux, 1986), x. Additional evidence regarding the Soviet Union and its satellites' training and financial support of the PLO was obtained during Israel's military raid of PLO headquarters in Lebanon in 1982, as documented in Raphael Israeli, ed., *PLO in Lebanon: Selected Documents* (London: Weidenfeld and Nicholson, 1983).

7. Israeli, *PLO in Lebanon,* 33–203.

8. *Title 22: Foreign Relations and Intercourse,* vol. 12 of *United States Code, 2000 Edition* (Washington, D.C.: U.S. Government Printing Office, 2001), ch 61, § 5201.

9. Rachel Ehrenfeld, *Evil Money* (New York: HarperBusiness, 1992), 5–7.

10. Nauru, a South Pacific island with eight thousand inhabitants, served as a major money laundering center. On June 13, 2003, the new head of state in Nauru, Willie Star, "revoked the offshore banking licenses of 139 banks, leaving only one for the Bank of Nauru." This move was made to remove the island from the blacklist of the Financial Action Task Force (FATF). "Nauru Ends Offshore Banking," *Corruption Watch* 3, no. 21 (June 19, 2003): *www.rferl.org/corruptionwatch/2003/06/21-190603.asp.*

11. Adams, *The Financing of Terror,* 83–107.

12. Sallah Dabbagh, quoted in Ralph Cwerman, "Narco Terror: Lebanon and the Bloody Politics of Drugs" (1987, typescript), 42, as cited in Rachel Ehrenfeld, *Narco-Terrorism* (New York: Basic Books, 1990), 69.

13. Adams, *The Financing of Terror,* 229.

14. Nathan M. Adams, "Drugs for Guns: The Bulgarian Connection," *Reader's Digest,* November 1983, 97.

15. U.S. Drug Enforcement Administration, Office of Intelligence, *Special Report: The Involvement of the People's Republic of Bulgaria in International Narcotics Trafficking,* May 1984, as cited in Ehrenfeld, *Narco-Terrorism,* 5.

16. Rachel Ehrenfeld, "Down and Out in Palestine," *Washington Times,* March 15, 2001.

17. App. B in National Criminal Intelligence Service (NCIS), "An Outline Assessment of the Threat and Impact by Organised/Enterprise Crime upon United Kingdom Interests" (1993, briefing paper).

18. Paraphrased in "Backgrounder: Corruption in the PLO's Financial Empire," *Middle East Digest* 9, no. 7 (July 1998): *www.cdn-friends-icej.ca/medigest/jul98/backgrnd.html.*

19. Adams, *The Financing of Terror,* 49–50, 93–95, 229–33.

20. "Major Milestones in the Peace Process," Center for Middle East Peace, *www. centerpeace.org/factsheets/fact-sheet-peaceprocess.htm.*

21. PA documents seized by the IDF, November 2002, trans. into Hebrew in Israel Defense Forces, *The Palestinian Preventive Security Force: A Corrupt Corporation* (doc. no. 688/0075, 2002).

22. PA Documents discovered by the IDF in Arafat's compound, May 2002, trans. into Hebrew in Israel Defense Forces, *International Financial Aid to the Palestinian Authority Redirected to Terrorist Elements* (doc. no. TR2-317-02, 2002).

23. Gil Feiler, "Donor Funding for the Palestinian Authorities, 1998–2001" (2003, forthcoming report).

24. IDF, *International Financial Aid to the Palestinian Authority Redirected to Terrorist Elements,* 2.

25. Feiler, "Donor Funding for the Palestinian Authorities, 1998–2001."

26. "European Commission Assistance to the Palestinians in 2000/2001," European Commission Technical Assistance Office, West Bank and Gaza Strip, *www.delwbg. cec.eu.int/en/partnership/assistance.htm.*

27. "Commission Approves EUR 29 Million in Support of Palestinian Reform Efforts and in Response to the Deteriorating Situation on the Ground," European Union On-Line, October 28, 2002, *europa.eu.int/comm/external_relations/gaza/news/ip02_ 1561.htm.*

28. The EU contributions to the PA for 1994–2001 amounted to €3.47 billion (U.S.$3.81 billion). "European Union Aid to the Palestinians, 1994–2001," European Commission Technical Assistance Office, West Bank and Gaza Strip, *www.delwbg.cec.eu.int/en/part-nership/02/aid.htm.*

29. "The MEDA Programme," European Union On-Line, *europa.eu.int/comm/ external_relations/euromed/meda.htm.*

30. "In 2000–2001, a total sum of €3.7 million was paid under Budget Lines B7-6000 (NGO co-financing), B7-6002 (Development Co-operation), and B7-7050 (EIDHR)." Request by 170 MEPs to the president of the European Parliament, "Request for the Constitution of a Temporary Committee of Inquiry (by Virtue of Article 151 of the Rules of Procedure) Concerning the EU Funding in the Middle East," February 4, 2003, *www.ilka.org/presse/pms/pms54anlagen/Request_EN_PDF.pdf,* 1, 1n.

31. EU Budget Line B7-2001 (ECHO). Ibid.

32. EU Budget Line B7-2000 (Food Aid). Ibid.

33. EU Budget Line B8-012/3 (CFSP). Ibid.

34. Commission of the European Communities, *Report from the Commission to the Council and the European Parliament: Annual Report of the MEDA Programme 2000* (Brussels: COM, 2001), 58.

35. UNRWA operates mainly in the Palestinian territories and elsewhere in the Middle East. UNRWA was established by the UN's General Assembly Resolution 302 (IV) of December 8, 1949. It began its operation on May 1, 1950, and its renewed mandate runs to June 30, 2005. "Questions and Answers," UNRWA, *www.un.org/unrwa/ about/qa.html.* The last donation of $15 million from the European Commission was announced on April 11, 2003. Khaled Abu Toameh, "Palestinian Refugees Receive European Funds," *Jerusalem Post,* April 12, 2003.

36. IDF, *International Financial Aid to the Palestinian Authority Redirected to Terrorist Elements*, 9.

37. Ibid, 10, 36.

38. Dani Naveh et al, *The Involvement of Arafat, PA Senior Officials and Apparatuses in Terrorism Against Israel, Corruption and Crime* (doc. no. 3, 2002), 22.

39. Ibid, 30–33.

40. Israel Defense Forces, *Iraqi Support of Palestinian Terrorism* (doc. no. TR2-656-02, 2002); Israel Defense Forces, *Large Sums of Money Transferred by Saudi Arabia to the Palestinians Are Used for Financing Terror Organizations (Particularly the Hamas) and Terrorist Activities (Including Suicide Attacks Inside Israel)* (doc. no. TR2-350-02, 2002); IDF, *International Financial Aid to the Palestinian Authority Redirected to Terrorist Elements*.

41. Memorandum from European Commission Technical Assistance Office, West Bank and Gaza Strip, to *Die Zeit*, July 26, 2002, *Die Zeit* Web archive, *www.zeit.de/2002/34/Politik/akten4.pdf*, 3.

42. IDF, *International Financial Aid to the Palestinian Authority Redirected to Terrorist Elements*, 12.

43. Israel Defense Forces, *The Palestinian Authority Employs Fatah Activists Involved in Terrorism and Suicide Attacks* (doc. no 688/0022, 2002).

44. Fax from Marwan Zallum to Yasser Arafat, August 6, 2001, trans. in "Absorption of Fatah Activists in the PA Manpower Ranks," App. A of IDF, *The Palestinian Authority Employs Fatah Activists Involved in Terrorism and Suicide Attacks*.

45. EU Commission, quoted in Thomas Kleine-Brockhoff, "With Unyielding Faith," trans. Stefan Sharkansky, *www.usefulwork.com/shark/arafatbombs2.html*; originally published as "Unbeugsame Gutgläubigkeit," *Die Zeit* 34/2002 (August 15, 2002).

46. "Released Palestinian Prisoners Speak on Prison Experience, Conditions," Foreign Broadcast Information Service, January 13, 2003, available through Independent Media Review Analysis, *www.imra.org.il/story.php3?id=15403*.

47. Isa Abu Qaraqi, quoted in "Released Palestinian Prisoners Speak on Prison Experience, Conditions."

48. David Hoffman, "Arafat Denounces Conditions Imposed on Foreign Aid," Washington Post Foreign Service, July 2, 1994.

49. Christopher Patten, testimony in Question Time, European Parliament, sitting of October 22, 2002, *www3.europarl.eu.int/omk/omnsapir.so/cre?FILE=20021022r&LANGUE=EN&LEVEL=DOC&NUMINT=2-166&LEG=L5*.

50. Christopher Patten to MEP Laschet, January 21, 2003, *europa.eu.int/comm/external_relations/mepp/eufundspa.htm*.

51. Christopher Patten, "EU Answers Back," letter to the editor, *Jerusalem Post*, July 18, 2002.

52. Memorandum from European Commission Technical Assistance Office, West Bank and Gaza Strip, to *Die Zeit*, July 26, 2002, 4.

53. International Monetary Fund, Fund Staff Representative, "The Palestinian Authority's Fiscal Situation, Policies, and Prospects," statement to the Ad Hoc Liaison Committee Meeting, Oslo, April 25, 2002, *Die Zeit* Web archive, *www.zeit.de/2002/34/Politik/akten6.pdf*, 9.

54. Thomas C. Dawson, "The IMF Responds," letter to the editor, *Wall Street Journal*, June 17, 2002.

55. George Abed, "Interview with George Abed: Middle East's Best Hope Lies in Urgently Tackling Economic and Social Reforms," interview by Laura Wallace, *IMF Survey* 31, no. 16 (September 2002): 2.

56. "Olaf Investigation Concerning Allegations of Misuse of EU Budgetary Support to the Palestinian Authority," European Anti-Fraud Office, February 5, 2003, *europa. eu.int/comm/anti_fraud/press_room/press_releases/2003/2003_03_en.html.*

57. "Investigating Arafat," editorial, *Wall Street Journal,* February 6, 2003.

58. Quoted in "Diplomats Say EU Knew Palestinians Misappropriated Cash to Finance Terrorism," trans. Independent Media Review Analysis, May 10, 2002, *www.imra. org.il/story.php3?id=11955;* originally published as "EU wist dat Arafat geld misbruikte," *Rotterdam NRC Handelsblad,* May 8, 2002.

59. Ambrose Evans-Pritchard, "Financial Watchdog Discloses EU Fraud and Error," *Daily Telegraph,* November 6, 2002.

60. "EU to Support Reform of Palestinian Authority with New Forms of Aid," European Union On-Line, April 30, 2003, *europa.eu.int/rapid/start/cgi/guesten.ksh?p_action. gettxt=gt&doc=IP/03/607|0|RAPID&lg=EN;* "EU to Refocus Palestinian Aid as Tax Dues Resume," Reuters, April 30, 2003, *www.alertnet.org/thenews/newsdesk/L30564340.htm.*

61. Christopher Patten, quoted in "PNA, EU Officials Discuss Reforms: EU Allocates €345 Million to Help Palestinians," Palestine Media Center, May 7, 2003, *www. palestine-pmc.com/details.asp?cat=1&id=773.*

62. The State Department added HAMAS to its Designated Foreign Terrorist Organization list in October 2001, recognizing the group's connections to al-Qaeda.

63. "EU: Hamas Must Accept Ceasefire or Face Blacklist," *Jerusalem Times* (Palestinian publication), June 19, 2003.

64. Feiler, "Donor Funding for the Palestinian Authorities, 1998–2001."

65. Total sum derived from UNRWA finances. "How Is UNRWA Financed?" UNRWA, *www.un.org/unrwa/finances/index.html.*

66. The U.S. has provided 30 percent of the UNRWA budget in recent years. "AIPAC Facts: UNWRA Camps Used as Terrorist Strongholds," American Israel Public Affairs Committee, May 20, 2002, *www.aipac.org/documents/aipacfacts16.html.*

67. Palestinian Ministry of Planning and International Cooperation, Aid Coordination Department, *MOPIC's 2001 First and Second Quarterly Monitoring Report of Donors' Assistance* (Ramallah: MOPIC, 2001).

68. Vernon Silver, "Arafat's New Finance Minister Hunts for His Boss's Billions," *Bloomberg Markets,* September 2002.

69. For the full text of the document, see "The Wye River Memorandum: October 23, 1998," Israel Ministry of Foreign Affairs, *www.mfa.gov.il/mfa/go.asp?MFAH07o10.*

70. Douglas Waller, "Coming in from the Cold," *TIME,* November 2, 1998.

71. Amira Hass, "CIA Begins Training Palestinian Officers," *Haaretz,* September 17, 2002.

72. Stacy Lakind and Yigal Carmon, "The PA Economy," part 2, *MEMRI Inquiry and Analysis Series* 11 (January 8, 1999).

73. Azmi Shuaibi, "Elements of Corruption in the Middle East and North Africa: The Palestinian Case," paper presented at the Ninth International Anti-Corruption Conference, Durban, South Africa, October 10–15, 1999.

74. George W. Bush, White House news conference, June 24, 2002, transcribed in "President Bush Calls for New Palestinian Leadership," White House Office of the Press Secretary, June 24, 2002, *www.whitehouse.gov/news/releases/2002/06/20020624-3.html.*

75. Condoleezza Rice, quoted in Susan Sevareid, "Palestinians Outline New Peace Plan," *Charlotte Observer*, June 17, 2002.

76. Jon Immanuel, "Playing His Hand," *Jerusalem Post*, February 26, 1997.

77. Ronen Bergman, "How Much Is the PLO Really Worth?" *Haaretz*, November 28, 1999.

78. "British National Criminal Intelligence Service Report" (1994, unpublished report), 28.

79. Task Force on Terrorism and Unconventional Warfare (October 28, 1991, unpublished report).

80. Sofya Vasilyeva and Serhey Podrazhansky, "The Black Budget of Yasser Arafat," *Moscow News*, October 2, 1997.

81. "Where Is the Money?" Israel Government Press Office, April 15, 1997.

82. Vasilyeva and Podrazhansky, "The Black Budget of Yasser Arafat."

83. Tom Gross, "Hackers Uncover Secret Billions of Arafat's PLO," *London Sunday Telegraph*, December 5, 1999.

84. Ibid.

85. Stacy Lakind and Yigal Carmon, "The PA Economy," part 1, *MEMRI Inquiry and Analysis Series* 10 (January 7, 1999).

86. Tuvia Blumenthal, "What Palestinians Could Learn from the Jews," *econ.bgu.ac.il/facultym/tuvia/news10e.pdf.*

87. Naveh et al, *The Involvement of Arafat, PA Senior Officials and Apparatuses in Terrorism Against Israel, Corruption and Crime*, 68.

88. Yoram Ettinger, "Should Congress Fund PLO Corruption and Violence?" *Jerusalem Cloakroom* 95 (December 14, 2000): *www.acpr.org.il/cloakrm/clk95.html.*

89. Shimon Shiffer, "Bashar Assad Is Playing with Fire," *Yediot Ahronot*, Sabbath Supplement, July 19, 2002.

90. Ettinger, "Should Congress Fund PLO Corruption and Violence?"

91. Lakind and Carmon, "The PA Economy," part 2.

92. Ibid.

93. David Bedein, ed., "PA Accountability," *Israel Resource Review*, November 22, 1999, *www.israelbehindthenews.com/Nov-22-99.htm.*

94. William Orme Jr., "Palestinian Investment Fund, No Longer Secret, Will Close," *New York Times*, July 7, 2000.

95. Ibid.

96. "Palestinian Authority Admits Squirreling Millions Away in Secret Slush Fund," Agence France Presse, July 5, 2000.

97. Blumenthal, "What Palestinians Could Learn from the Jews."

98. *Palestinian Authority and P.L.O. Non-Compliance with Signed Agreements and Commitments: A Record of Bad Faith and Misconduct*, Government of Israel, November 20, 2000, *www.unitedjerusalem.com/ON_THE_AGENDA/Barak_Gov_White_Paper/barak_gov_white_paper.asp.*

99. Lakind and Carmon, "The PA Economy," part 2.

100. Ibid.

101. Ibid.

102. Shiffer, "Bashar Assad Is Playing with Fire."

103. Jawad Ghussein, quoted in Laurie Copans, "Ex-Aide Accuses Arafat of Corruption," Associated Press, August 18, 2002.

104. Copans, "Ex-Aide Accuses Arafat of Corruption."

105. Quoted in Ronen Bergman and David Ratner, "The Man Who Swallowed Gaza," *Haaretz*, Weekend Supplement, April 4, 1997.

106. Bergman and Ratner, "The Man Who Swallowed Gaza."

107. Ibid.

108. Vernon Silver, "Hunt Is On for Arafat's Money Pots," *The Age*, August 24, 2002, *www.theage.com.au/articles/2002/08/23/1030052974940.html*.

109. "IDF Intelligence: Arafat's Wealth Estimated at 1.3 Billion US Dollars," *Jerusalem Post*, August 13, 2002.

110. Rachel Ehrenfeld, "Arafat's Stash: The Guy's a Billionaire," *National Review*, August 15, 2002.

111. Ginnosar's partner Uzrad Lev, quoted in "The Ginnosar File: Investigative Report in Israeli Media on Corruption Affair Involving High Ranking Israeli (and Palestinian) Officials," *MEMRI Special Dispatch* 453 (December 27, 2002).

112. Memorandum by Uzrad Lev, quoted in "The Ginnosar File."

113. "The Ginnosar File."

114. "Full Report on PNA Assets by Standard and Poor's and the Democracy Council," Palestine Media Center, March 3, 2003, *www.palestine-pmc.com/details.asp?cat=3&id=170*.

115. *Al-Watan*, June 7, 2002, quoted in "A Kuwaiti Daily Reports Arafat Deposited $5.1 Million from Arab Funds into His Personal Account," *MEMRI Special Dispatch* 390 (June 14, 2002).

116. Ibid.

117. "Arafat Cracks Down on His Critics," *Palestine Times* 103 (January 2000): *www.ptimes.org/issue103/comment.html*.

118. Muawiya al-Masri, interview in *al-Sabil*, July 3, 2002, trans. in "Palestinian Legislative Council Member: The PA Is Corrupt," *MEMRI Special Dispatch* 406 (August 2, 2002).

119. Khaled Abu Toameh, "PA Officials Stealing Aid, Own Documents Show," *Jerusalem Post*, January 2, 2003.

120. Abd al-Wahab al-Effendi, article in *al-Hayat*, August 6, 2002, trans. in "On the Struggle Against Corruption in the Arab Regimes," *MEMRI Special Dispatch* 411 (August 14, 2002).

121. Quoted in Amir Bohbot, "This Is How the Counterfeiting Industry Finances Terror," *Maariv Hayom*, August 14, 2002. Translation from Hebrew by the author.

122. Bohbot, "This Is How the Counterfeiting Industry Finances Terror."

123. Yoram Ettinger, "The US Funds the Most Corrupt/Oppressive Mideast Regime!" *Jerusalem Cloakroom* 108 (July 15, 2001): *www.acpr.org.il/cloakrm/clk108.html*.

124. Michael Widlanski, "Bulletin: Yasser Arafat's Headquarters Was Center for Counterfeiting Money," *Media Line*, April 1, 2002.

125. Author's field research, June 2002.

126. Yoram Ettinger, "Should Congress Fund PLO Corruption and Violence?" *Jerusalem Cloakroom* 95 (December 14, 2000): *www.acpr.org.il/cloakrm/clk95.html*.

127. "Operation Clean-up," *Deccan Herald*, July 11, 2002; Ettinger, "Should Congress Fund PLO Corruption and Violence?"

128. Ibid.

129. "PA probing alleged theft of $20mm," *Jerusalem Post*, September 4, 2002.

130. Eyalil Shahar, "Company Owned by Suha Arafat Suspected of Links to Stolen Cars," *Maariv*, January 31, 2003. Translation from Hebrew by the author.

131. "Casualties During 'Ebb and Flow' since 29.9.00," Israel Defense Forces, April 1, 2003, *www.idf.il/daily_statistics/english/1.gif;* "Monthly Analysis of All Terrorist Incidents Since September 2000," Israel Defense Forces, March 31, 2003, *www.idf.il/ daily_statistics/english/4.gif.*

132. During the two-week period between October 6 and October 20, 2002, the Israelis prevented twenty-seven attacks and arrested twenty-eight terrorists. "Terrorist Attacks Thwarted by Security Forces: 6–20 October 2002," Embassy of Israel, October 29, 2002, *www.israelemb.org/articals/2002/October/ 2002102900.htm.*

133. Israel Defense Forces, *PA Documents Exposing Corruption, Waste, and Use of the PA Budget to Encourage and Fund Terrorism* (doc. no. 688/0085, 2003), 3–32. Translation from Hebrew by the author.

134. Ibid.

135. App. A-2 of IDF, *PA Documents Exposing Corruption, Waste, and Use of the PA Budget to Encourage and Fund Terrorism*, 3–7.

136. App. A-7 of IDF, *PA Documents Exposing Corruption, Waste, and Use of the PA Budget to Encourage and Fund Terrorism*, 12–13.

137. App. A-3 of IDF, *PA Documents Exposing Corruption, Waste, and Use of the PA Budget to Encourage and Fund Terrorism*, 8–9.

138. Israel Defense Forces, *A Network of Arms Producing Workshops in the Gaza Strip Operated by the PA Preventive Security Apparatus* (doc. no. TR5-906-02, 2003), 2.

139. Ibid., 1.

140. Ahmed Yassin, interview with the Muslim Web site Alskifa, January 10, 2003, trans. in "'We Went to Cairo to Consolidate National Unity, Not to Wave the White Flag of Surrender at the Jewish Enemy,'" IDF Spokesperson, January 12, 2003, *www.idf.il/ newsite/english/0112-5.stm.*

141. "EU Urged to Stop Paying Barghouti Salary" Independent Media Review Analysis, September 10, 2002, *www.imra.org.il/story.php3?id=13580.*

142. IDF, *International Financial Aid to the Palestinian Authority Redirected to Terrorist Elements*, 55.

143. The letters were dated January 20, 2001, and April 5, 2001, respectively.

144. IDF, *International Financial Aid to the Palestinian Authority Redirected to Terrorist Elements*, 55–75.

145. *State of Israel v. Marwan bin Khatib Barghouti*, case no. 092134/02 (District Court of Tel Aviv and Jaffa 2002).

146. IDF, *The Palestinian Authority Employs Fatah Activists Involved in Terrorism and Suicide Attacks*, 2.

147. App. H of IDF, *PA Documents Exposing Corruption, Waste, and Use of the PA Budget to Encourage and Fund Terrorism*, 6566.

148. App. B, doc 8 of IDF, *The Palestinian Authority Employs Fatah Activists Involved in Terrorism and Suicide Attacks*.

149. Kleine-Brockhoff, "With Unyielding Faith."

150. App. B, doc 8 of IDF, *The Palestinian Authority Employs Fatah Activists Involved in Terrorism and Suicide Attacks.*

151. Zvi Harel, "Barghouti's Deputy Convicted of Fourteen Counts of Murder," *Haaretz,* May 1, 2003.

152. Yoram Yarkoni, "The Punishment of the TANZIM Commander: Fourteen Life Sentences for Fourteen Murders," *Yedioth Aharonot,* May 6, 2003. Translation from Hebrew by the author.

153. "The Palestinian Authority's Possession of Arms in Violation of International Agreements," IDF Spokesperson, *www.idf.il/project1/english/index.stm.*

154. IDF, *The Palestinian Authority Employs Fatah Activists Involved in Terrorism and Suicide Attacks,* 15, 17.

155. Naveh et al, *The Involvement of Arafat, PA Senior Officials and Apparatuses in Terrorism Against Israel, Corruption and Crime,* 50.

156. Israel Defense Forces, *The Appointment of Mahmud Awdallah as Fuad Shubaki's Replacement* (doc. no. TR2-907-02, 2002), 1–2.

157. Michael Widlanski, "Defiant Arafat, Palestinian Media Revving Up Attack on Israel, U.S.," *Media Line,* September 30, 2002.

158. Kuwaiti Arabic-language newspaper *Alzamin,* June 20, 2002.

159. Olara Otunnu, quoted in Melissa Radler, "UN Condemns Palestinians' Use of Children in Conflict," *Jerusalem Post,* January 15, 2003.

160. Ibid.

161. Declaration of Principles on Interim Self-Government Arrangements (Oslo Accords), September 13, 1993, *www.iap.org/oslo.htm.*

162. Joint Declaration by the European Parliament, the European Council, and the European Commission Against Racism and Xenophobia, paragraph 4, 11 June 1986, Annex 1 (OJ C 158, 25.6.1986), *www.europarl.eu.int/workingpapers/libe/102/text5_en.htm#annex1.*

163. Reuven Ehrlich, ed., "Incitement and Propaganda Against Israel and Zionism in the Educational System of the Palestinian Authority," *Center for Special Studies Information Bulletin* 3 (June 2002): 12.

164. UNRWA, "UNRWA Programme Budget for the Biennium 2002–2003," *www.un.org/unrwa/finances/pdf/summary.pdf.*

165. Prism Group, *Palestinian Children: What Are They Taught?* July 2003, *www.theprismgroup.org/education.htm.*

166. Quoted in Ehrlich, ed., "Incitement and Propaganda Against Israel and Zionism in the Educational System of the Palestinian Authority," *www.intelligence.org.il/eng/c_june.htm.*

167. Ibid., 16.

168. Ehrlich, ed., "Incitement and Propaganda against Israel and Zionism in the Educational System of the Palestinian Authority," 22. Official maps of the PA do not include Israel, either.

169. "Palestinian Schools Praise Suicide Bombers," IDF Spokesperson, *www.idf.il/newsite/english/010.stm.*

170. Saheil Alhinadi, July 6, 2001, paraphrased in Dani Naveh, "Inciting and Educating Children Towards Hate, Anti-Semitism and Violence in the Palestinian Authority,"

Israeli Prime Minister's Office, Spring 2002, *www.pmo.gov.il/english/nave/violence-5.html.*

171. Natan Sharansky et al, briefing at the National Media Center, Jerusalem, April 19, 2002, *www.mfa.gov.il/mfa/go.asp?MFAH0lla0.*

172. Paul McCann, quoted in Michael Wines, "Killing of U.N. Aide by Israel Bares Rift with Relief Agency," *New York Times,* January 4, 2003.

173. IDF and Palestinian sources.

174. Marc Ginsburg, interview by Brit Hume, *Special Report with Brit Hume,* Fox News, May 1, 2002, *www.foxnews.com/story/0,2933,51622,00.html.*

175. Michael Rubin, "The UN's Refugees," *Wall Street Journal,* April 18, 2002.

176. Julie Stahl, "US Tax Money Funding Palestinian Propaganda," CNSNews.com, August 28.

177. Ibid.

178. HAMAS killed at least five American citizens in the homicide bombing of the cafeteria at the Hebrew University of Jerusalem on July 31, 2002. ICT Casualties Database (Middle Eastern Terrorism), International Policy Institute for Counter-Terrorism, *www.ict.org.il/ARAB_ISR/incidentsearch2.cfm.*

179. "Hamas (Islamic Resistance Movement)," International Policy Institute for Counter-Terrorism (ICT), *www.ict.org.il/inter_ter/orgdet.cfm?orgid=13.*

180. George W. Bush, White House news conference, December 4, 2001, transcribed in "Bush Freezes Financial Assets of Three Groups Linked to Hamas," U.S. Department of Justice, December 4, 2001.

181. "Hamas (Islamic Resistance Movement)," ICT.

182. Ahmed Yassin, quoted in "Palestinian Authority Expresses Support for Saddam Hussein, Incitement Against US," IDF Spokesperson, January 17, 2003, *www.idf.il/newsite/english/0117-2.stm.*

183. "Palestinian Authority Expresses Support for Saddam Hussein, Incitement Against US."

184. Elie Rekhess, "The Terrorist Connection: The Islamic Jihad and Hamas," *Justice* 5 (May 1995): *www.fas.org/irp/world/para/docs/950500.htm.*

185. George W. Bush, December 4, 2001, transcribed in "Bush Freezes Financial Assets of Three Groups Linked to Hamas."

186. Matthew A. Levitt, testimony in "Role of Charities and NGOs in Terrorist Financing," hearing before the Senate Committee on Banking, Housing, and Urban Affairs, Subcommittee on International Trade and Finance, 107th Cong., 2nd sess., August 1, 2002.

187. IDF, *Large Sums of Money Transferred by Saudi Arabia to the Palestinians Are Used for Financing Terror Organizations and Terrorist Activities,* 21.

188. "The Holy Land Foundation for Relief and Development," Anti-Defamation League (ADL), *www.adl.org/israel/holyland.asp.*

189. Steven Emerson, testimony in "PATRIOT Act Oversight: Investigating Patterns of Terrorist Financing," hearing before the House Committee on Financial Services Subcommittee on Oversight and Investigations, 107th Cong., 2nd sess., February 12, 2002, serial 107-53 (Washington, D.C.: U.S. Government Printing Office, 2002), 132.

190. George W. Bush, December 4, 2001, transcribed in "Bush Freezes Financial Assets of Three Groups Linked to Hamas."

191. Emerson, testimony in "PATRIOT Act Oversight," 132.

192. FBI report, 2001, quoted in Emerson, testimony in "PATRIOT Act Oversight," 132. Bracketed interpolations in original.

193. "The Holy Land Foundation for Relief and Development," ADL.

194. Quoted in "The Holy Land Foundation for Relief and Development," ADL.

195. Levitt, testimony in "Role of Charities and NGOs in Terrorist Financing."

196. Quoted in "The Holy Land Foundation for Relief and Development," ADL.

197. Ibid.

198. Ibid.

199. Paraphrased in Steve McGonigle, "Ex-agent Says Criminal Probe of InfoCom Based on Holy Land Data," *Dallas Morning News*, December 20, 2002.

200. Quoted in Jim Bronskill and Rick Mofina, "Hamas Funded by Canadian Agency; Report: Aid Organization Accused of Sending Money to U.S. Charity Shut Down for Alleged Hamas Ties," *Ottawa Citizen*, December 6, 2001.

201. Bronskill and Mofina, "Hamas Funded by Canadian Agency."

202. Ronny Naftaniel, quoted in Sharon Sadeh, "Dutch Tolerance May Benefit Muslim Extremists," *Haaretz*, August 11, 2002.

203. AIVD spokesman Vincent Van Steen, quoted in Sadeh, "Dutch Tolerance May Benefit Muslim Extremists."

204. Sadeh, "Dutch Tolerance May Benefit Muslim Extremists."

205. Al-Aqsa Foundation official Web site, *www.aqsa.org.za*.

206. "Emergency Relief Aid," al-Aqsa Foundation, *www.aqsa.org.za/special.htm*.

207. The United States District Court for the District of Columbia, Civil Action, Case Number 1:02CV01616(JR), Third Amended Complaint, September 2002, 234. (This source is cited subsequently as "Civil Action.")

208. Emerson, testimony in "PATRIOT Act Oversight," 142.

209. Ibid., 142–43.

210. Jamie C. Zarate, quoted in Levitt, testimony in "Role of Charities and NGOs in Terrorist Financing."

211. Timothy L. O'Brien, "U.S. Presses Saudis to Police Accounts Used to Aid Palestinians," *New York Times*, June 24, 2003. For information on direct Saudi funding of HAMAS, see Memorandum from Yasser Arafat to Abu Mazen (Mahmoud Abbas) and Mustapha Dib, January 7, 2001, trans. in App. E3 of IDF, *Large Sums of Money Transferred by Saudi Arabia to the Palestinians Are Used for Financing Terror Organizations and Terrorist Activities*, 54.

212. Known in Arabic as *Harakat al-Jihad al-Islami al-Filastini*.

213. "Jenin: The Palestinian Suicide Capital," Israel Defense Forces, *www.idf.il/english/news/jenin.stm*.

214. "Islamic Jihad Terrorists Admit to Receiving Funds and Orders from Syrian HQ," IDF Spokesperson, February 5, 2003, *www.idf.il/newsite/english/0205-4.stm*. The U.S. State Department's annual *Patterns of Global Terrorism* report confirms Iran's support not only for the PIJ but also for HAMAS and Hizballah—the latter of which "receives substantial amounts of financial, training, weapons, explosives, political, diplomatic, and organizational aid from Iran." U.S. Department of State, *Patterns of Global Terrorism 2001*, May 2002, *www.state.gov/documents/organization/10319.pdf*, 65, 95.

215. Abd Allah al-Shami, interview in *al-Quds al-Arabi*, November 22, 2002, paraphrased

in Bill Samii, "Iran May Be Funding al-Aqsa Martyrs Brigade," *Iran Report* 5, no. 44 (December 2, 2002): *www.rferl.org/iran-report/2002/12/44-021202.html.*

216. Samii, "Iran May Be Funding al-Aqsa Martyrs Brigade."

217. Sean Rayment, "IRA Link to PLO Examined in Hunt for Deadly Sniper," *Daily Telegraph,* October 3, 2002.

218. Paul Collinson, paraphrased in David Bamber, "IRA Role Seen in Bombs in Jenin," *London Sunday Telegraph,* April 28, 2002.

219. Quoted in Bamber, "IRA Role Seen in Bombs in Jenin,"

220. Rachel Ehrenfeld, "IRA + PLO = Terror," *National Review Online,* August 21, 2002.

221. IDF, *Iraqi Support of Palestinian Terrorism,* part 1, 12.

222. In September 2002, Dr. Mustafa Barghouti claimed that 75 percent of the Palestinians live on $2 a day. Mustafa Barghouti, "The Current Situation," *Palestine Monitor* presentation, Palestine Media Center, Ramallah, West Bank. September 25, 2002, *www.palestinemonitor.org/mustafa/resentation_Sep_25_2002.htm.*

223. Ibrahim Barzak, "Saddam Gives Money to Palestinian Families," Associated Press, March 21, 2003.

224. Kenneth R.Timmerman, "Proof That Saddam Bankrolls Terrorism," *Insight,* November 26, 2002.

225. ALF/Baath party document, August 25, 2001, trans. in IDF, *Iraqi Support of Palestinian Terrorism,* part 2, 24.

226. Khaled Abu Toameh, "PA Confiscates Saddam's Donations for 'Martyrs,' Demolished Homes," *Jerusalem Post,* January 4, 2003.

227. Quoted in Abu Toameh, "PA Confiscates Saddam's Donations for 'Martyrs,' Demolished Homes."

228. Barzak, "Saddam Gives Money to Palestinian Families."

229. Tony Perry, "Possible Tie to Terror Found," *Los Angeles Times,* April 7, 2003.

230. Bill Gertz, "Guerrilla Fighters Seen as Threat to Allied Forces," *Washington Times,* April 15, 2003.

231. Mansoor Ijaz, "The Clinton Intelligence Record," *National Review Online,* April 29, 2003; Inigo Gilmore, "Ties Between al Qaeda, Saddam Revealed," *London Sunday Telegraph,* April 27, 2003.

232. Quoted in C. J. Chivers, "Instruction and Methods from al Qaeda Took Root in North Iraq with Islamic Fighters," *New York Times,* April 27, 2003.

233. Chivers, "Instruction and Methods from al Qaeda Took Root in North Iraq."

234. Ibid.

235. Fahd bin Abd al-Aziz, paraphrased in Donna Abu-Nasr, "Saudi Telethon Raising Millions for Families of Martyrs," Associated Press, April 12, 2002.

236. Nayef bin Abd al-Aziz, quoted in Abu-Nasr, "Saudi Telethon Raising Millions for Families of Martyrs."

237. Abu-Nasr, "Saudi Telethon Raising Millions for Families of Martyrs."

238. Ibid.

239. Saudi embassy press release, April 2001, quoted in Civil Action, 313

240. "Israeli Report Details Saudi Funding for Palestinian Militants," *World Tribune.com,* Thursday, July 4, 2002.

241. Ibid.

242. Ibid.

243. Ibid.

244. IDF, *Large Sums of Money Transferred by Saudi Arabia to the Palestinians Are Used for Financing Terror Organizations and Terrorist Activities*, 24–32.

245. Ibid.

246. "PLO Gets More Than SR 1.8 Million from the Popular Committee for Assisting the Palestinian Mujahideen," Saudi Press Agency, April 22, 2003, available through Independent Media Review Analysis, *www.imra.org.il/story.php3?id=16622.*

247. "Saudi Aid to 21,000 Palestinian Families," *Jerusalem Times* (Palestinian publication), April 17, 2003, available through Independent Media Review Analysis, *www.imra.org.il/story.php3?id=16576.*

248. App. E of IDF, *Large Sums of Money Transferred by Saudi Arabia to the Palestinians Are Used for Financing Terror Organizations and Terrorist Activities*, 44–68.

249. Abu Mazen (Mahmoud Abbas) to Salman bin Abd al-Aziz, December 30, 2000, trans. in App. E-2 of IDF, *Large Sums of Money Transferred by Saudi Arabia to the Palestinians Are Used for Financing Terror Organizations and Terrorist Activities*, 50.

250. News summary prepared for Yasser Arafat, January 7, 2001, trans. in App. E-3 of IDF, *Large Sums of Money Transferred by Saudi Arabia to the Palestinians Are Used for Financing Terror Organizations and Terrorist Activities*, 54.

251. Memorandum from Yasser Arafat to Abu Mazen (Mahmoud Abbas) and Mustapha Dib, January 7, 2001.

252. Quoted in "World Bank Paints Gloomy Picture of Palestinian Economy," *Haaretz*, March 5, 2003

253. James Phillips, testimony in "Are Yasser Arafat and the Palestinian Authority Credible Partners for Peace?" hearing before the House Armed Services Committee, Terrorism Oversight Panel, 107th Cong., 2nd sess., June 6, 2002.

254. Ibid.

255. George W. Bush, June 24, 2002, transcribed in "President Bush Calls for New Palestinian Leadership."

256. George W. Bush, White House news conference, March 14, 2003, transcribed in "President Discusses Roadmap for Peace in the Middle East," White House Office of the Press Secretary, March 14, 2003, *www.whitehouse.gov/news/releases/2003/03/20030314-4.html* .

257. George W. Bush, June 24, 2002, transcribed in "President Bush Calls for New Palestinian Leadership."

258. George W. Bush, March 14, 2003, transcribed in "President Discusses Roadmap for Peace in the Middle East."

259. Steven R. Weisman, "Bush, in Rebuff to Partners, Freezes Mideast Peace Plan," *New York Times*, March 9, 2003.

260. Yasser Arafat, quoted in "PA Cuts Off Formal Peace Talks with U.S.," Middle East Newsline, April 2, 2003.

261. "Quartet Envoys to Discuss Middle East 'Road Map,'" Reuters, April 2, 2003.

262. The idea to create the position of a Palestinian prime minister originated with Germany's foreign minister, Joschka Fische.

263. Mohammed Assadi, "Palestinian Legislature Approves Premiership," Reuters, March 10, 2003.

264. "Not New, Not Leadership," editorial, *Jerusalem Post,* March 11, 2003.

265. Ahmed Tibi, quoted in "PA Official: Arafat to Retain Control of Peace Talks, Security Forces," *Haaretz,* March 10, 2003.

266. Palestinian official, quoted in "PA Official: Arafat to Retain Control of Peace Talks, Security Forces."

267. Hatem Lufti, "PLC Gives Final Approval on Premiership Bill, Arafat Signs It into Law," *Jerusalem Times,* March 20, 2003.

268. "Palestinian Authority Reveals $600m in Investments," *Jerusalem Times,* March 8, 2003.

269. Lead auditor James Prince, interview by author, March 4, 2003.

270. "Palestinian National Authority Releases Data on Investments, Discloses Assets: Valuation and Transparency Report," Palestine Investment Fund, March 3, 2003, *www.pa-inv-fund.com/lpr.asp#march3-2003.* For the full report see Democracy Council and Standard and Poor's, *Palestine Investment Fund: Initial Report on Valuation and Transparency as of January 1, 2003,* Palestine Media Center, March 2, 2003, *www.palestine-pmc.com/details.asp?cat=3&id=170.*

271. Democracy Council and Standard and Poor's, *Palestine Investment Fund: Initial Report,* 83.

272. Bedein, ed., "PA Accountability."

273. James Prince, interview by author, March 4, 2003.

274. Israeli Foreign Ministry information.

275. Israel Defense Forces, *The Economic Reforms in the Palestinian Authority: Situation Assessment* (doc. no. GE2-133-03, 2003), 6.

276. Ibid., 6, 10.

277. Ibid., 9

278. Arnon Regular, "Analysis: Abu Mazen May Pull Out Rather Than Present Cabinet," *Haaretz,* April 8, 2003.

279. Tom DeLay, quoted and paraphrased in Jim VandeHei, "Bush Meets Resistance on Mideast Plan," *Washington Post,* Friday, April 4, 2003,

280. Khaled Abu Toameh, "Palestinian Parliament Approves Abu Mazen Cabinet," *Jerusalem Post,* April 29, 2003.

281. Amos Harel, "Arafat asks EU's Solana to Exert Pressure on Israel," *Haaretz,* May 16, 2003.

282. These forces are: Intelligence, the National Security Forces, Force 17, Military Intelligence, and the naval forces.

283. Mahmoud Abbas, interview in *Alsharak Alawast,* March 3, 2003, trans. in "Abu Mazen Justifies the 'Armed Struggle' Against Jewish Residents of the West Bank and Gaza Strip," IDF Spokesperson, March 3, 2003, available through Independent Media Review Analysis, *www.imra.org.il/story.php3?id=16113.*

284. Roni Singer and Haim Shadmi, "Tel Aviv Suicide Bomber Was British Citizen," *Haaretz,* April 30, 2003.

285. Amos Harel, "Terrorist Cell That Murdered Zion David Yesterday Sit in Arafat's Ramallah Office," *Haaretz,* May 12, 2003.

286. Khaled Abu Toameh, "PA Pays Salaries of Aksa Brigades Members," *Jerusalem Post,* May 15 2003.

287. "New Violence Halts Mideast Peace Effort," Fox News, May 19, 2003, *www.foxnews.com/story/0,2933,87191,00.html.*

288. Barry Schweid, "Powell, Egyptians Disagree on Arafat," Associated Press, May 12, 2003.

289. **"Cabinet Approves Mideast Road Map, but Adds Own Conditions,"** *Haaretz,* May 25, 2003.

290. Colin L. Powell, quoted in Tom Rose, "Road Rage," *Weekly Standard* 8, no. 40 (June 23, 2003): *www.weeklystandard.com/Content/Public/Articles/000/000/002/808cywgl.asp.*

Chapter 4

1. Slogan of the Movement of the Deprived, quoted in "The Imam Musa Sadr," al-Manar Television, 1997, *almashriq.hiof.no/lebanon/300/320/324/324.2/musa-sadr.*

2. AMAL is Arabic for "hope," and an acronym for *Afwaj al-Muqawamah al-Lubnaniyyah,* or "Lebanese Resistance Detachments." See *www.globalsecurity.org/military/world/para/amal.htm.*

3. "The Imam Musa Sadr."

4. Rachel Ehrenfeld, *Evil Money* (New York: HarperBusiness, 1992), 187. Hizballah is also known as Islamic Jihad, Revolutionary Justice Organization, Organization of the Oppressed on Earth, and Islamic Jihad for the Liberation of Palestine.

5. U.S. Department of State, *Patterns of Global Terrorism 2001,* May 2002, *www.state.gov/documents/organization/10319.pdf.*

6. "Hizballah (Party of God)," International Policy Institute for Counter-Terrorism, *www.ict.org.il/inter_ter/orgdet.cfm?orgid=15.*

7. Ibid.

8. Dick Armey, testimony in "U.S. Policy Toward Syria and the Syria Accountability Act," hearing before the House Committee on International Relations, Subcommittee on the Middle East and South Asia, 107th Cong., 2nd sess., September 18, 2002, serial 107-119 (Washington, D.C.: U.S. Government Printing Office, 2002), 6.

9. "Hizballah (Party of God)."

10. Jeffrey Goldberg, "In the Party of God," part 1, *New Yorker,* October 14, 2002, *www.newyorker.com/fact/content/?021014fa_fact4.*

11. James Risen, "$25m Wanted Man Linked with Iran," *New York Times,* January 18, 2002; Defense and Foreign Affairs/International Strategic Studies Association, "Russian SVR Officer Claims to Know a Potentially Key Figure in September 11, 2001, Attacks," *Defense and Foreign Affairs Daily,* November 1, 2001.

12. Ibid.

13. Task Force on Terrorism and Unconventional Warfare (October 28, 1991, unpublished report).

14. Ehrenfeld, *Evil Money,* 196–200.

15. Claudia Rosett, "Pining for Freedom: Syrian Occupation Suffocates Lebanon, and the World Shrugs," OpinionJournal, February 5, 2003, *www.opinionjournal.com/columnists/cRosett/?id=110003028.*

16. Goldberg, "In the Party of God," part 1.

17. Yossef Bodansky, *Bin Laden: The Man Who Declared War on America* (Rocklin, Calif.: Forum, 1999), 153.

18. Ibid., 407.

19. Library of Congress, Federal Research Division, "A Global Overview of Narcotics-Funded Terrorist and Other Extremist Groups" (May 2002, draft).

20. Joseph Farah, "Hezbollah to Attack Israel During Iraq War," WorldNetDaily, February 10, 2003, *www.worldnetdaily.com/news/article.asp?ARTICLE_ID=30964*.

21. Hassan Nasrallah, al-Manar Television, March 8, 2002, trans. in Israel Defense Forces, *Hizballah and Terrorism: Ideological Foundations; Operational Methods; Terrorism Policy* (doc. no. TR5-496-02, 2002), 19.

22. Library of Congress, "A Global Overview of Narcotics-Funded Terrorist and Other Extremist Groups."

23. Intellicom, "Hezbollah—The Party of God: A Middle East Threat Analysis," United States Committee for a Free Lebanon, February 2002, *www.freelebanon.org/articles/a226.htm*.

24. "Dossier: Hassan Nasrallah."

25. *Britannica Student Encyclopedia*, 2003, s.v. "Mussawi, 'Abbas al-'"

26. "Dossier: Hassan Nasrallah."

27. Ibid.

28. Michael Rubin, "No Change: Iran Remains Committed to Israel's Destruction," *National Review Online*, July 1, 2002.

29. Matthew Levitt, "The Political Economy of Middle East Terrorism," *Middle East Review of International Affairs (MERIA) Journal* 6, no. 4 (December 2002): *meria.idc.ac.il/journal/2002/issue4/jv6n4a3.html*; Matthew Levitt, *Fletcher Forum of World Affairs* 27, no. 1 (Winter/Spring 2003).

30. Bodansky, Bin Laden, 364. In addition, in July 2003 President Bush declared, "Today, Syria and Iran continue to harbor and assist terrorists. This behavior is completely unacceptable and states that support terror will be held accountable." George W. Bush, remarks in press availability, July 21, 2003, transcribed in "President Bush, PM Berlusconi Discuss Iraq and War on Terrorism," White House Office of the Press Secretary, July 21, 2003, *www.whitehouse.gov/news/releases/2003/07/20030721.html*.

31. The Arab Bank stands out as the main money channel for such terrorist organizations. Israel Defense Forces, Military Intelligence, *Iran and Syria as Strategic Support for Palestinian Terrorism (Based on Interrogations of Arrested Palestinian Terrorists and Captured Palestinian Authority Documents)* (doc. no. TR6-548-02, 2002), 30.

32. "Is Sudan Terrorism's New Mecca?" Marine Corps University Command and Staff College, 1997, *www.globalsecurity.org/military/library/report/1997/Littleton.htm*.

33. David Ignatius, "U.S. Fears Sudan Becoming Terrorists' 'New Lebanon,'" *Washington Post*, January 31, 1992.

34. IDF, *Hizballah and Terrorism*, 11.

35. Rubin, "No Change"; Hillary Mann, "Iranian Links to International Terrorism—the Khatemi Era," *PolicyWatch* 296 (January 28, 1998): *www.washingtoninstitute.org/watch/Policywatch/policywatch1998/296.htm;* "Iran and Hizbullah," Israel Foreign Ministry, Information Division, April 25, 1998, available through International Policy Institute for Counter-Terrorism, *www.ict.org.il/articles/articledet.cfm?articleid=15*.

36. Ely Karmon, "Hizballah and the War on Terror," *PolicyWatch* 642 (July 30, 2002): *www.washingtoninstitute.org/watch/Policywatch/policywatch2002/642.htm*.

37. IDF, *Hizballah and Terrorism*.

38. Task Force on Terrorism and Unconventional Warfare.

39. Ibid.

40. French intelligence sources, interview by author, July 2002.

41. Ehrenfeld, *Evil Money,* 198–199.

42. Task Force on Terrorism and Unconventional Warfare.

43. Quoted in Task Force on Terrorism and Unconventional Warfare.

44. Task Force on Terrorism and Unconventional Warfare.

45. "Iran and Hizbullah."

46. Muhammad Khatami, quoted in Yossef Bodansky, *The High Cost of Peace: How Washington's Middle East Policy Left America Vulnerable to Terrorism* (Roseville, Calif.: Forum, 2002), 250.

47. Bodansky, *The High Cost of Peace,* 250; "Iran and Hizbullah"; IDF, *Hizballah and Terrorism,* 10.

48. Bodansky, *The High Cost of Peace,* 327.

49. Ibid.

50. Ibid., 328.

51. Ibid.

52. Ibid., 328; IDF/MI, *Iran and Syria as Strategic Support for Palestinian Terrorism,* 35–37; Liza Porteus, "Profile: Palestinian Islamic Jihad," Fox News, February 20, 2003, *www.foxnews.com/story/0,2933,79131,00.html.*

53. Raymond van Doornik, "Iran's Links to European Terrorists," *International Review,* Winter 1995–96, *www.geocities.com/Paris/Rue/4637/terr10a.html.*

54. Amos Harel, "Wounded Palestinians Treated in Iran Received Military Training," *Haaretz,* December 12, 2002.

55. Ibid.

56. Abolghassem Mesbahi, paraphrased in Martin Edwin Andersen, "Did Menem Tango with Terrorists?" *Insight,* February 4, 2003.

57. Abolghassem Mesbahi, quoted in Andersen, "Did Menem Tango with Terrorists?"

58. "Menem Faces New Investigations," Swissmoney Research, July 26, 2002, *www.swissmoney.net/jul02.htm.*

59. Marc Perelman, "Argentina Set to Indict Iran Agents," *Forward,* October 4, 2002.

60. Ibid.

61. "Iran as a State Sponsoring and Operating Terror," Center for Special Studies, Intelligence and Terrorism Information Center, April 2003, 80–81.

62. Ira Stoll, "Iran Giving Safe Haven to al Qaeda Kingpins," *New York Sun,* May 7, 2003.

63. "Argentine Court Issue International Warrant Against Khameneh'i," Iran Press Service, February 23, 2003.

64. Yoram Schweitzer, "Iranian Transnational Terrorism," International Policy Institute for Counter-Terrorism, *www.ict.org.il/articles/articledet.cfm?articleid=362.*

65. Benjamin Gilman, testimony in "U.S. Policy Toward Syria and the Syria Accountability Act," 3; IDF, *Hizballah and Terrorism,* 10.

66. Matthew Levitt, testimony in "U.S. Policy Toward Syria and the Syria Accountability Act," 48.

67. IDF/MI, *Iran and Syria as Strategic Support for Palestinian Terrorism,* 8.

68. Levitt, testimony in "U.S. Policy Toward Syria and the Syria Accountability Act," 1.

69. IDF, *Hizballah and Terrorism*, 11–12.

70. Hassan Nasrallah, quoted in Karmon, "Hizballah and the War on Terror." Elision in original.

71. Elias Saadi, testimony in "U.S. Policy Toward Syria and the Syria Accountability Act," 32.

72. Quoted in IDF/MI, *Iran and Syria as Strategic Support for Palestinian Terrorism*, 1.

73. Ramadan Shalah, quoted in IDF/MI, *Iran and Syria as Strategic Support for Palestinian Terrorism*, 14.

74. Amin al-Hindi, Palestinian intelligence report, December 10, 2000, paraphrased in IDF/MI, *Iran and Syria as Strategic Support for Palestinian Terrorism*, 15.

75. Jibril Rajoub, Palestinian intelligence report, October 31, 2001, quoted in IDF/MI, *Iran and Syria as Strategic Support for Palestinian Terrorism*, 15.

76. Ibid. Bracketed interpolation in original.

77. IDF/MI, *Iran and Syria as Strategic Support for Palestinian Terrorism*, 22.

78. Ibid.

79. Ibid., 23.

80. David Rudge, "Hizbullah 'A-Team' of International Terror?" *Jerusalem Post*, May 23, 2003.

81. Eitan Glikman, "A School for Terror" (in Hebrew), *Yedioth Aharonot*, May 23, 2003.

82. Ibid., 25–26.

83. "Syria Contributes 4.94 Million to Support the Palestinian Resistance," Official Syrian News Agency, March 12, 2003, available through Independent Media Review Analysis, *www.imra.org.il/story.php3?id=16121*.

84. Dafna Vardi, "Hizballah Has Chemical Warheads," *Ma'ariv*, January 30, 2003.

85. "Hizballah" (in Hebrew), part A, Intelligence and Terrorism Information Center at the Center for Special Studies, March 2003, 72.

86. Levitt, "Political Economy of Middle East Terrorism."

87. "Hizballah" (in Hebrew), part A, 72–74.

88. "U.S. Drug Ring Tied to Aid for Hizballah," *Transnational Threats Update* 1, no. 1 (September 2002): *www.csis.org/tnt/ttu/ttu_0209.pdf*, 3.

89. Library of Congress, "A Global Overview of Narcotics-Funded Terrorist and Other Extremist Groups."

90. "Hizballah" (in Hebrew), part A, 72, 73–74

91. Ibid, 75–76.

92. "Hezbollah Seeking to Acquire Berlin Premises: German Press," zawya.com, June 22, 2002.

93. "Hizballah" (in Hebrew), part A, 72, 76–78.

94. David Cohen, federal court document, September 12, 2002, quoted in Ira Stoll, "Fifth Avenue Charity is 'Totally Controlled' by Iran, NYPD Says," *New York Sun*, December 5, 2002.

95. Khalil Osman, "Key Aspects of the Modus Operandi of Lebanon's Hizbullah-led Islamic Resistance," *Crescent International*, September 16–30, 2000.

96. *Al-Sharq al-Awsat*, June 8, 2002, trans. in "Iran Increases Funding and Training for Suicide Bombings; Islamic Jihad Leader: The Intifada Foiled the American Plots

Against Iraq; A Hizbullah Leader on the Iranian-Syrian-Lebanese-Palestinian Axis," *MEMRI Special Dispatch* 387 (June 11, 2002).

97. William Samii, "Iran: Teheran Supports Hezbollah in Lebanon," Radio Free Europe Radio Liberty, November 10, 1999, *www.rferl.org/nca/features/1999/11/F.RU. 991110134517.html.*

98. Matthew Levitt, "Stemming the Flow of Terrorist Financing: Practical and Conceptual Challenges," lecture given at program sponsored by U.S. Embassy Vienna, Austria, Vienna, Graz, and Bregenz, January 20–23, 2003, *www.usembassy.at/en/embassy/ photo/lev_lecture.htm.*

99. Ibid.

100. Ibid.

101. "Two Men in United States Convicted of Aiding Hizballah," International Policy Institute for Counter-Terrorism, June 23, 2002, *www.ict.org.il/spotlight/det.cfm?id=797.*

102. *United States v. Mohamad Youssef Hammoud et al.,* case no. 00-CR-147 (W.D. N.C. filed July 20, 2000, amended March 28, 2001) Superseding Bill of Indictment, ¶3.

103. Larry D. Thompson, testimony in "The Administration's National Money Laundering Strategy for 2002," hearing before the Senate Committee on Banking, Housing, and Urban Affairs, 107th Cong., 2nd sess., October 3, 2002.

104. "Two Men in United States Convicted of Aiding Hizballah."

105. Phil Fairbanks, "Al-Qaida's Money Trail is Built on Stealth," *Buffalo News,* October 13, 2002; "Alleged Hizballah Support Ring Arrested in United States," *Charlotte Observer,* July 21, 2000.

106. Jeffrey Goldberg, "In the Party of God," part 2, *New Yorker,* October 28, 2002, *www.newyorker.com/fact/content/?021028fa_fact2.*

107. "Alleged Hizballah Support Ring Arrested in United States."

108. Amelia Hill, "Bin Laden's $20m African 'Blood Diamonds' Deals," *Observer,* October 20, 2002.

109. Matthew Levitt, "Banning Hizballah Activity in Canada," *PolicyWatch* 698 (January 6, 2003): *www.washingtoninstitute.org/watch/Policywatch/policywatch2003/ 698.htm*; Karmon, "Hizballah and the War on Terror."

110. Steven Emerson, testimony in "PATRIOT Act Oversight: Investigating Patterns of Terrorist Financing," hearing before the House Committee on Financial Services Subcommittee on Oversight and Investigations, 107th Cong., 2nd sess., February 12, 2002, serial 107-53 (Washington, D.C.: U.S. Government Printing Office, 2002), 139.

111. Levitt, "Banning Hizballah Activity in Canada."

112. "Alleged Hizballah Support Ring Arrested in United States."

113. Evidence presented at trial, quoted in Levitt, "Banning Hizballah Activity in Canada."

114. Goldberg, "In the Party of God," part 2.

115. Quoted in "Alleged Hizballah Support Ring Arrested in United States."

116. Federal affadavit, quoted in "Alleged Hizballah Support Ring Arrested in United States."

117. Michael Chertoff, testimony in "Financial War on Terrorism: New Money Trails Present Fresh Challenges," hearing before the Senate Committee on Finance, 107th Cong., 2nd sess., October 9, 2002, S Hrg. 107-880 (Washington, D.C.: U.S. Government Printing Office, 2002), 29.

118. Levitt, "Banning Hizballah Activity in Canada"; John Mintz and Douglas Farah, "Small Scams Probed for Terror Ties," *Washington Post*, August 12, 2002.

119. Mintz and Farah, "Small Scams Probed for Terror Ties."

120. Karmon, "Hizballah and the War on Terror."

121. Quoted in "Alleged Hizballah Support Ring Arrested in United States."

122. Quoted in Karmon, "Hizballah and the War on Terror."

123. Quoted in David E. Kaplan, "Homegrown Terrorists: How a Hezbollah Cell Made Millions in Sleepy Charlotte, N.C.," *U.S. News and World Report*, March 10, 2003, 30–33.

124. Kaplan, "Homegrown Terrorists."

125. Levitt, "Banning Hizballah Activity in Canada."

126. Quoted in "U.S. Drug Ring Tied to Aid for Hizballah."

127. Kaplan, "Homegrown Terrorists."

128. Mintz and Farah, "Small Scams Probed for Terror Ties."

129. Richard Rohde, testimony in "Foreign Terrorists in America: Five Years After the World Trade Center," hearing before the Senate Committee on the Judiciary, Subcommittee on Technology, Terrorism, and Government Information, 105th Cong., 2nd Sess., February 24, 1998.

130. Ibid.

131. Mintz and Farah, "Small Scams Probed for Terror Ties."

132. Quoted in Bodansky, *Bin Laden*, 322.

133. Levitt, "Political Economy of Middle East Terrorism."

134. Library of Congress, "A Global Overview of Narcotics-Funded Terrorist and Other Extremist Groups."

135. Reuven Erlich, "Terror and Crime in Lebanon: The Removal of Syria and Lebanon from the US Department List of Countries Selling Drugs," International Policy Institute for Counter-Terrorism, April 24, 1998, *www.ict.org.il/articles/articledet.cfm? articleid=7.*

136. Tom Knowlton, "Al Qaeda and Hezbollah Plot a Dangerous Alliance," *DefenseWatch*, January 1, 2003, *www.sftt.org/dwa/2003/1/1/4.html.*

137. Ibid.

138. Ibid.; Erlich, "Terror and Crime in Lebanon."

139. Ibid.

140. U.S. intelligence sources, interview by author, fall 2002.

141. Library of Congress, "A Global Overview of Narcotics-Funded Terrorist and Other Extremist Groups."

142. Knowlton, "Al Qaeda and Hezbollah Plot a Dangerous Alliance."

143. Ibid.

144. Quoted in Knowlton, "Al Qaeda and Hezbollah Plot a Dangerous Alliance."

145. Library of Congress, "A Global Overview of Narcotics-Funded Terrorist and Other Extremist Groups."

146. Jerry Seper, "Terror Cell on Rise in South America," *Washington Times*, December 18, 2002.

147. "Iran as a State Sponsoring and Operating Terror," 73–74.

148. Goldberg, "In the Party of God," part 2.

149. Library of Congress, "A Global Overview of Narcotics-Funded Terrorist and Other Extremist Groups."

150. Alberto Cardoso, *Correio Brasiliense* Web site, November 9, 2001, quoted in "Brazil: Official Admits Triborder Money Laundering May Fund Terrorism," BBC Monitoring Service, November 22, 2001.

151. Library of Congress, "A Global Overview of Narcotics-Funded Terrorist and Other Extremist Groups."

152. Levitt, "Political Economy of Middle East Terrorism."

153. Goldberg, "In the Party of God," part 2.

154. Roberto Cosso, "Extremistas receberam US$50 mi de Foz do Iguaçu" (Extremists Received U.S.$50 Million from Foz do Iguaçu), *Folha de S. Paolo*, December 3, 2001.

155. Library of Congress, "A Global Overview of Narcotics-Funded Terrorist and Other Extremist Groups."

156. Blanca Madani, "Hezbollah's Global Finance Network: The Triple Frontier," *Middle East Intelligence Bulletin* 4, no. 1 (January 2002): *www.meib.org/articles/0201_l2.htm.*

157. "Commandos terroristas se refugian en la triple frontera" (Terrorist "Commandos" Hide in the Tri-Border Region), *El Pais* (Colombia), November 9, 2001, cited in Library of Congress, "A Global Overview of Narcotics-Funded Terrorist and Other Extremist Groups."

158. *ABC Color* (Paraguay), November 5, 2001, trans. in Foreign Broadcast Information Service, "Barchini's Calls Under Scrutiny, New Antiterrorist Officials," LAP20011105000019, November 5, 2001.

159. Ibid.

160. Anthony Faiola, "U.S. Terrorist Search Reaches Paraguay; Black Market Border Hub Called Key Finance Center for Middle East Extremists," *Washington Post*, October 13, 2001.

161. Madani, "Hezbollah's Global Finance Network"; Ricardo Galhardo Enviado, "Paraguai pede a prisão de libanês no Brasil" (Paraguay Sentences a Lebanese in Brazil to Prison), *O Globo* (Brazil), November 6, 2001.

162. Marc Perelman, "U.S. Hand Seen in Paraguay's Pursuit of Terrorism Suspect," *Forward*, January 17, 2003.

163. Enviado, "Paraguai pede a prisão de libanês no Brasil."

164. Carlos Altenburger, quoted in Perelman, "U.S. Hand Seen in Paraguay's Pursuit of Terrorism Suspect."

165. Stan Lehman, "Wanted by Paraguay, Hezbollah Supporter Is Free in Brazilian Town Across the Border," Associated Press, December 12, 2001.

166. Ibid.

167. "Barakat Resorted to Blackmail to Get Money," *Última Hora* (Asunción, Paraguay), December 6, 2001, trans. in Foreign Broadcast Information Service, "Media on Efforts to Combat Terrorist Financial Activity in Triborder Area," LAP20011210000096, December 10, 2001.

168. Ibid.

169. "Brazil Detains Alleged Hezbollah Supporter Wanted in Paraguay," Associated Press Worldstream, June 22, 2002.

170. Ana Felicia Linares, quoted in Perelman, "U.S. Hand Seen in Paraguay's Pursuit of Terrorism Suspect."

171. Library of Congress, "A Global Overview of Narcotics-Funded Terrorist and Other Extremist Groups."

172. Ibid.; Madani, "Hezbollah's Global Finance Network."

173. Cosso, "Extremistas receberam US$50 mi de Foz do Iguaçu."

174. Goldberg, "In the Party of God," part 2.

175. Orrin Hatch, testimony in "Narco-Terrorism: International Drug Trafficking and Terrorism—a Dangerous Mix," hearing before the Senate Committee on the Judiciary, 108th Cong., 1st sess., May 20, 2003, *www.senate.gov/~judiciary/member_statement. cfm?id=764&wit_id=51.*

176. Sergo Gobetti, "PF investiga ligacao de prefeito con Bin Laden," Oestadao.com.br, September 12, 2001.

177. Claire Sterling, *Octopus: The Long Reach of the International Sicilian Mafia* (New York: W.W. Norton and Company, 1990), 136–38.

178. International Consortium of Investigative Journalists, "Latin America" in *Tobacco Companies Linked to Criminal Organizations in Cigarette Smuggling*, Center for Public Integrity, March 3, 2001.

179. Jose Meirelles Passos, "The Shadow of Bin Laden in Latin America," *O Globo* (Brazil), Internet edition, October 29, 2001, trans. in Foreign Broadcast Information Service, "Brazil: Daily Notes US Views Triborder as al-Qaidah Center for L.A.," LAP20011029000036, October 29, 2001.

180. Library of Congress, "A Global Overview of Narcotics-Funded Terrorist and Other Extremist Groups."

181. Fabio Castillo, with research by Leydi Herrera, "The Hizballah Contact in Colombia," part 3 of "Tracking the Tentacles of the Middle East in South America," *El Espectador*, December 9, 2001, trans. in Foreign Broadcast Information Service, "Alleged Hizballah Ties in Colombia Investigated," LAP20011210000036, December 10, 2001.

182. Richard Armitage, prepared remarks to U.S. Institute of Peace, Washington, D.C., September 5, 2002, transcribed in "Conditions Underlying Conflict Must Be Addressed, Armitage Says," U.S. Department of State, Office of International Information Programs, September 5, 2002, *usinfo.state.gov/regional/nea/sasia/text/0905amtg.htm.*

183. U.S. Department of State, *Patterns of Global Terrorism 2002*, April 2003, *www.state.gov/documents/organization/20177.pdf,* 52.

Chapter 5

1. Bernard Lewis, *The Assassins: A Radical Sect in Islam* (New York: Oxford University Press, 1987), 35–36.

2. George P. Shultz, prepared remarks to the Greater Miami Chamber of Commerce, September 14, 1984, quoted in Helga Silva, "Communist Nations Aiding Terrorists, Latin Drug Traffickers, Shultz Says," *Miami Herald,* September 15, 1984.

3. Mark Edington, "Taking the Offensive: The Case for Major Changes in the Way the United States Confronts Terrorism," *Atlantic Monthly* 269 (June 1992): 40–50.

4. Colin L. Powell, testimony in "Foreign Affairs Budget," hearing before the Senate Committee on Foreign Relations, 108th Cong., 1st sess., February 6, 2003, *www.state.gov/secretary/rm/2003/17423.htm.*

5. Quoted in Yossef Bodansky, *Bin Laden: The Man Who Declared War on America* (Rocklin, Calif.: Forum, 1999), 322.

6. Hubert Hering, *A History of Latin America* (New York: Knopf, 1964), 497–511.

7. John Dorschner and Jim McGee, "The Case Against Cuba," *Tropic* (*Miami Herald* Sunday magazine), November 20, 1983.

8. U.S. Drug Enforcement Administration, "Involvement in Drug Trafficking by the Government of Cuba," (July 1971, classified report, declassified March 31, 1982).

9. Steven W. Casteel, testimony in "Narco-Terrorism: International Drug Trafficking and Terrorism—a Dangerous Mix," hearing before the Senate Committee on the Judiciary, 108th Cong., 1st sess., May 20, 2003, *www.senate.gov/~judiciary/ testimony.cfm?id=764&wit_id=2111.*

10. "Four Killed, Twenty-seven Injured in Colombia Car Bomb," Agence France-Presse, January 16, 2003.

11. U.S. Department of State, *Patterns of Global Terrorism 1983* (Washington D.C.: U.S. Government Printing Office, 1984).

12. Library of Congress, Federal Research Division, "A Global Overview of Narcotics-Funded Terrorist and Other Extremist Groups" (May 2002, draft).

13. U.S. Department of State, "Cuba's Renewed Support for Violence in Latin America," Special Report 90 (December 14, 1981).

14. Roger W. Fontaine, *Terrorism: The Cuban Connection* (New York: Crane, Russack and Co., 1998), 95–99.

15. Rachel Ehrenfeld, *Narco-Terrorism* (New York: Basic Books, 1990), 79.

16. U.S. General Accounting Office, *Drug Control: U.S. Assistance to Colombia Will Take Years to Produce Results* (doc. no. GAO-01-26, 2000), 13.

17. Ibid., 15.

18. Jerry Seper, "DEA Ties Rise in U.S. Heroin Use to Colombian Groups," *Washington Times,* December 24, 2002.

19. Since there is no bookkeeping for illegal activities, it is difficult to know how profitable the illegal drug trade actually is. One can estimate, however, that it provides Colombian narco-terrorists with revenue from as little as $750 million to as much as several billion dollars annually. These estimates are based on how much overall illegal drug trading is taking place in Colombia, according to Colombian and American sources.

20. Library of Congress, "A Global Overview of Narcotics-Funded Terrorist and Other Extremist Groups."

21. Douglas Farah, "U.S. Widens Colombia Counter-Drug Efforts," *Washington Post,* July 10, 1999.

22. Andres Pastrana, *Clarin* (Argentine newspaper), 2000, quoted in Rachel Ehrenfeld, testimony in "Terrorism and Threats to U.S. Interests in Latin America," hearing before the House Committee on Armed Services, Special Oversight Panel on Terrorism, 106th Cong., 2nd sess., June 29, 2000, *armedservices.house.gov/testimony/106th congress/00-06-29ehrenfeld.html.*

23. Ehrenfeld, testimony in "Terrorism and Threats to U.S. Interests in Latin America."

24. Barry McCaffrey, quoted in Bill Rodgers, "Background Report: Colombia FARC—Drugs," Voice of America, August 8, 1999, available at *www.fas.org/man/ dod-101/ops/war/1999/08/990818-colombia1.htm.*

25. "U.S. Targets Colombian Cocaine Crop," Associated Press, July 25, 2000.

26. Ehrenfeld, testimony in "Terrorism and Threats to U.S. Interests in Latin America"; U.S. Department of State, *Patterns of Global Terrorism 1999*, April 2000, *www.state.gov/www/global/terrorism/1999report/patterns.pdf.*

27. Vanessa Arrington, "Country Collapses In on Bishop," Associated Press, November 14, 2002.

28. "Colombia's Uribe Rejects Rebel Demand for DMZ," Voice of America, April 16, 2003.

29. Jeremy McDermott, "Colombia Land-for-Peace Deal Extended," BBC News, December 7, 2000.

30. Alma Guillermoprieto, "Colombia's Child Army," *N.Y. Review of Books*, May 11, 2000.

31. "The EU's Relations with Colombia: Overview," European Union On-Line, *europa. eu.int/comm/external_relations/colombia/intro.*

32. "Chronology of Peace Process in Colombia 1998–2001," U.K. Foreign and Commonwealth Office, February 28, 2001.

33. "DEA Director Announces Arrest of FARC Member," Drug Enforcement Administration, June 19, 2002, *www.usdoj.gov/dea/pubs/pressrel/pr061902.html.*

34. Casteel, testimony in "Narco-Terrorism: International Drug Trafficking and Terrorism—a Dangerous Mix."

35. Dan Burton, quoted in Jerry Seper, "U.S. Fails to Achieve Anti-Drug Goal in Colombia," *Washington Times,* January 16, 2003.

36. Benjamin A. Gilman, quoted in Seper, "U.S. Fails to Achieve Anti-Drug Goal in Colombia."

37. "Colombia Secures $2bn IMF Aid," BBC News, January 16, 2003.

38. Charlene Porter, "U.S., Colombia Investigate Expansion of Terrorist Alliances," U.S. Department of State, April 25, 2002, *usinfo.state.gov/regional/ar/colombia/ 02042501.htm.* For more details on IRA's involvement with the FARC, see "International Global Terrorism: Its Links with Illicit Drugs as Illustrated by the IRA and Other Groups in Colombia," hearing before the House Committee on International Relations, 107th Cong., 2nd sess., April 24, 2002, serial 107-87 (Washington, D.C.: U.S. Government Printing Office, 2002).

39. Henry McDonald, "'New Proof' Links IRA to Drug Terror," *Observer,* December 9, 2001.

40. Jeremy McDermott, "Colombian Attacks 'Have Hallmark of IRA,'" BBC News, August 11, 2002.

41. José Cadena, quoted in Library of Congress, "A Global Overview of Narcotics-Funded Terrorist and Other Extremist Groups." A similar statement was made by Colombia's former police chief, General Rosso Jose Serrano, in interviews with the author. See also Martin Arostegui, "Search for bin Laden Links Looks South," United Press International, October 12, 2001.

42. "Egyptian Suspect in Luxor Attack Arrives in Ecuador," *Daily Telegraph,* October 21, 1998.

43. Spain's official EFE press agency, paraphrased in Bill Samii, "Iranians Out of Colombia," *Iran Report* 2, no. 51 (December 7, 1999): *www.rferl.org/iran-report/ 1999/12/-271299.html.*

44. Jose Meirelles Passos, "The Shadow of Bin Laden in Latin America," *O Globo* (Brazil), Internet edition, October 29, 2001, trans. in Foreign Broadcast Information

Service, "Brazil: Daily Notes US Views Triborder as al-Qaidah Center for L.A.," LAP20011029000036, October 29, 2001.

45. "Accusations Fly Between Venezuela, Colombia," CNN.com, April 21, 2003.

46. Library of Congress, "A Global Overview of Narcotics-Funded Terrorist and Other Extremist Groups."

47. Ibid.

48. U.S. Department of State, *Patterns of Global Terrorism 2001*, May 2002, *www.state.gov/documents/organization/10319.pdf*, 88.

49. Library of Congress, "A Global Overview of Narcotics-Funded Terrorist and Other Extremist Groups."

50. Ibid.

51. Robert Frank and James Hookway, "Manila Police Say Rebels Have Links to Bin Laden," *Wall Street Journal*, September 25, 2001.

52. Library of Congress, "A Global Overview of Narcotics-Funded Terrorist and Other Extremist Groups."

53. Joshua Kurlantzick, "Opening Up a Second Front," *U.S. News and World Report*, December 24, 2001, 24.

54. Following the arrest of Jemaah Islamiyah operatives in Thailand in June 2003, security officials throughout Asia have been voicing growing concerns about the group's activities . Jemaah Islamiyah advocates the establishment of a Muslim state that includes Indonesia, Malaysia, Singapore, Thailand, and the Philippines. "Thai Arrests Show Terrorism Links in Asia," *Wall Street Journal*, June 12, 2003.

55. Phil Zabriskie, and Mark Thompson, "Picking a Fight: The U.S. Takes Its War on Terrorism to the Philippines. But Is It Taking On the Right Bad Guys?" *Time International*, February 25, 2002, 23.

56. Based on information from "The Abu Sayyaf Group," *Jane's World Insurgency and Terrorism* 13 (2001).

57. Hamsiraji Sali, quoted in Marc Lerner, "Philippine Terrorists Claim Link to Iraq," *Washington Times*, March 4, 2003.

58. Library of Congress, "A Global Overview of Narcotics-Funded Terrorist and Other Extremist Groups."

59. Donna S. Cueto, "Philippine Police Officer Links Abu Sayyaf to Drug Trafficking," *Manila Philippine Daily Inquirer*, Internet edition, July 17, 2000.

60. Library of Congress, "A Global Overview of Narcotics-Funded Terrorist and Other Extremist Groups."

61. The LTTE comprises: the World Tamil Association (WTA), World Tamil Movement (WTM), the Federation of Associations of Canadian Tamils (FACT), and the Ellalan Force.

62. "The Tamil people of the island of Ceylon (now called Sri Lanka) constitute a distinct nation. They form a social entity, with their own history, traditions, culture, language and traditional homeland. The Tamil people call their nation Tamil Eelam." Tamil Eelam official Web site, *www.eelam.com*.

63. Rohan Gunaratna, "Lanka's Conflict and Global Ethnopolitics," prepared remarks to the Bandaranaike Centre for International Studies, June 17, 1999, available through SPUR Online, *www.spur.asn.au/island_990617_E.htm*.

64. Alex Perry, "A Rumor of Peace: Sri Lanka's Rebel Leader Talks of Ending Conflict for

the Cameras—While Continuing to Stock Arms Behind the Scenes," *Time Asia,* April 22, 2002, *www.time.com/time/asia/magazine/article/0,13673,501020422-230450,00.html.*

65. Rohan Gunaratna, "LTTE in South Africa," *Frontline* 15, no. 24 (November 21–December 4, 1998): *www.flonnet.com/fl1524/15240500.htm.*

66. The PKK was created in 1974 by Abdullah Ocalan as a revolutionary socialist organization committed to establishing an independent Kurdish state. According to the DEA, "The PKK . . . possibly control[s] a significant portion of the heroin market in Europe." Casteel, testimony in "Narco-Terrorism: International Drug Trafficking and Terrorism—a Dangerous Mix."

67. Gunaratna, "LTTE in South Africa."

68. Ibid.

69. "Tamil Tiger Arms Smugglers Blow Up Ship and Themselves," *Wall Street Journal,* February 7, 2003.

70. U.S. intelligence sources.

71. "Liberation Tigers of Tamil Eelam (LTTE)," International Policy Institute for Counter-Terrorism, *www.ict.org.il/inter_ter/orgdet.cfm?orgid=22.*

72. "Tigers Adopt New Tool of Terror," *Bangkok Post,* October 29, 1997.

73. Rand Beers, testimony in "Narco-Terror: The Worldwide Connection Between Drugs and Terrorism," hearing before the Senate Committee on the Judiciary, Subcommittee on Technology, Terrorism, and Government Information, 107th Cong, 2nd sess., March 13, 2002, *www.senate.gov/~judiciary/testimony.cfm?id=196&wit_id=331.*

74. "Tigers Adopt New Tool of Terror."

75. Quoted in "Tigers Adopt New Tool of Terror."

76. Ashok K. Mehta, "The LTTE, Once Rooted in Jaffna, Will Pose a Serious Threat to South India," rediff.com, September 21, 2000, *www.rediff.com/news/2000/sep/21ashok.htm.*

77. "Tamil Tiger Arms Smugglers Blow Up Ship and Themselves."

78. "Tamil Tigers Call Off Peace Talks," BBC News, April 21, 2003.

79. George W. Bush, remarks upon signing Drug-Free Communities Act Reauthorization Bill, Omni Shoreham Hotel, Washington, D.C., December 14, 2001.

80. "National Household Survey on Drug Abuse: DEA's Response to Results," Drug Enforcement Administration, September 6, 2002, *www.dea.gov/pubs/pressrel/pr090602.html.*

81. Steven Casteel, prepared remarks to National Symposium on Narco-Terrorism, DEA headquarters, Arlington, Va., December 4, 2001.

82. Raphael Perl, testimony in "Narco-Terrorism: International Drug Trafficking and Terrorism—a Dangerous Mix," *www.senate.gov/~judiciary/testimony.cfm?id=764&wit_id=2115.*

Chapter 6

1. George W. Bush, address to joint session of Congress, September 20, 2001, transcribed in "Address to a Joint Session of Congress and the American People," White House Office of the Press Secretary, September 20, 2001, *www.whitehouse.gov/news/releases/2001/09/print/20010920-8.html;* George W. Bush, remarks upon signing Executive Order on Terrorist Financing, White House, September 24, 2001, transcribed in

"President Freezes Terrorists' Assets," White House Office of the Press Secretary, September 24, 2001, *www.whitehouse.gov/news/releases/2001/09/20010924-4.html*.

2. Rachel Ehrenfeld, "The Palestinian Authority: Where Does the Money Go?" B'nei Brith Europe, October 23, 2002.

3. Barry Schweid, "Powell, Egyptians Disagree on Arafat," Associated Press, May 12, 2003.

4. The Saudi refusal to cooperate with U.S. investigators regarding terror attacks on American targets inside and outside the kingdom is nothing new. They refused to do so after the attacks on the American embassies in Kenya and Tanzania, and have continued in their refusal to the time of this writing (July 2003). Yet, according to Senator Bob Graham, a member of the 2002 joint House/Senate intelligence committee, the Bush administration refused to declassify sections in the committee's 2002 inquiry related to the Saudis (and other foreign governments) involvement in the funding of terrorism against the U.S., including September 11. Michael Isikoff, "Exclusive—The 9-11 Report: Slamming the FBI," *Newsweek*, July 28, 2003.

5. Douglas Jehl and David E. Sanger, "Five Requests to Saudis Went Unheeded, U.S. Says," *New York Times*, May 16, 2003.

6. Ibid.

7. Jeffrey Donovan, "Saudi Arabia: Officials Vow to 'Redouble' Antiterrorist Efforts, Though Doubts Linger," Radio Free Europe Radio Liberty, May 19, 2003, *www.rferl.org/nca/features/2003/05/19052003165952.asp*.

8. Dore Gold, *Hatred's Kingdom* (Washington D.C.: Regnary Publishing, 2003), 2

9. Jean-Charles Brisard, "Terrorism Financing: Roots and Trends of Saudi Terrorism Financing" (report prepared for the president of the UN Security Council, December 19, 2002). Brisard, the French investigator who authored this report, lost a libel case brought against him in London by Khalid bin Mahfouz, based on allegations made against the Saudi billionaire in Brisard's report. However, Brisard told the author that the judgement was by default, since he didn't have the financial means to defend himself against the Saudi billionaire.

10. Gold, *Hatred's Kingdom;* Alex Alexiev, "Among the Wahhabis," *Commentary* 115, no. 5 (May 2003).

11. Susan Katz Keating, "The Wahhabi Fifth Column," *FrontPageMagazine. com*, December 30, 2002.

12. Rosie Cowan, "Adams Says No to Colombia Hearing," *Guardian*, April 24, 2002.

13. Michael Casey, "Al Qaeda Active in Indonesia," Associated Press, October 15, 2002; Cindy Wockner, "Terror Suspect Trained Recruits," *Herald Sun* (Australia), June 8, 2003.

14. Indonesia's candidacy was confirmed by a source requesting anonymity.

15. "Texas Islamic Group Busted by Feds," CBSNEWS.com, December 18, 2002.

16. Diana Lynne, "Suspected Financiers Tied to 'Charity' Arrested," WorldNet Daily.com, December 18, 2002, *www.worldnetdaily.com/news/article.asp?ARTICLE_ ID=30063*.

17. Cuba, a country that has sponsored terrorism for decades and is involved in drug trafficking, is off the radar, but should be looked at. See José Antonio Friedl Zapata, *El Gran Engaño: Fidel Castro y su intima relación con el narcotráfico internaciona,* forthcoming in Spanish.

18. Paraphrased in Alex Alexiev, "A Failing Ally: Lessons from Pakistan" (Center for Security Policy, Washington. D.C., March 2003, draft); this draft is the expanded version of Alex Alexiev, "The Pakistani Time Bomb" *Commentary* 115, no. 3 (March 2003).

19. "Treaty on Suppression of Financing of Terrorism Comes into Force," United Nations Department of Public Information, April 5, 2002, *www.un.org/News/Press/docs/2002/LT4366.doc.*

20. Ibid.

21. Ibid.

22. The Convention on Fighting Bribery of Foreign Officials in Transnational Business Transactions was signed on December 17, 1997, in Paris, by the member countries of the Organisation for Economics Cooperation and Development, as well as some non-member countries. "Transnational Bribery: OECD Convention," World Policies, *www.worldpolicies.com/english/tb_oecd_convention.html.*

23. The Inter-American Convention Against Corruption was adopted by the member states of the Organization of American States at the third plenary session, March 29, 1996. The text of the agreement is available through Organization of American States, *www.oas.org/EN/PINFO/CONVEN/corrupt.htm.*

24. "Corruption," UN Office on Drugs and Crime, *www.unodc.org/unodc/corruption. html.*

25. Matthew Levitt, "Stemming the Flow of Terrorist Financing: Practical and Conceptual Challenges," lecture given at program sponsored by U.S. Embassy Vienna, Austria, Vienna, Graz, and Bregenz, January 20–23, 2003, *www.usembassy.at/en/embassy/photo/lev_lecture.htm.*

26. Maurice R. Greenberg et al, "Terrorist Financing: Report of an Independent Task Force Sponsored by the Council on Foreign Relations," Council on Foreign Relations, October 2002, *www.cfr.org/pdf/Terrorist_Financing_TF.pdf,* 4.

27. Levitt, "Stemming the Flow of Terrorist Financing."

28. George W. Bush, State of the Union Address, U.S. Capitol, January 28, 2003, transcribed in "President Delivers 'State of Union,'" White House Office of the Press Secretary, January 28, 2003, *www.whitehouse.gov/news/releases/2003/01/20030128-19.html.*

29. Ibid.

30. "By 2000, the [annual] economic cost of drug abuse is projected to be $160.7 billion." *The Economic Costs of Drug Abuse in the United States, 1992–1998* (Washington, D.C.: Executive Office of the President, 2001), 4.

31. Charlene Porter, "Burma, Guatemala, Haiti Failed in Drug War Cooperation, U.S. Says," Washington File, January 31, 2003.

32. The listed countries are: Afghanistan, the Bahamas, Bolivia, Brazil, Burma, China, Colombia, the Dominican Republic, Ecuador, Guatemala, Haiti, India, Jamaica, Laos, Mexico, Nigeria, Pakistan, Panama, Paraguay, Peru, Thailand, Venezuela, and Vietnam. Ibid.

33. Juan Forero and Tim Weiner, "Latin American Poppy Fields Undermine U.S. Drug Battle," *New York Times,* June 8, 2003.

34. Planned meeting of Multistate Research Project S-1001, "Development of Plant Pathogens as Bioherbicides for Weed Control," Reno, Nev., February 10, 2002, minutes available through University of Florida, Institute of Food and Agricultural Sciences, *plantpath.ifas.ufl.edu/s1001/minutes/Min2021.htm.*

35. Steven Casteel, prepared remarks to National Symposium on Narco-Terrorism, DEA headquarters, Arlington, Va., December 4, 2001.

36. Rachel Ehrenfeld, "Fighting International Graft, Lending Bodies Can Bolster War on Corruption." *Washington Times,* September 29, 1999.

37. For information on Wolfensohn's anticorruption initiatives, see "Tackling Corruption," World Bank Group, Office of the President, *web.worldbank.org/WBSITE/ EXTERNAL/EXTABOUTUS/ORGANIZATION/PRESIDENTEXTER NAL/0,,contentMDK: 20094290~menuPK:232057~pagePK:139877~piPK:199692~theSitePK:227585,00.html.*

38. Horst Köhler, "The Continuing Challenge of Transition and Convergence," prepared remarks at the conference "Completing Transition: The Main Challenges," Vienna, Austria, November 6, 2000.

39. Paul O'Neill, prepared remarks to the Detroit Economic Club, June 27, 2001, quoted in Stephen Fidler, "Who's Minding the Bank?" *Foreign Policy*, September/ October 2001, *www.foreignpolicy.com/issue_SeptOct_2001/fidler.html.*

40. Unpublished internal report, World Bank, Fall 2000.

41. William Easterly, "The Failure of Development," *Financial Times*, July 3, 2001.

42. Claudia Rosett, "My Job Is to Tell You He's Not Available: The World Bank Tries to Silence a Critic," *Wall Street Journal*, November 8, 2001.

43. David Adams, "Crackdown Costs Officials U.S. Visas: The U.S. Has Revoked Visas in Ten Countries in Latin America Due to Corruption Concerns," *St. Petersburg Times*, November 1, 2002.

44. According to the PATRIOT Act, entry visas into the U.S. cannot be issued to anyone involved with either terrorism or drug trafficking. Ricardo Soberón Garrido, "Corruption, Drug Trafficking and the Armed Forces: An Approximation for Latin America," Transnational Institute/Acción Andina, *Crime in Uniform: Corruption and Impunity in Latin America* (Cochabamba, Bolivia: CEDIB, 1997), *www.tni.org/drugs/folder3/ soberon.htm.* The story about Paz Zamora's renewed visa to the U.S. was conveyed by a high-ranking former State Department official who requested anonymity.

45. Adrian Karatnycky, "The 2001–2002 Freedom House Survey of Freedom: The Democracy Gap," Freedom House, *www.freedomhouse.org/research/freeworld/ 2002/akessay.pdf,* 10

46. Bernard Lewis, *What Went Wrong?* (New York: Oxford University Press, 2002), 159.

47. Karatnycky, "The 2001–2002 Freedom House Survey of Freedom," 7.

48. United Nations Development Programme and the Arab Fund for Economic and Social Development, *Arab Human Development Report 2002 (AHDR)* (New York: United Nations Publications, June 2002).

49. Tom Masland and Jeffery Bartholet, "Tracking Abacha's Billions," *Newsweek,* March 13, 2000.

50. *Japanese ODA Newsletter,* October 14–27, 2000, *www.euroact.co.jp/ oda-japan/Newsletter/Newsletter_Archive/newsletter_archive.html.*

51. Ibid.

52. Abdul Razak Zulkifli, "Poison Control: War on Drugs Derailed by Afghan Imperative," *New Straits Times* (Malaysia), February 2, 2003.

53. "Ambassador Paul Bremer Named Presidential Envoy to Iraq," U.S. Department of State, May 6, 2003, *usinfo.state.gov/topical/rights/democracy/03050603.htm.*

54. "The Bremer Regency," editorial, *Wall Street Journal*, May 16, 2003.

55. George W. Bush, prepared remarks to Inter-American Development Bank, Washington, D.C., March 14, 2002, transcribed in "President Proposes $5 Billion Plan to Help Developing Nations," White House Office of the Press Secretary, March 14, 2002, *www.whitehouse.gov/news/releases/2002/03/20020314-7.html.*

56. George W. Bush, videotaped remarks to African Growth and Opportunity Act

Forum, January 15, 2003, transcribed in "President Addresses African Growth and Opportunity Act Forum," White House Office of the Press Secretary, January 15, 2003, *www.whitehouse.gov/news/releases/2003/01/20030115.html*.

57. "Fact Sheet: Millennium Challenge Account Update," United States Agency for International Development, June 3, 2002, *www.usaid.gov/press/releases/2002/fs_mca.html*.

58. Rachel Ehrenfeld, "Don't Bank on Corruption: Lending Integrity Is a Prime U.S. Interest," *Washington Times,* December 29, 2000. For more on the International Integrity Standard, see the American Center for Democracy official Web site, *www.public-integrity.org*.

59. Claudia Rosett, "Oil for Food, Money for Kofi," *Weekly Standard* 8, no. 29 (April 7, 2003): *www.weeklystandard.com/Content/Public/Articles/000/000/002/459pqvob.asp*. For the UN office's own statements, see its official Web site, *www.un.org/Depts/oip*.

60. Conflict Securities Advisory Group official Web site, *www.conflictsecurities.com*

61. Carrie Satterlee, "Facts on Who Benefits from Keeping Saddam Hussein in Power," WebMemo 217, Heritage Foundation, February 28, 2003, *www.heritage.org/Research/MiddleEast/wm217.cfm*.

62. Massimo Calabresi, Jamil Hamad, and Adam Zagorin, "Hamas' French Funds?" *TIME,* June 30, 2003.

63. Jack Straw, statement to the UN Security Council, New York, May 5, 2003.

64. Lewis, *What Went Wrong?* 159.

Epilogue

1. John Ashcroft, remarks to press conference, Washington, D.C., May 26, 2004, quoted in "Feds: Al Qaeda Plans to 'Hit the U.S. Hard,'" Fox News, May 27, 2004, *www.foxnews.com/story/0,2933,120956,00.html*.

2. Mark Huband and David Buchan, "Al-Qaeda 'May Have 18,000 Operatives,'" *Financial Times Online,* May 25, 2004.

3. "Remarks by Secretary of Homeland Security Tom Ridge Regarding Recent Threat Reports," U.S. Department of Homeland Security, Office of the Press Secretary, August 1, 2004, *www.dhs.gov/dhspublic/display?content=3870*.

4. "Report: Al-Qaida has 18,000 Ready to Strike," Associated Press, May 25, 2004.

5. Huband and Buchan, "Al-Qaeda 'May Have 18,000 Operatives.'"

6. Samuel W. Bodman, testimony in "Counterterror Initiatives and Concerns in the Terror Finance Program," hearing before the Senate Committee on Banking, Housing, and Urban Affairs, 108th Cong., 2nd sess., April 29, 2004, *www.senate.gov/~banking/_files/bodman.pdf,* 6.

7. Curt Anderson, "Broader Law Sought on Terror Financing," *Washington Post,* May 5, 2004.

8. "Feds Face Questions on Terror Financing," Associated Press, April 29, 2004.

9. Juan Zarate, head of the Office of Terrorism and Financial Intelligence at the Treasury Department. "Over 170 jurisdictions have issued blocking orders, and we have built a tighter international financial net through which suspect funds may be captured." Testimony in "Saudi Arabia and the Fight Against Terrorism Financing," hearing before the House Committee on International Relations, Subcommittee on the Middle East and Central Asia, 108th Cong., 2nd sess., March 24, 2004, serial 108-109 (Washington, D.C.: U.S. Government Printing Office, 2004), 19.

10. Matthew Rosenberg, "Al-Qaida Continues to Siphon Charities," Associated Press, June 6, 2004.

11. However, instead of bringing suspected terrorists to justice, a strange practice of deporting militant Muslims and suspected terrorists has been adopted in many countries such as Canada, France, South Africa, the U.K., the U.S., Italy, and the Netherlands. It is difficult to understand why these terrorists are not being tried, sentenced, incarcerated, and removed from circulation under long prison terms. Deportation enables them to continue their activities with wider respectability and recognition among their cohorts, because they already have been acknowledged by the authorities for their unlawful activities. Craig Pyesjosh Meyer and William C. Rempe, "Terrorists Use Bosnia as Base and Sanctuary," *Los Angeles Times*, October 7 2001; "Montrealer Suspected of al-Qaeda Ties," *National Post* (Canada), May 22, 2003; "France Deports Islamic Mosque Leader," Associated Press, May 20, 2004; Edwin Lombard, "'Police Wanted Me to Be Informer,'" *Sunday Times* (S. Africa), June 6, 2004; "Radical Cleric Fights Deportation," BBC News, April 26, 2004, *news.bbc.co.uk/1/hi/england/london/3658761.stm;* "US Threatens Mass Expulsions," BBC News, June 10, 2003, *news.bbc.co.uk/2/hi/americas/2974882.stm;* "France's Crackdown on Islamic Radicals," *Business Week*, June 7, 2004, *www.businessweek.com/magazine/content/04_23/b3886073.htm;* Michael Isikoff and Mark Hosenball, "Behind Bars—Briefly," *Newsweek*, January 8, 2004.

12. David D. Aufhauser, written testimony in "Counterterror Initiatives in the Terror Finance Program," hearing before the Senate Committee on Banking, Housing, and Urban Affairs, 108th Cong., 1st sess., September 25, 2003, *www.senate.gov/~banking/_files/aufhausr.pdf,* 5.

13. Marcy Gordon, "Bank Fined $25M for Saudi Transactions," Associated Press, May 13, 2004.

14. Saudi Embassy spokesman, April 2004, quoted in "Feds Face Questions on Terror Financing."

15. Peter Finn, "Al-Qaeda link to Saudi National Guard," *The Age*, May 20, 2003, *www.theage.com.au/articles/2003/05/19/1053196523425.html.*

16. "Saudis Search for Clues After Militant Attack," MSNBC News, May 31, 2004, *msnbc.msn.com/id/5089558.*

17. Timothy L. O'Brien and David D. Kirkpatrick, "Nonpolitical Study of Terror Is Caught Up in Politics," *New York Times*, June 12, 2004.

18. National Commission on Terrorist Attacks upon the United States, *The 9/11 Commission Report* (Washington, D.C.: U.S. Government Printing Office, 2004), 171. *See also* Susan Schmidt, "Saudi Arabia Did Not Directly Finance 9/11, Panel Says," *Washington Post*, June 17, 2004.

19. Anonymous, *Imperial Hubris* (Washington, D.C.: Brassey's, 2004), xi.

20. A. La Guardia, "'Terror Link' Saudi Prince to be Envoy in Britain," *Daily Telegraph*, December 5, 2002.

21. Quoted in Schmidt, "Saudi Arabia Did Not Directly Finance 9/11, Panel Says."

22. Dore Gold, "Saudi Arabia's Dubious Denials of Involvement in International Terrorism," *Jerusalem Viewpoints* 504 (October 2003): 1.

23. Ibid. On July 6, 2004, a lawsuit was filed in a federal court in New York claiming that, for many years, the Arab Bank used its New York branch to launder Saudi money sent to Palestinian terrorists. According to the lawsuit, the branch converted the Saudi riyal into dollars and then transferred it to its different branches in the West Bank and Gaza Strip. That money was later distributed to family members of HAMAS and the

Palestinian Islamic Jihad who carried out homicide bombings against Israelis, the lawsuit claims. Lesser amounts were allegedly given to wounded and captured terrorists and their beneficiaries. *Courtney Linde et al v. Arab Bank, PLC* (E.D. N.Y., July 6, 2004), 26–33. *See also* Justin Glanville, "U.S. Lawsuit Accuses Arab Bank of Aiding Terrorists," Associated Press, July 6, 2004.

24. "New Heights for Saudi's Banks."

25. *Al-Jazira,* April 11, 2002, *www.suhuf.net.sa/2002jaz/apr/11/fe3.htm.* Translation from Arabic and summary by Yoni D. Halevy.

26. Ibid.

27. Quoted in Michael Isikioff and Mark Hosenball, "A Legal Counterattack," *Newsweek,* April 16, 2004.

28. Quoted in "Al Qaeda Militants Say They Were Helped by Saudi Forces," CNN.com, June 20, 2004.

29. Zarate, testimony in "Saudi Arabia and the Fight Against Terrorism Financing"; "Saudi Cabinet Approves Anti–Money Laundering Law," Reuters, August 19, 2003.

30. IDF intelligence sources, interviews by author, May 2004.

31. Josh Meyer, "U.S., Saudis Block Assets of Charity Group," *Los Angeles Times,* June 3, 2004; Les Zaitz, "Terror-Linked Charity Cut Off," *Oregonian,* June 3, 2004.

32. Jeannine Aversa, "Saudis to Tighten Control over Charities," Associated Press, June 3, 2004.

33. "Saudi Crackdown? Move May Have Less Than Meets the Eye," editorial, *Dallas Morning News,* June 7, 2004.

34. National Commission on Terrorist Attacks, *The 9/11 Commission Report,* 171.

35. Lt. Gen. Thomas McInerney and Maj. Gen. Paul Vallely, *Endgame: The Blueprint for Victory in the War on Terror* (Washington, D.C.: Regnery, 2004), 82–85.

36. National Commission on Terrorist Attacks, *The 9/11 Commission Report,* 169.

37. Ibid.

38. Scott Wheeler, "Alleged Terror Threat Operates in DC Suburb," CNSNews.com, July 12, 2004, *www.cnsnews.com/ViewSpecialReports.asp?Page=/SpecialReports/archive/200407/SPE20040712a.html.*

39. See MAS official Web site, *www.masnet.org.*

40. See ICNA official Web site, *www.icna.net.*

41. See INTERPAL official Web site, *www.interpal.org.*

42. See WAMY official Web site, *www.wamy.co.uk.*

43. Timothy L. O'Brien, "Lockboxes, Iraqi Loot and a Trail to the Fed," *New York Times,* June 6, 2004.

44. "A senior investigator with the Swiss Federal Banking Commission and several others briefed on the matter," paraphrased in O'Brien, "Lockboxes, Iraqi Loot and a Trail to the Fed."

45. "Oil-for-Fraud," *The Economist Global Agenda,* April 22, 2004, *www.economist.com/agenda/displayStory.cfm?story_id=2618260.*

46. Therese Raphael, "The Oil-for-Food Scandal," *Wall Street Journal,* March 11, 2004.

47. Nimrod Raphaeli, "The Saddam Oil Vouchers Affair," *MEMRI Inquiry and Analysis Series* 164 (February 20, 2004).

48. "How to End-Run Kofi's Coverup," *New York Post,* May 6, 2004.

49. "Oil-for-Fraud."

50. Interview with author, December 2002.

51. Benjamin Fulford, "North Korea: Another Outcropping of Terrorism," *Forbes*, September 18, 2001, *www.forbes.com/2001/09/18/0918fulford.html.*

52. Graham H. Turbiville Jr., "Drug Trafficking May Fund North Korean Regime," *Special Warfare* 7, no. 4 (October 1994): *fmso.leavenworth.army.mil/soffissues/oct94.htm.*

53. Andrew Ward, "North Korea: US Accused N. Korea of Links to Narcotics Trade," *Financial Times,* December 3, 2002.

54. Japan seems to be a major target for North Korean methamphetamines; 1.1 tons from North Korea were seized by the Japanese between 1999 and 2001. Mari Yamaguchi, "Japan Says Cash-Strapped North Korea Plying Trade in Illegal Stimulants," Associated Press, March 2, 2003.

55. Jay Solomon and Jason Dean, "Heroin Busts Point to Source of Funds for North Koreans," *Wall Street Journal,* April 23, 2003.

56. Barbie Dutter, "North Korean Heroin Ship Is Seized by SAS," *Daily Telegraph,* April 21, 2003, *www.telegraph.co.uk/news/main.jhtml?xml=/news/2003/04/21/whaul21.xml.*

57. Andrew Ward, "US Accuses N. Korea of Links to Narcotics Trade," *Financial Times,* December 3, 2002.

58. Bertil Lintner and Steve Steclow, "Trail of Paper Illuminates North Korea's Arms Trading," *Wall Street Journal,* February 10, 2003.

59. Douglas Farah, *Blood from Stones: The Secret Financial Network of Terror* (New York: Broadway Books, 2004).

60. National Commission on Terrorist Attacks, *The 9/11 Commission Report,* 171.

61. Quoted in Charlene Porter, "Drug Trade is Primary Income Source for Taliban, DEA Says," U.S. Department of State, Office of International Information Programs, October 3, 2001, *usinfo.state.gov/topical/pol/terror/01100311.htm.*

62. Quoted in Porter, "Drug Trade is Primary Income Source for Taliban, DEA Says."

63. Independent Task Force on Terrorist Financing, *Update on the Global Campaign Against Terrorist Financing* (New York: Council on Foreign Relations, 2004), 7. Elision and bracketed interpolation added.

64. Quoted in Jerry Seper, "U.S. Set to Target Afghan Opium," *Washington Times,* January 22, 2004.

65. The White House, *2002 National Drug Control Strategy* (Washington, D.C.: Office of National Drug Control Policy, 2002), 25.

66. "Department of Homeland Security Announces FY 2005 Budget in Brief," U.S. Department of Homeland Security, Press Office, February 2, 2004, *www.dhs.gov/dhspublic/display?content=3133.*

67. Matthew Beard, "Karzai Promises to Rid His Country of Drug Trade," *Independent* (U.K.), January 7, 2002.

68. "Foreign Operations, Export Financing, and Related Programs Appropriations Bill, 2005," report to the Committee of the Whole House on the State of the Union, 108th Cong., 2nd sess., July 13, 2004, serial 108-599 (Washington, D.C.: U.S. Government Printing Office, 2004); Robert B. Charles, testimony in "Afghanistan: Are the British Counternarcotics Efforts Going Wobbly?" hearing before the House Committee on Government Reform, Subcommitte on Criminal Justice, Drug Policy, and Human Resources, 108th Cong., 2nd sess., April 1, 2004, *reform.house.gov/UploadedFiles/Charles%20testimony.pdf.*

69. "IMF Warns Afghanistan Risks Becoming 'Narco-State,'" Agence France-Presse, September 22, 2003.

70. Paraphrased in "Afghan Army Seizes a Ton of Opium Poppies," *RFE/RL Newsline* 8, no. 134, part 3 (July 16, 2004): *www.hri.org/news/balkans/rferl/2004/04-07-16.rferl.html.*

71. Charles, testimony in "Afghanistan: Are the British Counternarcotics Efforts Going Wobbly?"

72. Quoted in "Afghan Opium Boom Spreads to Traditional Farmers," Reuters, May 6, 2004.

73. "Mycoherbicides," Agricultural Research Council of South Africa , Plant Protection Research Institute, *www.arc.agric.za/institutes/ppri/main/divisions/weedsdiv/ mycoherbicides.htm.*

74. "Clinton Signs Bill Funding Colombia, Kosovo Efforts," CNN.com, July 13, 2000.

75. "Transcript: G8 Leaders to Call for Middle East Reforms at Sea Island Summit," Washington File, June 7, 2004.

76. Quoted in "Bush Seeks Wider NATO Role in Iraq" Associated Press, June 9, 2004.

77. Egypt has received a total of $52.875 billion in U.S. aid since 1975: $32.5 billion in military aid and $20.375 billion in economic aid. Charles Levinson, "$50 Billion Later, Taking Stock of US aid to Egypt," *Christian Science Monitor,* April 12, 2004.

78. "Bush Seeks Wider NATO Role in Iraq."

79. "Gaza Withdrawal and the Road Ahead to Mideast Peace," statement of the G8 Summit, Sea Island, Ga., June 10, 2004,

80. Quoted in Edith M. Lederer, "Envoy: Palestinian Authority May Collapse," *Washington Post,* July 13, 2004.

81. According to the IDF, the PA received $105.8 million from Saudi Arabia, $116 million from the EU, $20 million from the World Bank, $10 million from Libya, $12 million from Norway, $10 million each from Canada and Japan, a few million more from the U.K. and the Gulf States, and $400,000 from USAID. David R. Sands, "U.S. Aid Goes to Terrorism Backers," *Washington Times,* June 16, 2004.

82. Mark Beunderman, "Investigations into EU-Financed Palestinian Terror Allegations Not Over, Says OLAF," *EUobserver,* June 9, 2004, *www.euobserver.com/?sid=24 &aid=16549.*

83. Quoted in Rachel Ehrenfeld, "Aid Donors Turn a Blind Eye to Palestinian Terror," *Wall Street Journal Europe,* December 11, 2003.

84. Al-Aqsa Martyrs Brigades commander Hani Uwaidah, quoted in Khaled Abu Toameh, "Fatah Acknowledges Aksa Brigades link," *Jerusalem Post,* June 15, 2004.

85. Jonathan Schanzer, "Tunnel Vision," *Daily Standard,* August 14, 2003, *www. weeklystandard.com/Content/Public/Articles/000/000/002/994qvpoj.asp.*

86. "A Weapon-Smuggling Tunnel Uncovered in Rafah," IDF Spokesperson, June 2, 2004, available through Independent Media Review Analysis, *www.imra.org.il/story. php3?id=21041.*

87. "Parliament Votes to Dismiss Palestinian Monetary Authority Governor," *Jerusalem Times* (Palestinian publication), May 13, 2004.

88. Quoted in Dan Ephron, "'Someone Was Going to Kill,'" *Newsweek,* June 21, 2004.

89. Conal Urquhar, "Palestinian PM Offers to Resign," *Observer,* July 18, 2004; "Palestinian PM Threatens to Quit," *Sunday Telegraph,* September 9, 2004.

90. "Demonstrations in Gaza Against the 'Symbol of Corruption,' *Yedioth Aharonot,*

July 17, 2004. Translation from Hebrew by the author. "Arafat Announces Security Shake-Up amid Turmoil," CNN.com, July 17, 2004.

91. Paul Richter and Warren Vieth, "U.S. Puts Onus on Palestinians," *Los Angeles Times,* November 13, 2004.

92. James D. Wolfensohn, foreword to *Helping Countries Combat Corruption: The Role of the World Bank,* World Bank Group, September 1997, *www1.worldbank.org/publicsector/anticorrupt/corruptn/corrptn.pdf,* 2.

93. James D. Wolfensohn, remarks to press conference, Dubai, United Arab Emirates, September 19, 2003, transcribed in "Press Conference with James D. Wolfensohn," World Bank Group, *web.worldbank.org/WBSITE/EXTERNAL/NEWS/0,,contentMDK: 20128705~menuPK:34477~pagePK:34370~piPK:34424~theSitePK:4607,00.html.*

94. Mark Palmer, *Breaking the Real Axis of Evil* (New York: Rowman and Littlefield., 2003), 319–21.

95. John Byrne, quoted in Kathleen Day and Terence O'Hara, "Obstacles Block Tracking of Terror Funding," *Washington Post,* July 14, 2004.

96. Quoted in "Grassley and Baucus Call for 'Fundamental Reform' Within War on Terrorist Financing," U.S. Senate Committee on Finance, March 29, 2004, *www.senate.gov/~finance/press/Gpress/2004/prg032904a.pdf,* 1.

97. Andrew C. McCarthy, "The War That Dare Not Speak Its Name," *National Review Online,* May 13, 2004.

Appendix B

1. Image in and trans. adapted from Israel Defense Forces, *Arafat's and the PA's Involvement in Terrorism (According to Documents Captured During Operation Defensive Wall),* (doc. no. 688/0023, 2002), 7.

2. Image in and trans. adapted from Israel Defense Forces, *The Personal Involvement of Arafat and His Financial Aide, Shubaki, in a Secret Deal for the Procurement of Arms for PA Entities,* (doc. no. TR1-861-02, 2002), 3–4.

3. Images in and trans. adapted from Israel Defense Forces, *The Palestinian Authority Financed "Fatah" Branch Activities from Its Official Budget,* (doc. no. TR3-337-02, 2002), 5–7.

4. Image in and trans. adapted from Israel Defense Forces, *The Appointment of Mahmud Awdallah as Fuad Shubaki's Replacement,* (doc. no. TR2-907-02, 2002), 3–5.

INDEX